Quicken 5 For Macs Fo~

M000268087

Some cool date-editing tricks

If the selection cursor is on a date field, you can

Press	What happens
+	Adds 1 day to the date shown
–	Subtracts 1 day from the date shown
y	Changes the date to the first date in the year
r	Changes the date to the last day in the year
m	Changes the date to the first date in the month
h	Changes the date to the last day in the month
t	Changes the data to today's date

Three things that every Quicken user should do

1. Use the Retirement Planner to estimate when and how you can retire.

2. Create a category list that makes it easy to track your spending and tax deductions.

3. Use the Reconcile command to balance bank accounts each month with only a few minutes of effort.

A Dozen Macintosh Tricks

You can use these in Quicken for the Macintosh—and just about any other Macintosh program, too.

1. To move a document window, drag its title bar.
2. To move quickly to list box entries starting with a letter—such as X—type the letter.
3. To select a list box entry and choose dialog box's suggested command button, double-click.
4. To move the insertion bar to the beginning of a field, press Home.
5. To move the insertion bar to the end of a field, press End.
6. To close a window or dialog box, click on its close box. (The close box is the box in the upper left corner of the window.)
7. To get help on the active application, press ⌘+?. You can also choose one of the Help menu's commands.
8. To quit the active application, press ⌘+q.
9. To cancel a printing job, press ⌘+. (That looks funny, but what it means is that you press both the ⌘ key and the period key.)
10. To resize a window, drag the size box. (The size box is the box in the lower right corner of the window.)
11. To activate a window, click it.
12. To alternative increase and decrease a window's size, click its zoom box. (The zoom box is the box in the upper right corner of the window.)

. . . For Dummies: #1 Computer Book Series for Beginners

Quicken 5 For Macs For Dummies

Cheat Sheet

Iconbar Icon Descriptions: Almost a dozen sneaky shortcuts for busy people.

Icon	Description
Help	An electronic yelp for help — do this when you get into trouble
Accounts	Displays a window that lists all the accounts you've set up
Register	Displays the Register window for the account. Do this when you want to enter transactions for an account
Checks	Displays the Write Checks window so that you can record and print a check
Prn Chks	Prints any checks you've entered into the Write Checks window
Calendar	Shows Quicken's Financial Calendar
QuickFill	Displays a list of memorized transactions that Quicken can and will use to QuickFill fields and even entire transactions
Cat	Shows a list of categories and accounts so that you can select one
Transfer	Displays a dialog box that you can use to easily record transfers between accounts
Reconcile	Let's reconcile an account, dude
Quick	Displays a dialog box you can use to create a QuickReport

Speedy shortcuts that'll save you scads of time

Shortcut	Why you should try darn hard to remember this
⌘+E	Displays Splits dialog box so that you can use more than one category to describe a payment or deposit
⌘+X	Moves the selected text in a field to the Clipboard (so that you can paste it into some other field)
⌘+C	Copies the selected text in a field to the Clipboard (so that you can paste it into some other field)
⌘+V	Pastes what's on the Clipboard into the selected field
⌘+'	Pastes the current system date into a date field
⌘+Z	Yikes! Quicken, please undo what I just typed
⌘+R	Displays the Register window
⌘+J	Displays the Write Checks window
⌘+A	Displays the My Accounts window
⌘+L	Displays the Categories window
⌘+[	Goes to the other side of a transfer transaction

. . . *For Dummies: #1 Computer Book Series for Beginners*

 TM

References for the Rest of Us

COMPUTER BOOK SERIES FROM IDG

Are you intimidated and confused by computers? Do you find that traditional manuals are overloaded with technical details you'll never use? Do your friends and family always call you to fix simple problems on their PCs? Then the ... *For Dummies*™ computer book series from IDG is for you.

... *For Dummies* books are written for those frustrated computer users who know they aren't really dumb but find that PC hardware, software, and indeed the unique vocabulary of computing make them feel helpless. ... *For Dummies* books use a lighthearted approach, a down-to-earth style, and even cartoons and humorous icons to diffuse computer novices' fears and build their confidence. Lighthearted but not lightweight, these books are a perfect survival guide to anyone forced to use a computer.

> **"I like my copy so much I told friends; now they bought copies."**
> **Irene C., Orwell, Ohio**

> **"Quick, concise, nontechnical, and humorous."**
> **Jay A., Elburn, IL**

> **"Thanks, I needed this book. Now I can sleep at night."**
> **Robin F., British Columbia, Canada**

Already, hundreds of thousands of satisfied readers agree. They have made ... *For Dummies* books the #1 introductory level computer book series and have written asking for more. So if you're looking for the most fun and easy way to learn about computers, look to ... *For Dummies* books to give you a helping hand.

IDG BOOKS

QUICKEN 5 FOR MACS

FOR

DUMMIES™

QUICKEN 5 FOR MACS FOR DUMMIES™

by Stephen L. Nelson

IDG BOOKS

IDG Books Worldwide, Inc.
An International Data Group Company

San Mateo, California ♦ Indianapolis, Indiana ♦ Boston, Massachusetts

Quicken 5 For Macs For Dummies

Published by
IDG Books Worldwide, Inc.
An International Data Group Company
155 Bovet Road, Suite 310
San Mateo, CA 94402

Library of Congress Catalog Card No.: 94-78902

ISBN 1-56884-211-2

Printed in the United States of America

10 9 8 7 6 5 4 3 2 1

1B/QZ/SX/ZU

Distributed in the United States by IDG Books Worldwide, Inc.

Distributed in Canada by Macmillan of Canada, a Division of Canada Publishing Corporation; by Computer and Technical Books in Miami, Florida, for South America and the Caribbean; by Longman Singapore in Singapore, Malaysia, Thailand, and Korea; by Toppan Co. Ltd. in Japan; by Asia Computerworld in Hong Kong; by Woodslane Pty. Ltd. in Australia and New Zealand; and by Transworld Publishers Ltd. in the U.K. and Europe.

For general information on IDG Books in the U.S., including information on discounts and premiums, contact IDG Books 800-434-3422 or 415-312-0650.

For information on where to purchase IDG Books outside the U.S., contact Christina Turner at 415-312-0633.

For information on translations, contact Marc Jeffrey Mikulich, Foreign Rights Manager, at IDG Books Worldwide; FAX NUMBER 415-286-2747.

For sales inquiries and special prices for bulk quantities, write to the address above or call IDG Books Worldwide at 415-312-0650.

For information on using IDG Books in the classroom, or ordering examination copies, contact Jim Kelly at 800-434-2086.

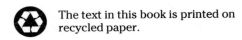

is a registered trademark of
IDG Books Worldwide, Inc.

The text in this book is printed on recycled paper.

About the Author

Stephen L. Nelson

Steve Nelson is a CPA with a masters degree in finance. As corny as it sounds, Steve truly enjoys writing books that make using personal computers easier and more fun. In fact, a substantiated rumor says Steve has written over 40 computer books.

Steve is the best-selling author on the Quicken product, having sold something like 300,000 books on Quicken.

Welcome to the world of IDG Books Worldwide.

IDG Books Worldwide, Inc., is a subsidiary of International Data Group, the world's largest publisher of business and computer-related information and the leading global provider of information services on information technology. IDG was founded more than 25 years ago and now employs more than 5,700 people worldwide. IDG publishes more than 200 computer publications in 63 countries (see listing below). Forty million people read one or more IDG publications each month.

Launched in 1990, IDG Books is today the fastest-growing publisher of computer and business books in the United States. We are proud to have received 3 awards from the Computer Press Association in recognition of editorial excellence, and our best-selling ...For Dummies series has more than 10 million copies in print with translations in more than 20 languages. IDG Books, through a recent joint venture with IDG's Hi-Tech Beijing, became the first U.S. publisher to publish a computer book in the People's Republic of China. In record time, IDG Books has become the first choice for millions of readers around the world who want to learn how to better manage their businesses.

Our mission is simple: Every IDG book is designed to bring extra value and skill-building instructions to the reader. Our books are written by experts who understand and care about our readers. The knowledge base of our editorial staff comes from years of experience in publishing, education, and journalism — experience which we use to produce books for the '90s. In short, we care about books, so we attract the best people. We devote special attention to details such as audience, interior design, use of icons, and illustrations. And because we use an efficient process of authoring, editing, and desktop publishing our books electronically, we can spend more time ensuring superior content and spend less time on the technicalities of making books.

You can count on our commitment to deliver high-quality books at competitive prices on topics customers want to read about. At IDG, we value quality, and we have been delivering quality for more than 25 years. You'll find no better book on a subject than an IDG book.

John J. Kilcullen

John Kilcullen
President and CEO
IDG Books Worldwide, Inc.

Acknowledgments

Hey, reader, a lot of people spent a lot of time working on this book to make Quicken easier for you. You should know who these people are in case you ever meet them in the produce section of the local grocery store squeezing cantaloupe.

The editorial folks are: Mary Bednarek, Diane Steele, Sandy Blackthorn, Tracy Barr, and Colleen Rainsberger. Thanks also to the production staff of Cindy Phipps, Michelle Worthington, Chris Collins, Tyler Connor, Carla Radzikinas and Gina Scott.

Special thanks to Tom Ware for his technical assistance and superb attention to detail. Thanks also to Michael Hart for his help!

(The publisher would like to give special thanks to Patrick J. McGovern, without whom this book would not have been possible.)

Credits

Publisher
David Solomon

Managing Editor
Mary Bednarek

Acquisitions Editor
Janna Custer

Production Director
Beth Jenkins

Senior Editors
Tracy L. Barr
Sandra Blackthorn
Diane Graves Steele

Production Coordinator
Cindy L. Phipps

Pre-Press Coordinator
Steve Peake

Associate Acquisitions Editor
Megg Bonar

Project Editor
Colleen Rainsberger

Technical Reviewer
Tom Ware

Production Staff
Chris Collins
J. Tyler Connor
Carla Radzikinas
Patricia Reynolds
Gina Scott

Proofreader
Michelle Worthington

Indexer
David Heiret

Book Design
University Graphics

Cover Design
Kavish + Kavish

Contents at a Glance

Cartoons at a Glance

By Rich Tennant

page 211

page 47

page 7

page 241

page 264

page 18

page 173

page 230

page 70

page 139

Table of Contents

Introduction

You aren't a dummy, of course. But, here's the deal. You don't have to be some sort of techno-geek or financial wizard to manage your financial affairs on a Macintosh. You have other things to do, places to go, and people to meet. And that's where Quicken for the Macintosh for Dummies comes in.

In the pages that follow, I give you the straight scoop on how to use Quicken for the Macintosh, without a lot of extra baggage, goofy tangential information, or misguided advice.

About This Book

This book isn't meant to be read cover to cover like some Tom Clancy page turner. Rather, it's organized into tiny, no sweat descriptions of how you do the things you'll need to do. If you're the sort of person who just doesn't feel right not reading a book from cover to cover, you can, of course, go ahead and read this thing from front to back.

I can only recommend this, however, for people who have already checked the TV listings. There may, after all, be a "Rockford Files" rerun on.

About The Author

If you're going to spend your time reading what I have to say, you deserve to know what my qualifications are. So let me take just a minute or so to do that.

I have an undergraduate degree in accounting and a masters degree in finance and accounting. I am also a certified public accountant (CPA).

I've spent most of the last ten years helping businesses set up computerized financial management systems. I started with Arthur Andersen & Co., which is one of the world's largest public accounting and system consulting firms. More recently, I've been working as a sole proprietor. When I wasn't doing financial systems work, I served as the controller of a small, 50-person computer software company.

One other thing. I've used Quicken for my business and for my personal record-keeping for several years.

None of this makes me sound like the world's most exciting guy, of course. I doubt you'll be inviting me to your next dinner party. Hey, I can deal with that.

But knowing a little something about me should give you a bit more confidence in applying the stuff talked about in the pages that follow. All joking aside, we're talking about something that's extremely important: *your money.*

How to Use This Book

I always enjoyed reading those encyclopedias my parents bought for me and my siblings. You could flip open, say, the E volume, look up *Elephants*, and then learn just about everything you need to know about elephants for a fifth grade report: where elephants lived, how much they weighed, and why they ate so much.

You won't read anything about elephants here. But you should be able to use this book in the same way. If you want to learn about something, look through the table of contents or index and find the topic - *check printing*, for example. Then flip to the correct chapter or page and read as much as you need or enjoy. No muss. No Fuss.

If there's anything else you want to learn about, of course, you just repeat the process.

What You Can Safely Ignore

Sometimes I had to provide step-by-step descriptions of tasks. I feel very bad that I had to do this. To make things easier for you, I described the tasks using bold text. That way you'll know exactly what you're supposed to do. I also provided a more detailed explanation in regular text. You can skip the regular text that accompanies the step-by-step descriptions if you already understand the process.

Here's an example that shows what I mean:

1. **Press Return.**

   Find the key that's labeled *Return*. Extend your index finger so that it rests ever so gently on the Return key. In one sure, fluid motion, press the Return key using your index finger. Then release your finger.

OK, that's kind of an extreme example. I never actually go into that much detail. But you get the idea. If you know how to press Return, you can just do that and not read further. If you need help - say with the finger part or something - just read the nitty-gritty details.

Is there anything else you can skip? Let me see now. . . . You can skip the Technical stuff, too. That information is really only here for those of you who like that kind of stuff.

For that matter, I guess the Tip stuff can be safely ignored, too. If you're some-one who enjoys trying it another way, go ahead and read the Tips.

What You Should Not Ignore (Unless You're a Masochist)

Don't skip Warning text. It's the text flagged with the picture of the nineteenth century bomb. It describes some things you really shouldn't do.

Out of respect for you, I'm not going to put stuff in these Warnings like, "Don't smoke." I figure that you're an adult. You can make your own lifestyle decisions.

So I'll reserve the Warnings for more urgent and immediate dangers — things akin to: "Don't smoke while you're filling the car with gasoline."

Three Foolish Assumptions

I'm going to assume just three things:

- You have a Macintosh.
- You know how to turn it on.
- You want to use Quicken.

By the way, if you haven't already installed Quicken and need some help, see Appendix A. It describes how to install Quicken if you're really lazy or really busy.

How This Book Is Organized

This book is organized into five mostly coherent parts.

Part I: Zen, Quicken, and the Big Picture

Part I, "Zen, Quicken, and the Big Picture," covers some up-front stuff you need to take care of. I promise I won't waste your time here. I just want to make sure that you get off on the right foot.

Part II: The Absolute Basics

This second part of Quicken for Macintosh For Dummies explains the core knowledge that you need to keep a personal or business checkbook with Quicken: using the checkbook, printing, balancing your bank accounts, and using the Quicken calculators.

Some of the stuff isn't very exciting compared to MTV. I'll work hard to make things more fun for you.

Part III: Home Finances

Part III talks about the sorts of things you may want to do with Quicken if you're using it at home: credit cards, loans, mutual funds, stocks and bonds. You get the idea. If you don't ever get this far—hey, that's cool.

If you do get this far, you'll find that Quicken provides some tools that eliminate not only the drudgery of keeping a checkbook, but also the drudgery of most other financial burdens.

While we're on the subject, I also want to categorically deny that Part III contains any secret messages if you read it backwards. (planner savings retirement the try to sure be, way the by, else anything for Quicken use don't you If.)

Part IV: Serious Business

The "Serious Business" section helps people who use Quicken in a business.

If you're pulling your hair out because you're using Quicken in a business, postpone the hair-pulling—at least for the time being. Read Part IV first. It will tell you about preparing payroll, tracking the amounts that customers owe you, and other wildly exciting stuff.

Part V: The Part of Tens

Gravity isn't just a good idea, it's also the law.

By tradition, the same is true for this part of a *...For Dummies* book. "The Part of Tens" provides a collection of ten-something lists: ten things you should do if you get audited, ten things you should do if you own a business, ten things to do when you next visit Acapulco—oops, sorry about that last one. Wrong book.

Appendixes

It's an unwritten rule that computer books have appendixes, so I included two. Appendix A tells you how to install Quicken in 10 easy steps. Appendix B is a glossary of key financial and Quicken terms.

Conventions Used in This Book

To make the best use of your time and energy, you should know about the conventions used in this book.

When I want you to type something such as **Hydraulics screamed as the pilot lowered his landing gear**, I'll put it in bold letters. When I want to type something that's short and uncomplicated, like **Jennifer**, it will still appear in bold type.

By the way, with Quicken you don't have to worry about the case of the stuff you type. If I tell you to type Jennifer, you can type **JENNIFER**. Or you can follow e. e. cummings lead and type **jennifer**.

Whenever I describe a message or information that you'll see on the screen, I present it as follows:

```
Surprise! This is a message on-screen.
```

Special Icons

Like many computer books, this book uses icons, or little pictures, to flag things that don't quite fit into the flow of things. ...*For Dummies* books use a standard set of icons that flag little digressions, such as:

This icon points out nerdy technical material that you may want to skip (or read, if you're suddenly feeling a bit, well, nerdy).

This icon points out some nugget of knowledge that will make your life easier.

This icon points out a friendly reminder to do something.

This icon points out a friendly reminder *not* to do something.

This icon points out information you may want to take special notice of.

Where to Next?

If you're just getting started, flip the page and start reading the first chapter.

If you've got a special problem or question, use the table of contents or the index to find out where the topic is covered and then turn to that page.

Part I
Zen, Quicken, and the Big Picture

The 5th Wave   By Rich Tennant

"THE IMAGE IS GETTING CLEARER NOW...I CAN ALMOST SEE IT...YES! THERE IT IS—THE GLITCH IS IN A FAULTY CELL REFERENCE IN THE FOOTBALL POOL SPREADSHEET."

In this part...

When you go to a movie theater, there are some prerequisites for making the show truly enjoyable. And I'm not referring to the presence of Sharon Stone or Arnold Schwarzenegger. Purchasing a bucket of popcorn is essential, for example. One should think strategically both about seating and about soda size. And one may even have items of a, well, personal nature to take care of — like visiting the little boys or girls room.

I mention all this stuff for one simple reason. To make getting started with Quicken as easy and fun as possible, there are some prerequisites, too. And this first part of Quicken For Windows For Dummies — "Zen, Quicken, and the Big Picture" — talks about these sorts of things.

Chapter 1

Setting Up Shop

● ●

In This Chapter

▶ Starting Quicken for the first time

▶ Setting up a bank account if you're a first-time user

▶ Retrieving existing Quicken data files

● ●

*I*f you haven't ever used Quicken, begin here. The next section tells you how to start the program for the first time.

You also learn how you go about setting up Quicken accounts to track banking activities — specifically, the money that goes into and out of a checking or savings account.

If you have already begun to use Quicken, don't waste any time reading this chapter unless you want the review. You already know the stuff it covers.

By the way, I assume you know a little bit about using your Macintosh. No, you don't have to be some sort of expert. Shoot, you don't even have to be all that proficient. You do need to know how to start programs (such as Quicken). It'll also help immensely if you know how to choose commands from menus and how to enter stuff into windows and dialog boxes.

If you don't know how to do these kinds of things, find the user guide that came with your Macintosh and skim through the first chapter or two. Or if you'd like to help a struggling author buy groceries, trot down to the same bookstore where you bought this book and pick up a copy of David Pogue's *Macs For Dummies.*

Starting Quicken for the First Time

The very first time you start Quicken, you'll see a little message box asking you to personalize your copy of Quicken, as shown in Figure 1-1. To do this, you're supposed to enter your name in the text box provided. Do this and click OK. If you don't feel comfortable doing this, you can also give Quicken someone else's name. Perhaps your neighbor's.

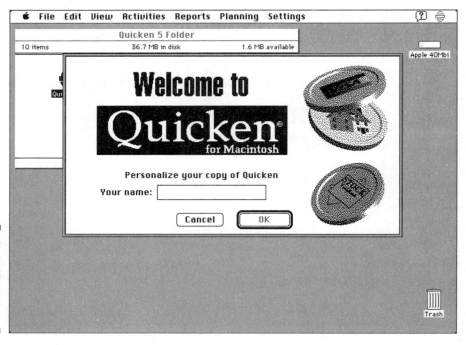

Figure 1-1:
You use this
dialog box
to give
Quicken
your name.

Quicken next displays the Introduction to Quicken window. If you read through the window text, you'll learn that Quicken wants you to learn how to get help, the difference between files and accounts, and what categories are. If you have the time, you can click the Continue button to see a little tutorial on what this stuff all means. Or you can click Skip. I don't really get a vote in what you do, but I don't think it would be a bad idea if you take the time to step through the tutorial. I'll wait right here.

Done with the tutorial? Okay, good. Quicken next displays a dialog box that asks you to name a new Quicken data file (see Figure 1-2). Quicken also displays this dialog box any time you choose the New command from the File menu. To name a new data file, just enter a name in the File For Your Accounts text box. If you want to locate the file someplace other than in the Quicken 5 folder, you also need to activate the pop-up menu at the top of the dialog box and select the other folder.

Once you've got the name thing figured out, click New.

Quicken next adds a few things to its desktop: a toolbar-iconbar kind of thing; a window that lists the accounts you've set up (you haven't set up any yet, so don't worry that you've missed something); a dialog box called the Set Up Account dialog box; and even a Qcard. A *Qcard* is Quicken's own, special version of Balloon help. When you move the selection cursor from field to field on a dialog box or window, Quicken displays a pop-up message box that offers suggestions and tips (such as "Type something-or-other here" and "Plant your

corn early this year"). Figure 1-3 shows the Quicken application window with
some new windows displayed.

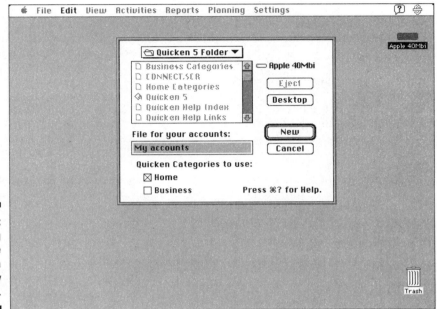

Figure 1-2:
The dialog
box you use
to create a
brand new
Quicken file.

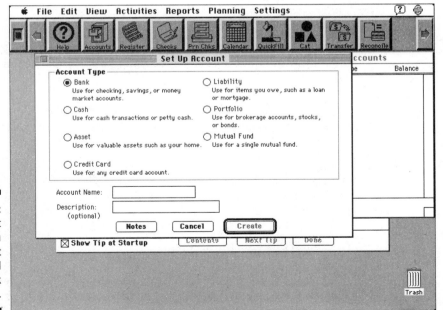

Figure 1-3:
The first
time you
start
Quicken, it'll
almost look
like this.

You won't be able to see it in the figure, but Quicken also displays a tip dialog box. This tip dialog box provides you with juicy nuggets of knowledge. You just read the tip and click Done. When you're tired of the whole tip thing and want to be left alone, simply unmark the check box. These tip boxes are called *Qcards*.

Quicken's Qcards present me, your new friend, with a dilemma. Oh sure. Qcards are really neat for new users — and you're probably a new user of Quicken. But darn it, if I leave the Qcards showing while I'm taking pictures of the screens for this book, the Qcards make things messy. So I turned off the Qcards for all the pictures in this book.

When you get tired of a Qcard, as you undoubtedly will, you can turn it off by clicking the close box in the Qcard's upper left corner.

I should mention an interesting little quirk of Qcards here, too. Qcards appear the first time you use a window or dialog box. If you turn off Qcards for one window or dialog box, for example, you'll still see Qcards for your other windows. To turn all the Qcards back on, just choose the Show Qcards command from the Help menu.

Setting Up a Bank Account for First-Time Users

Okay, let's say that you're new in town. Let's say that you haven't used Quicken before. What you need to do first is set up a bank account and tell Quicken which categories list you want to use.

The Set Up Account dialog box should still be showing if you've just started Quicken for the first time. If it isn't, choose the New Account command from the Edit menu. Follow these steps:

1. **Tell Quicken you want to set up a bank account.**

   Click the Bank option button to select it if it isn't already selected. (Option buttons are also known as *radio buttons.*)

2. **Name the account.**

   With the cursor in the Account Name text box, give the name of the bank account. You can name the account just about anything you want. I usually go for something that names the bank or that describes the account type, as in "First National" or "Checking."

3. **(Optional) Describe the account.**

   If the name you provide in step 2 just isn't enough, you can also provide a description. I don't think you need to worry about this field, but you can still use it. Perhaps you might use this field for the account number. Yeah. That wouldn't be a bad idea.

4. Click Create.

You know how this works, right? You move the mouse so that the pointer rests ever so gently over the Create button. Then you press the mouse button.

Quicken displays the register window for the account you've just created, as shown in Figure 1-4. You're almost in business. The opening balance will show as 0.00 — something we'll need to fix before we go any further.

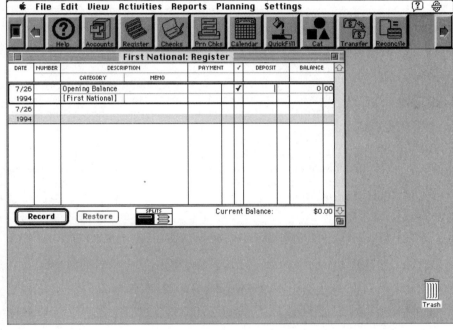

Figure 1-4:
The Quicken application window with a register window for your new account.

5. Find your checkbook.

Check your purse, your jacket, your desk, your briefcase, and so on. Wait a minute. I don't need to be telling you this stuff. Sorry.

6. Enter the account balance into the Deposit column.

This isn't as tough as it sounds. First of all, Quicken has already moved the selection cursor to the Deposit column. All you need to do is type a number. And the balance thing is pretty easy, too. This balance is the amount of money in your account on the date you want to begin your financial record-keeping. If you had four dollars and sixteen cents in your checking account on the date you choose, for example, type **4.16**.

By the way, the folks at Quicken really want you to use the ending balance from a bank statement. Let's not beat around the bush here. If your financial records are a mess, go ahead and follow Quicken's suggestion. If your financial records are as clean as a whistle, enter the balance your checkbook shows.

7. (Optional) Enter the date from which you want to begin your financial record-keeping.

Quicken uses the date from your Mac's internal clock as the date for the opening balance. But this may be wrong. If it is, move the cursor to the Date column for the Opening Balance row of the register — this will be the amount you just entered — and then enter a date using the MM/DD/YY format. If the date is January 1, 1994, for example, type **1/1/94**.

Some of the most valuable things you may want to do with Quicken require a full year of financial information. Because it won't take you that long to enter your checking transactions — even if it's for the whole year — I think it really makes more sense to use January 1 as the starting date and, therefore, the January 1 account balance as the starting balance.

8. Click Record.

Quicken records the opening balance transaction into the register. It also highlights the next row of the register by drawing a dark border around it. Figure 1-5 shows the register window after this opening balance transaction is entered.

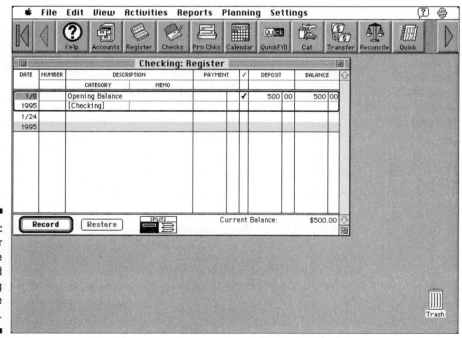

Figure 1-5:
The register after you've recorded the opening balance transaction.

About the iconbar

The iconbar is not a place where icons go to "tie one on." The iconbar is a set of command icons located at the top of the Quicken application window (refer to Figure 1-5). You can easily choose a common Quicken command by clicking one of these icons with the mouse.

I refer to the iconbar icons by their names in the pages that follow. If you want to see a list of the iconbar icons along with descriptions of what they do, flip open the front cover of this book.

Setting Up Quicken if You've Used Quicken before

Let's say that you're not new in town. Suppose that you're a Quicken veteran. An old hand. A long-time friend. Well, anyway, you get the idea.

If you used an earlier version of Quicken for the Macintosh, you need to either start from scratch or convert your old files. Starting from scratch is described earlier in this chapter. Converting your old files is described in the Quicken user documentation — but not here. (If you need more help with this, consult the documentation.)

Using the Open File command

To select and open your existing Quicken files, you use the Open File command on the File menu. Here's how:

1. **Choose the Open File command from the File menu.**

   Click File and then click Open File. Figure 1-6 shows the Open a Quicken Data File dialog box that appears after you choose the command. Quicken uses this dialog box to ask the burning question, "Hey, buddy, what file you wanna open?"

2. **Tell Quicken which folder the files are stored in.**

   If the correct folder isn't the one already shown in the pop-up menu in the Open a Quicken Data File dialog box, tell Quicken which folder is the correct one. Click the down arrow at the end of the pop-up menu. When you do, Quicken displays a list of the disks and folders your computer has. When the list of disks and folders appear, click the one where you've stored your Quicken files.

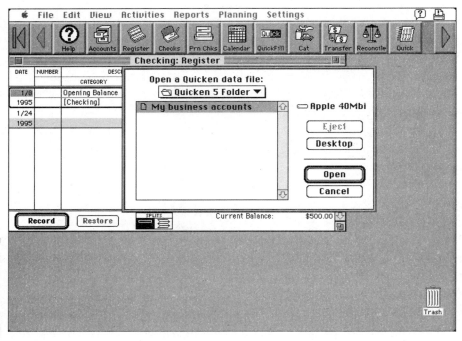

3. **Select the file from the File Name list box. (It's the only list box on the dialog box.)**

   After you tell Quicken on which disk and in which folder you stored your data files, the Quicken files in that location appear in the list box beneath the pop-up menu. Just click the file you want. If the list is long, click the first file in the list and then use the Page Up and Page Down keys or mouse to scroll through the list.

4. **Click Open.**

   After you find the file, click the Open button. Quicken opens the file and displays the active account in the register window.

Did you upgrade?

When you start Quicken for the first time, it may display the dialog box used to open a file, shown in Figure 1-6, rather than the dialog box used to create a file, shown in Figure 1-2. This happens because Quicken thinks that you've previously used Quicken and that you may have a Quicken file floating around someplace on your disk.

What if you can't find the Quicken file?

Uh-oh. This is a problem. But don't worry. You're not out of luck. What you need to do is to look through each of the folders on the disk. Or if you've got more than one hard disk, look through each of the directories on each of the hard drives.

Bummer, huh? Maybe this is a reasonable place to bring up a point. If you're a new user, it's best to just go with whatever an application (such as Quicken) suggests. If Quicken suggests that you use the Quicken 5 folder — this is the suggestion, by the way — just do it. If Quicken suggests that you view its tutorial about Help and the history of Quicken, just do it. If Quicken suggests that you take all your money, put it in a coffee can, and bury the can in your backyard. . . . Whoa, wait a minute. Bad idea.

Maybe there's a better rule. Hmmm. . . . How about this? While you shouldn't follow suggestions blindly and without thinking, you also shouldn't ignore Quicken's suggestions unless you have a good reason. And "Just because. . . ," "I don't know," and "For the heck of it" aren't good reasons.

Command shortcuts

If you look closely at any menu, including the File menu, you will notice that a key combination follows many menu names. After the File menu's Close Window command, for example, you can see ⌘+W. And after the File menu's Print Checks command, you can see ⌘+P. Key combinations such as ⌘+W and ⌘+P represent command shortcuts. By simultaneously pressing the two keys, you choose the command. Pressing ⌘+W, for example, is equivalent to choosing the Close Window command from the File menu.

The 5th Wave — By Rich Tennant

"I THINK I'VE FOUND YOUR FILE, MARGARET! IT FEELS LIKE A SPREADSHEET! RIGHT?! RIGHT?!"

Chapter 2
Introduction to the Big Picture

- -

- -

*B*efore you spend a bunch of time and money on Quicken, you must understand the big picture. You need to know what Quicken can do. You need to know what you actually want to do. And, as a practical matter, you need to tell Quicken what you want it to do.

Boiling Quicken Down to Its Essence

When you boil Quicken down to its essence, it does four things:

✔ *It lets you track your tax deductions.*

This makes preparing your personal or business tax return easier for you or your poor accountant, Cratchit.

✔ *It lets you monitor your income and outgo either on-screen or by using printed reports.*

Usually this stuff is great fodder for discussions about the family finances.

✔ *It lets you print checks.*

This device is mostly a time-saver, but it can also be useful for people who are neat-freaks.

✔ *It lets you track the things you own.*

It let's you track things such as bank accounts, investments, and real estate and the debts you owe, such as home mortgage principal, car loan balances, and credit card balances.

You can do some of these things or all of these things with Quicken.

Tracking tax deductions

To track your tax deductions, make a list of the deductions you want to track. To do so, pull out last year's tax return. Note which lines you filled in. This tactic works because there's a darn good chance that the tax deductions you claimed last year will also be the tax deductions you'll claim in the future.

A little bit later in the chapter you'll learn about Quicken's categories, which are used to track your tax deductions.

Monitoring spending

At our house we (Sue, my wife, and I, your humble author) use Quicken to monitor our spending on the little necessities of life — groceries, TV Guide, clothing, VCR rentals, baby food, cable television, and, well . . . you get the picture. (Yeah, I do watch too much TV.) To keep track of how much we spend on various items, we use Quicken's categories. Is the suspense building?

If there is a spending category you want to monitor, it's really easier to decide up front what it is. Your list of spending categories, by the way, shouldn't be an exhaustive list of super-fine pigeon-holes like "Friday-night Mexican food," "Fast food for lunch," and so on. To track your spending or eating out, one category named something like "Meals" or "Grub" usually is easiest.

In fact, I'm going to go out on a limb. You can probably get away with half a dozen categories or less:

- Household Items (food, toiletries, cleaning supplies)
- Car
- Rent (or mortgage payments)
- Entertainment and Vacation
- Clothing
- Work Expenses

Of course, you can expand this list if you want. Heck, you can include dozens and dozens of categories. My experience, though, is that you'll probably use only a handful of categories.

Do you want to print checks?

You can use Quicken to print checks. And this little trick provides a couple of benefits: it's really fast if you have a lot of checks to print, and your printed checks look very neat and darn professional.

To print checks you need to do just two things. First, look through the check supply information that comes with Quicken and pick a check form that suits your style. Then order the form. (The check forms that come with remittance advices — or check stubs — work well for businesses.)

You'll notice that the preprinted check forms aren't cheap. If you're using Quicken at home with personal-style checks (like those that go in your wallet), using computer checks may not be cost-effective. Even if you're using Quicken for a business where you are used to buying those outrageously expensive business-style checks, you'll still find computer checks a bit more expensive.

I'm pretty much a cheapskate, so I don't use printed checks at home or in my business. I should admit, however, that I also don't write very many checks.

By the way, I've "checked" around. Although you can order Quicken check forms from other sources (such as your local office supplies store), they're about the same price from Intuit (the maker of Quicken).

Tracking bank accounts, credit cards, and other stuff

You must decide which bank accounts and credit cards you want to track. In most cases, you want to track each bank account you use and any credit card on which you carry a balance.

You may also want to track other assets and liabilities. *Assets* are just things you own — investments, cars, a house, and so on. *Liabilities* are things you owe — margin loans from your broker, car loans, a mortgage, and so on.

Shoot, I suppose that you could even track the things your neighbor owns — or perhaps just those things you especially covet. I'm not sure that this is a very good idea, though. Maybe a healthier approach is to track just those things your neighbor owns that you've borrowed.

Setting Up Additional Accounts

When you start Quicken for the first time, you set up a bank account, such as a checking account. If you want to track any additional bank accounts — a savings account, for example — you must set them up, too.

Setting up an additional bank account

To set up a bank account, give the account a name and then its balance as of a set date. Here's how:

1. Choose the Accounts icon.

You can also choose Accounts from the View menu. Quicken displays the My Accounts list, as shown in Figure 2-1.

2. Choose the New button from the My Accounts window.

Quicken displays the Set Up Account dialog box (see Figure 2-2).

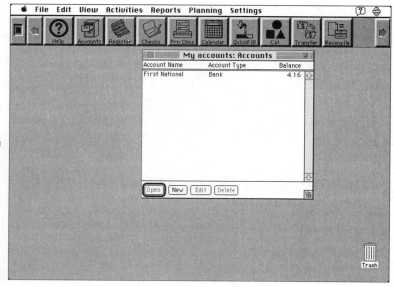

Figure 2-1:
Quicken displays a list of your accounts in a window. How thoughtful.

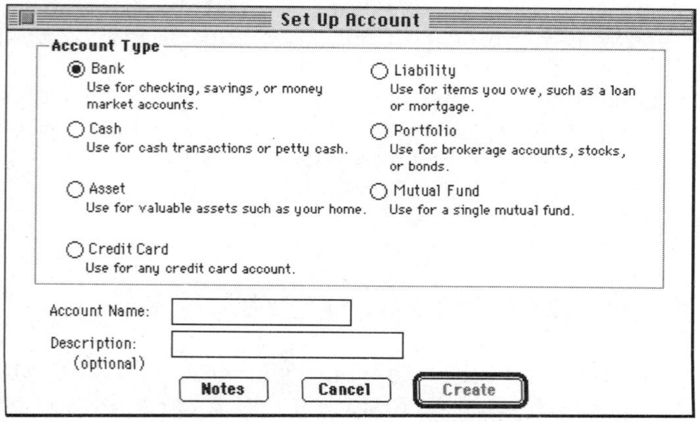

Figure 2-2:
The Set Up Account dialog box collects the information Quicken needs to create a new account.

3. Select the type of account.

Tell Quicken which type of account you want to set up by marking the Bank option button. I'm assuming that at this point you're just doing bank accounts. I'll discuss why and when you use the remaining account types later in the book.

Wondering about those other accounts? If the suspense is just killing you, look ahead. Chapter 10 describes how to set up and use credit card accounts. Chapter 14 describes how to set up and use a cash account. Chapter 11 describes how to set up and use liability accounts. Chapters 12 and 13 describe how to set up and use Investment accounts. And finally, Chapter 16 describes how to set up and use assets accounts.

4. Name the account.

With the cursor positioned in the Account Name text box, enter a name.

5. Enter the account description.

Move the cursor to the Description text box and type whatever you want to use to describe the account. Your favorite color, the name of your first boyfriend or girlfriend, or anything else you want. Heck, you may even want to follow the pack and type a description of the account here. (Some people get really crazy and enter the account number.)

6. Click Create.

Quicken displays a new register window, as shown in. Figure 2-3.

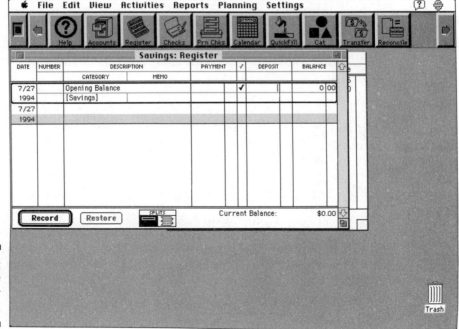

Figure 2-3:
The new register window.

7. Enter the bank account balance.

With the cursor positioned in the Deposit column — it should already be there — enter the balance using the number keys. (The folks at Intuit, by the way, really want you to use the balance from your bank statement. If you have terrible financial records — you haven't reconciled your account since Ronald Reagan left office, for example — this idea is probably good advice. If you have neat, accurate financial records, go ahead and use your check register balance.)

If you use the bank statement balance as your starting balance, enter all the transactions that cleared after the bank statement balance date. This should make sense, right? If a check or deposit isn't reflected in the bank statement figure, you must enter it later.

8. Enter the account balance date.

Enter the date you'll start keeping records for the bank account with Quicken. Move the cursor to the Date column and type the month number, a slash, the day number, a slash, and the year number. If you start on January 1, 1995, for example, type **1/1/95**.

9. Choose Record.

Quicken records the transaction into the register and updates the account balance, as shown in Figure 2-4.

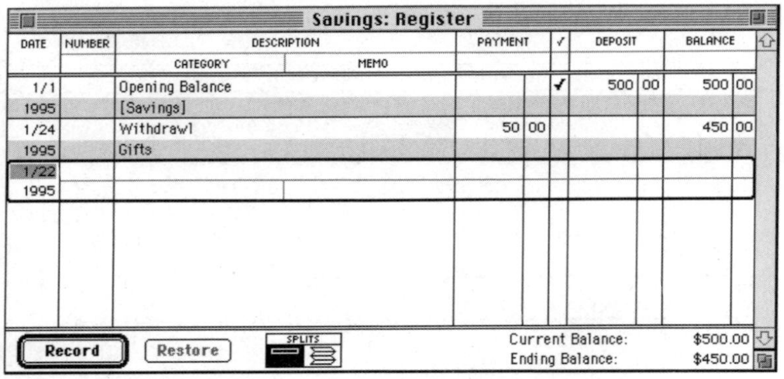

		Savings: Register					
DATE	NUMBER	DESCRIPTION		PAYMENT	✓	DEPOSIT	BALANCE
		CATEGORY	MEMO				
1/1		Opening Balance			✓	500 00	500 00
1995		[Savings]					
1/24		Withdrawl		50 00			450 00
1995		Gifts					
1/22							
1995							

Figure 2-4: Quicken updates the account balance once you record the transaction.

Record   Restore   SPLITS

Current Balance: $500.00
Ending Balance: $450.00

Hey, Quicken, I want to use that account!

If you've been reading this missive since Chapter 1, you now know you can have more than one account open at one time. You also may have guessed that because only one account appears in a register window, you work with one account at a time. The logic is simple: In Quicken you record income and expense for a particular account — a specific checking account, savings account, and so on.

And all this raises an interesting question. How do you tell Quicken which account you want to work with? You just use the My Accounts window to tell Quicken which account you want to work with (refer to Figure 2-1).

As a reminder, to display the My Accounts dialog box, you just choose the Accounts icon or choose the Accounts from the View menu. If you're experiencing a sense of *déjà vu* right now, it's probably because I've already told you about these commands earlier in the chapter.

After you display the My Accounts dialog box, highlight the account you want by using the up- and down-arrow keys or by using the mouse. Then press Enter or choose Open. Quicken selects the account and displays either the register window or the Write Checks window. Chapter 4 describes how to enter checking account transactions.

If the My Accounts window gets in your way after you display it, you can remove it from the application window by clicking its close box. The close box is that little square that appears in the upper left corner of the window.

Whipping Your Category Lists into Shape

When you set up Quicken (at least if you followed the approach described in Chapter 1), Quicken sets up a list of predefined categories.

The predefined categories lists may be just what you want. Then again, they may not. Table 2-1 shows the categories list, which focuses more on personal stuff than business stuff. Quicken's list of predefined categories is a great starting point for someone using Quicken at home, but maybe not so great for someone using Quicken in a small business.

If you are going to use Quicken in a business, you can choose the New File command from the File menu to create an entirely new file. (I describe how you do this in Chapter 8.) In this case, Quicken lets you say, "Provide me with the business categories," and uses the categories list shown in Table 2-2 instead. If you are using Quicken in a business, take a look at Table 2-2. If it shows the categories you want, flip ahead to Chapter 8 so that you can use the New File command.

Take a minute to look through the lists. If you find categories you don't need, cross them off the list in the book. You'll be able to delete them in a minute or so on your computer. If you need categories you don't see, add them at the bottom of the list. You'll be able to add them shortly.

Remember that determining whether you need or don't need a category is pretty simple:

- ✔ To track a certain income or spending item for income tax purposes, you need a Quicken category.

- ✔ To track a certain income or spending item because you're just interested in how much you really spend (renting VCR tapes, for example), you need a Quicken category.

- ✔ Because you also budget by categories, you need a category for any income or spending item you want to budget.

Table 2-1	The Predefined Categories
Category	*Description*
Income Categories	
Bonus	Bonus Income
CPP	Canadian Pension
Div Income	Dividend Income
Gift Received	Gift Received
Interest Earned	Interest Income
Old Age Pension	Old Age Pension
Other Inc	Other Income
Salary	Salary Income
Expense Categories	
Auto	Automobile Expenses
Fuel	Auto Fuel
Service	Auto Service
Bank Charges	Bank Charge
Charity	Charitable Donations
Childcare	Childcare Expense
Clothing	Clothing
Dining	Dining Out
Education	Education
Entertainment	Entertainment
Gifts	Gift Expenses
Groceries	Groceries
Home Repair	Home Repair & Maintenance

Category	Description
Household	Household Miscellaneous Expense
Insurance	Insurance
Auto	Automobile Insurance
Home	Homeowners Insurance
Interest Paid	Interest Expense
Investment Exp	Investment Expense
Medical	Medical Expense
Miscellaneous	Miscellaneous
Mortgage Int	Mortgage Interest Expense
Recreation	Recreation Expense
RRSP	Reg Retirement Savings Plan
Subscriptions	Subscriptions
Supplies	Supplies
Taxes	Taxes
Federal	Federal Tax
Medicare	Medicare Tax
Other	Miscellaneous Taxes
Property	Property Tax
Soc Sec	Social Security Tax
State	State Tax
UIC	Unemployment Insurance Commission
Utilities	Water, Gas, Electric
Gas & Electric	Gas and Electricity
Water	Water

Table 2-2	The Predefined Business Categories
Category	**Description**
Income Categories	
Gross Sales	Sales or service income
Interest Earned	Interest Income
Rent Income	Rental property income

(continued)

Table 2-2 *(continued)*

Category	Description
Expense Categories	
Ads	Advertising
Bad Debt	Advertising
Bank Charges	Bank Service Charges
Benefits	Employee Benefits
Car & Truck	Car and Truck Expenses
Commissions	Sales Commissions
Cost of Goods	Cost of Goods Sold
Labor	Cost of direct labor used to make items sold
Materials	Cost of materials used to make items sold
Other	Other costs of making items sold
Depletion	Natural Resources Depletion Expense
Depreciation	Depreciation Expense
Dues	Professional Dues
Entertainment	Entertainment Expense
Freight	Freight
Insurance	Business Insurance
Interest Paid	Interest Expense
Janitorial	Janitorial and Cleaning Expense
L&P Fees	Legal and Professional Fees
Late Fees	Late Payment Fees
Miscellaneous	A Catchall Category
Office	Office Expenses
Pensions	Employee Pension Expense
Repairs	Repairs
Returns	Returns and Allowances
Services	Other Services Expenses
Supplies	Supplies: paperclips, pens, etc.
Taxes	Federal and State Taxes
Telephone	Local and Long Distance Charges

Category	Description
Travel	Travel Expenses
Utilities	Water, Gas, Electric, and Garbage Expenses
Wages	Wages and Job Credits

Subcategories . . . yikes, what are they?

One of the things I'm trying to do with this book is make Quicken easier for you to use. A big part of this goal is telling you which features you can ignore if you're feeling a bit overwhelmed. Subcategories are among those things I think you can ignore.

"Subcategories," you say. "Yikes, what are they?"

Subcategories are categories within categories. If you look at the Taxes expense category in Table 2-1, for example, you'll notice a bunch of categories that follow the Tax category and are slightly indented: Federal (Federal Tax), Medicare (Medicare Tax), Other (Miscellaneous Taxes), Property (Property Tax), Soc Sec (Social Security Tax), and State (State Tax).

When you use subcategories, you can tag a transaction that pays, for example, federal taxes; you can further break down this category into subcategories such as federal income tax, Medicare tax, and Social Security tax. If you want to see a list of the ways you've spent your money, Quicken summarizes your spending both by category and, within a category, by subcategory. On a Quicken report, you can see this level of detail:

Taxes

Federal Tax	900
Medicare	100
Soc Sec	700
Total Taxes	1700

Subcategories are useful tools. There's no doubt about it. But they make working with Quicken a little more complicated and a little more difficult. As a practical matter, though, you usually don't need them. If you want to track a spending category, it really belongs on your list as a full-fledged category. For these reasons, I'm not going to get into subcategories here.

If you get excited about the topic of subcategories later on — after you have the hang of Quicken — you may want to peruse the Quicken documentation for more information.

If you want to use Quicken's subcategories, don't delete the subcategories shown in Table 2-1. If you don't want to use the subcategories, go ahead and delete them.

Supercategories . . . Double Yikes!

Supercategories are a recent innovation of the Intuit development people. The supercategory feature appears only in the most recent versions of the DOS, Windows, and Macintosh products. Supercategories combine categories into sets you can use in your reports and budgeting. Sure, they're sort of cool. But you don't need to worry about them if you're just starting with Quicken.

Three tips on categorization

I have just three tips for categorizing:

✔ *Cross off any category you won't use.*

If you're a Canadian, get rid of the United States tax categories. If you're a U.S. Citizen, get rid of the Canadian tax categories. Extra, unneeded categories just clutter your list. I think it's great if you can get down to just a handful of categories.

✔ *Don't be afraid to lump similar spending categories together.*

Take your utilities expense, for example. If you pay water, natural gas, electricity, and sewer, why not use a single Utilities category? If you pay different utility companies for your water, natural gas, electricity, and sewer, you'll still be able to see what you spent on just electricity, for example, even with a single, catch-all category for utilities.

✔ *Be sure to categorize anything that may be a tax deduction.*

Categorize medical and dental expenses, state and local income taxes, real estate taxes, personal property taxes, home mortgage interest and points, investment interest, charitable contributions, casualty and theft losses, moving expenses, unreimbursed employee expenses, and all those vague miscellaneous deductions. By the way, the foregoing is the complete list of itemized deductions at the time this book was being written.

Ch-ch-changing a category list

OK, you should now be ready to fix any category list problems. Basically, you will do three things: add categories, remove categories, and change category names and descriptions.

Adding categories you'd love to use

Adding categories is a snap. Here's all you have to do:

1. **Choose the Cat icon.**

   Quicken displays the Categories window (see Figure 2-5). This window lists the categories available and the accounts you've set up. You can also access this window by choosing Categories & Transfers command from the View menu.

2. **Click the New button in the Categories window.**

   Quicken, dutifully following your every command, displays the Set Up Categories dialog box (see Figure 2-6). It probably won't surprise you to learn that you use this puppy to describe the new category.

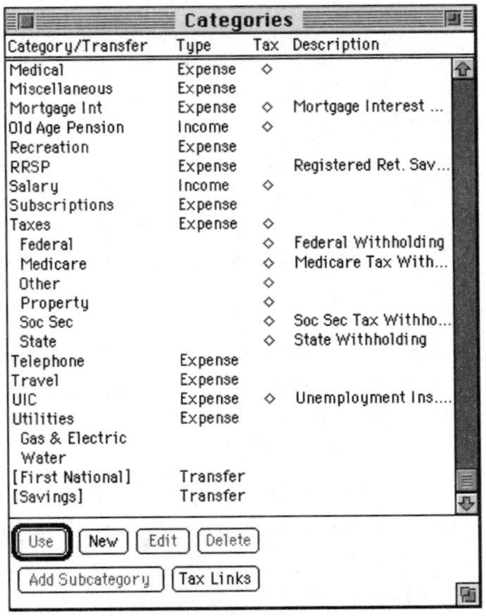

Figure 2-5:
The Categories window shows a list of your categories.

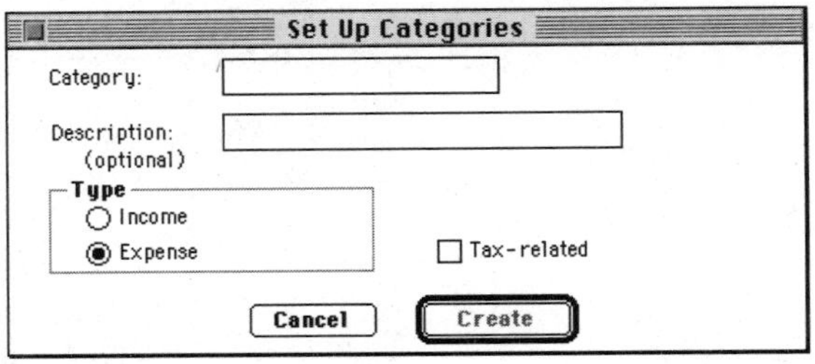

Figure 2-6:
The Set Up Categories dialog box.

3. Enter a short name for the category.

With the cursor positioned in the Category text box, enter a name. Although you can use up to 15 characters, use as short a name as possible to clearly identify the category. Why? Because you'll need to use this category name every time you want to tag a transaction to fall into the category.

4. Enter a description for the category.

Move the cursor to the Description text box and then describe the category. Here's where you can get long-winded if you want. If you don't enter a description, Quicken uses the category name on reports that show the category.

5. Indicate whether the category is an income category or an expense category.

Use your furry little friend, the mouse, to select the appropriate Income or Expense option button.

6. Indicate whether the category tracks an amount you will use on an input line on next year's tax return. (By line, I mean the actual tax form line — such as line 7 on the 1040 form.)

Move the cursor to the Tax-Related check box and then mark the check box if the category is tax-related, or unmark the check box if the category isn't tax-related. Just to clear up any confusion, vacationing in Hawaii isn't a tax deduction — even if the guy on Channel 22 promises it is.

7. Choose Create.

Quicken adds the new category to the Categories window shown in Figure 2-5 and then redisplays the window. Now that you understand the stuff in the Categories window, note that it shows the category name, its type, the notation that a category is tax-related, and, golly darn, even its description.

Adding a Subcategory

I know a lot of computer book writers feel differently, but my feeling is that I'm supposed to be working for you, the reader. My job — if you want to call it that — is to help you get started and up-to-speed with Quicken. And sure, it's OK if I offer up some suggestions and every once in a while share a little advice. But the truth is, you're the boss, and I'm the lackey.

Which brings up the point of subcategories. If you've totally blown off my admonition not to use subcategories, you may want to know how to work with these babies. Here's the straight scoop. With the Categories window displayed, select the category to which you want to add a subcategory. Then click the Add Subcategory button. Quicken will display the Set Up Categories dialog box — yes, the same one shown in Figure 2-6. Enter the subcategory name in the Category text and a description for the new subcategory in the Description text box. Mark the Tax-related check box if the category tracks taxable income or a tax deductible expense. Then click Create.

Removing categories you loathe

Removing categories takes only a couple of keystrokes or mouse actions. With the Categories window displayed, use the arrow keys or the mouse to highlight the category you want to remove. Then click the Delete button. Quicken displays a message that asks you to confirm your decision. Assuming that you want to remove the selected category, select Yes; otherwise, select No.

Changing category names and descriptions

In case you later discover you made some mistake, such as misspelling a word in a description, Quicken lets you change a category name, its type, its description, and its tax-related setting.

To do so, display the Categories window. Use the arrow keys or click your mouse to highlight the category you want to change. Then click the category and choose the Edit button. In a surprise move, Quicken displays a dialog box which is cleverly labeled Edit Categories (see Figure 2-7). The text boxes and option buttons within the dialog box describe the selected category's information: name, description, type, and tax-related status.

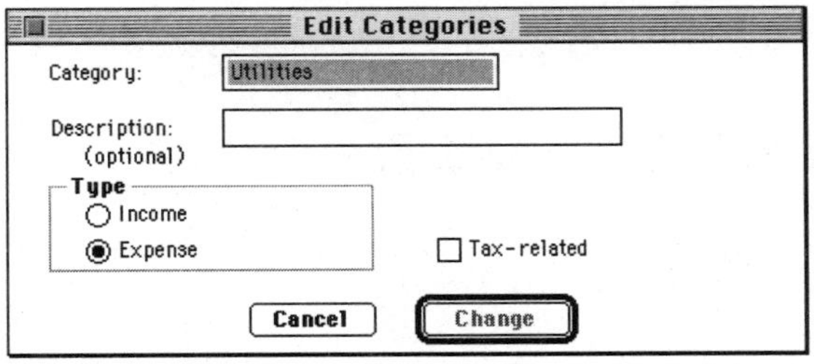

Figure 2-7:
The Edit
Categories
dialog box.

```
┌──────────────── Edit Categories ────────────────┐
│  Category:    [ Utilities             ]          │
│                                                  │
│  Description: [                                ] │
│  (optional)                                      │
│  ┌─ Type ──────────────────────────────────────┐ │
│  │  ○ Income                                    │ │
│  │  ● Expense          □ Tax-related            │ │
│  └──────────────────────────────────────────────┘ │
│            ( Cancel )   ( Change )               │
└──────────────────────────────────────────────────┘
```

Make the changes you want by replacing text box contents or changing option button settings. Then choose OK to save your changes and return to the Categories window.

The Small Matter of Income Taxes

If you're planning to take the financial information you collect with Quicken and export it to a tax preparation package such as MacNTax or TaxCut, there's one final thing you need to fiddle-faddle with. You need to tell Quicken on which tax forms and tax form lines the information from a category gets plopped. For example, you may know that you need to report your total salary and wages on the first line of the 1040 form. But Quicken doesn't know that. You need to tell it.

To do this, open the Categories window and then click Tax Links. Quicken displays the Assign Tax Links dialog box, shown in Figure 2-8.

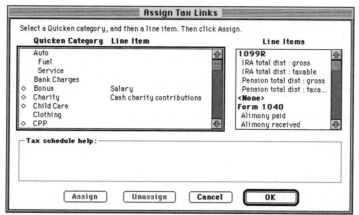

Figure 2-8:
The Assign
Tax Links
dialog box.

To tell Quicken on which tax form and tax form line a category total goes, select the category from the Quicken Category/Line Item list box shown on the left half of the dialog box. Then select the tax form and tax form line from the Line Items list box shown on the right half of the dialog box.

Do You Need a Little Class?

Categories aren't the only way you can summarize your financial records. Quicken provides a second tool, called *classes*.

I have mixed feelings about classes, and I'll tell you why. I use them — with good success — to track the types of gross income that my business produces (writing, consulting, teaching, and so on) and the types of expenses my business incurs in these activities. (In fact, *Writing*, *Consulting*, and *Teaching* are the names of three of my classes.)

Classes present a couple of problems, however. First, you can't budget by classes. (Before you say, "Ah, Steve, I don't want to budget," please read the next chapter.) Second, you need to remember to tag transactions with their classes. In comparison, Quicken will remind you to include a category.

Because I really don't think you'll use it now, I'm not going to describe how you use classes. But if you get really comfortable with Quicken's categories and you want a way to organize your financial information across categories, consider using Quicken's classes. You can flip to the Quicken documentation to get this information.

Chapter 3
Maximum Fun, Maximum Profits

● ●

● ●

I don't think a budget amounts to financial handcuffs and neither should you. A budget is really a plan that outlines the way people need to spend their money to achieve the maximum amount of fun or the way businesses need to spend their money to make the most profit.

Should You Even Bother?

A budget, as you probably know, is just a list of the ways you earn and spend your money. And if you've created a good, workable categories list, you're halfway to a good solid budget. In fact, the only step left is to specify how much you earn in each income category and how much you spend in each expense category.

Does everybody need a budget? No, of course not. Maybe at your house, you're already having a bunch of fun with your money. Maybe in your business, you make your money so effortlessly that there's really no reason to plan your income and outgo.

For everyone else, though, a budget improves your chances of getting to wherever it is you want to go financially. In fact, I'll stop calling it a budget. The word has such negative connotations. I know — I'll call it *The Secret Plan*.

Serious Advice about Your Secret Plan

Before I walk you through the mechanics of outlining your secret plan, I want to give you a few tips.

Your personal secret plan

You can do certain things to make it more likely that your secret plan will work. Here are four things:

✔ *Plan your income and expenses as a family.*

When it comes to this sort of planning, two heads are invariably better than one. What's more, though I don't really want to get into marriage counseling here, a family's budget — oops, I mean secret plan — needs to reflect the priorities and feelings of everyone who has to live within the plan. Don't use a secret plan as a way to minimize what your spouse spends on clothing or on long-distance telephone charges talking to relatives in the old country. You need to resolve clothing and long-distance charges issues before you finalize your secret plan anyway.

✔ *Include some cushion in your plan.*

In other words, don't budget to spend every last dollar (or if you're German, every last *deutsche mark*). If you plan from the start to spend every dollar you make, you'll undoubtedly have to fight the mother of all financial battles: paying for unexpected expenses when you don't have any money. (You know the sort of things I mean: car repairs, medical expenses, or that cocktail dress or tuxedo you absolutely must have for a special party.)

✔ *Regularly compare your actual income and outgo to your planned income and outgo.*

This is probably the most important part and also what Quicken will help you with the most. As long as you use Quicken to record what you receive and spend, you'll be able to print reports showing what you planned and what actually occurred.

✔ *Make adjustments as necessary.*

When there are problems with your secret plan — and there will be — you'll know that your plan isn't working. You can then make adjustments, by spending a little less calling the old country, for example.

Your business secret plan

These tips for personal secret plans also apply to businesses. But I've also got a special tip for small businesses using Quicken. (I'm going to write very quietly now so that no one else hears. . . .)

Here's the secret tip: go to the library, ask for the Robert Morris & Associates Survey, and look up the ways that other businesses like yours spend money.

This is really cool. Robert Morris & Associates surveys bank lending officers and then creates a summary of the information these bankers receive from their customers and publishes the results. For example, you can look up what percentage of sales the average tavern spends on beer and peanuts.

Plan to take an hour or so at the library. It takes a while to get used to the way the Robert Morris & Associates information is displayed. There won't actually be a line on the tavern's page labeled "beer and peanuts," for example. It'll be called "cost of goods sold" or some similarly vague accounting term. You have to love those accountants, huh?

Remember to make a few notes so that you can use the information you glean to better plan your own business financial affairs.

Two things that really goof up secret plans

Because we're talking about you-know-what, let me touch on a couple of things that really goof up your financial plans: windfalls and monster changes.

The problem with windfalls

Your boss smiles, calls you into his office, and then gives you the good news. You're getting a bonus — $5,000! *Yippee!* You think to yourself. Outside, of course, you maintain your dignity. You act grateful, but not gushy. Then you call your husband.

Here's what happens next. Bob (that's your knucklehead husband's name) gets excited, congratulates you, and tells you he'll pick up a bottle of wine on the way home to celebrate.

On your drive home you mull over the possibilities and conclude that you can use the $5,000 as a big down payment for that new family van you've been looking at. (With the trade-in and the $5,000, your payments will be a manageable $200 a month.)

Bob, on his way home, stops to look at those golf clubs he's been coveting for about three years, charges $800 on his credit card, and then, feeling slightly guilty, buys you the $600 set. (Let's say that you're just starting to play golf.)

You may laugh at this scenario, but suppose that it really happened. Furthermore, pretend that you really do buy the van. At this point, you've spent $6,400 on a van and golf clubs, and you've signed up for what you're guessing will be another $200-a-month payment.

This doesn't sound all that bad now, does it?

Here's the problem. When you get your check, it's not going to be $5,000. You're probably going to pay roughly $400 of Social Security and Medicare taxes, maybe around $1500 in federal income taxes, and then probably some state income taxes.

There may be other money taken out, too, for forced savings plans (like a 401K plan) or for charitable giving. After all is said and done, you'll get maybe half the bonus in cash — say $2,500.

Now you see the problem, of course. You've got $2,500 in cold, hard cash, but with Bob's help you've already spent $6,400 and signed up for $200-a-month payments.

In a nutshell, there are two big problems with windfalls. Problem one is that you never get the entire windfall — yet it's easy to spend like you will. Problem two is that windfalls, by their very nature, tend to get used for big purchases (often as down payments) that ratchet up your living expenses. Boats. New houses. Cars.

Regarding windfalls, my advice to you is simple:

- ✔ Don't spend a windfall until you actually hold the check in your hot little hand. (It's even better to wait, say, six months. That way Bob can really think about whether he needs those new golf clubs.)

- ✔ Don't spend a windfall on something that increases your monthly living expenses without redoing your budget.

About monster income changes

If your income changes radically, it becomes *really* hard to plan.

Suppose that your income doubles. One day you're cruising along making $35,000 and the next you're suddenly making $70,000. (Congratulations, by the way.)

I'll tell you what you'll discover should you find yourself in this position. You'll find that $70,000 a year isn't as much money as you might think.

Go ahead. Laugh. But for one thing, if your income doubles, your income taxes almost certainly more than quadruple.

One of the great myths about income taxes is that the rich don't pay very much or that they pay the same percentage. Poppycock. If you make $30,000 a year and you're an average family, you probably pay about $1,500 in federal income taxes. If you make $200,000 a year, you'll pay about $45,000 a year. So if your salary increases by roughly seven times, your income taxes increase by about thirty times. I don't bring this up to get you agitated about whether it's right or fair to make the rich pay more. I bring it up so that you can better plan for any monster income changes you experience.

Another thing — and I know it sounds crazy — but you'll find it hard to spend, for example, $70,000 smartly when you've been making a lot less. And if you start making some big purchases like houses and cars and speedboats, you'll not only burn through a lot of cash, you'll also ratchet up your monthly living expenses.

Monster income changes that go the other way are even more difficult. If you've been making, say, $70,000 a year and then see your salary drop to a darn respectable $35,000, it's going to hurt, too. And probably more than you think.

That old living-expenses ratcheting effect comes into play here, of course. Presumably, if you've been making $70,000 a year, you've been spending it — or most of it.

But there are some other reasons why it's very difficult — at least initially — to have a monster salary drop. You've probably chosen friends (nice people, like the Joneses), clothing stores, and hobbies that are in line with your income.

Another thing is sort of subtle. You probably denominate your purchases in amounts related to your income. Make $35,000 and you think in terms of $5 or $10 purchases. But make $70,000 a year and you think in terms of $10 or $20 purchases.

This all makes perfect sense. But if your income drops from $70,000 down to $35,000, you'll probably still find yourself thinking of those old $20 purchases.

So what to do? If you do experience a monster income change, redo your secret plan. Be particularly careful and thoughtful, though.

Zen and monster income changes

To conclude this secret plan business, I'll make a philosophical digression.

At the point you've provided yourself and your family with the creature comforts — a cozy place to live, adequate food, and comfortable clothes — more stuff won't make the difference you think.

I don't mean to minimize the challenges of raising a family of four on, say, $14,000 a year. But, hey, I work with a fair number of wealthy people. What continually surprises me is that when you get right down to it, someone who makes $300,000 or $600,000 a year doesn't live a better life than someone who makes $30,000.

Sure, they spend more money. They buy more stuff. They buy more expensive stuff. But they don't live better. They don't have better marriages. Their kids don't love them more. They don't have better friends or more considerate neighbors.

But you already know all this. I know you do.

Setting Up a Secret Plan

OK, enough metaphysical stuff. Let's set up your budget — er, I mean, secret plan.

Getting to the Set Up Budgets window

To get to the window in which you'll enter your budget, just choose the Budget command from the Planning menu. Quicken displays the Budget window shown in Figure 3-1.

There's nothing very complicated about the window. The income and expense categories you've created appear down the left edge of the screen. There are subtotals for any categories with subcategories (if you have these), for the total inflows and for the total outflows.

Across the top of the screen, there's a row of icons that makes your budgeting job easier. (I'll describe the more useful commands in a few paragraphs and provide brief descriptions of those that aren't quite as useful.)

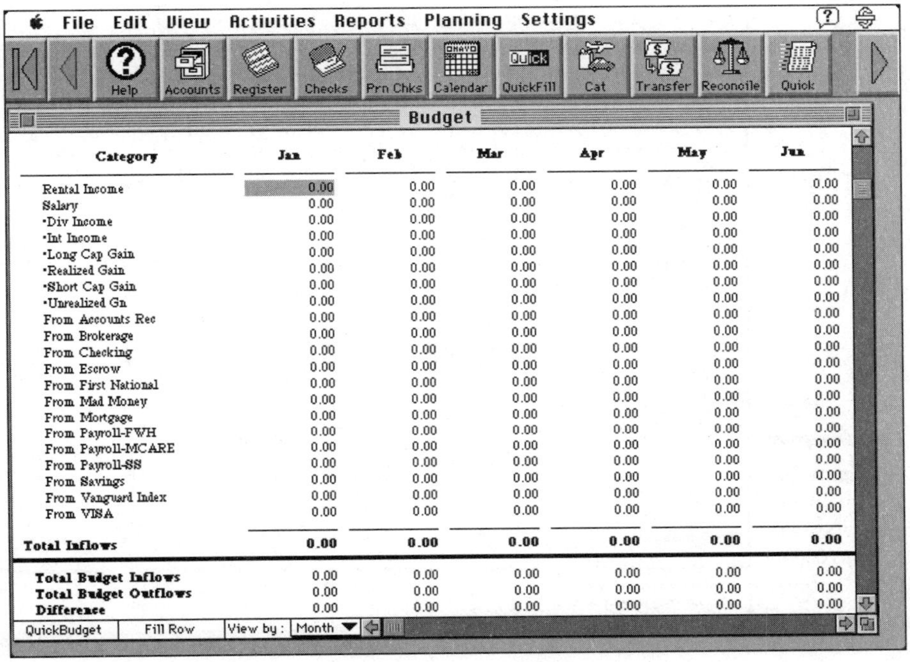

Figure 3-1:
The Budget,
er, I mean,
Secret Plan
window.

Entering budgeted amounts the simple way

Here's the two-step way to enter budgeted amounts — not to be confused with the Texas Two-Step:

1. **Select the amount you want to budget.**

   Highlight the income or expense amount for which you want to enter a budgeted amount either by using the arrow keys or by clicking the zeros with the mouse. To select the January Income budget field, for example, click it with the mouse. Or use the arrow keys to move the highlight to the field. (You're doing this so that you can enter the budgeted amount.)

2. **Enter the budgeted amount.**

   Type the amount you've budgeted. Suppose that you've already selected the January Salary budget amount field and now need to enter a value. Say that you take home $3,000 a month. To use this figure as the January Salary budget, type **3000**.

   After you press Enter, Quicken updates any subtotals and grand totals that use the Salary amount, as shown in Figure 3-2. For example, look at the Total Inflows subtotal just under the Salary row. And look at the Total column along the right edge of the window.

| ⌘ | File | Edit | View | Activities | Reports | Planning | Settings | ⑦ | 🖶 |

[toolbar: Help | Accounts | Register | Checks | Prn Chks | Calendar | QuickFill | Cat | Transfer | Reconcile | Quick]

Budget

Category	Jan	Feb	Mar	Apr	May	Jun
Rental Income	0.00	0.00	0.00	0.00	0.00	0.00
Salary	3,000.00	3,000.00	3,000.00	3,000.00	3,000.00	3,000.00
•Div Income	0.00	0.00	0.00	0.00	0.00	0.00
•Int Income	0.00	0.00	0.00	0.00	0.00	0.00
•Long Cap Gain	0.00	0.00	0.00	0.00	0.00	0.00
•Realized Gain	0.00	0.00	0.00	0.00	0.00	0.00
•Short Cap Gain	0.00	0.00	0.00	0.00	0.00	0.00
•Unrealized Gn	0.00	0.00	0.00	0.00	0.00	0.00
From Accounts Rec	0.00	0.00	0.00	0.00	0.00	0.00
From Brokerage	0.00	0.00	0.00	0.00	0.00	0.00
From Checking	0.00	0.00	0.00	0.00	0.00	0.00
From Escrow	0.00	0.00	0.00	0.00	0.00	0.00
From First National	0.00	0.00	0.00	0.00	0.00	0.00
From Mad Money	0.00	0.00	0.00	0.00	0.00	0.00
From Mortgage	0.00	0.00	0.00	0.00	0.00	0.00
From Payroll-FWH	0.00	0.00	0.00	0.00	0.00	0.00
From Payroll-MCARE	0.00	0.00	0.00	0.00	0.00	0.00
From Payroll-SS	0.00	0.00	0.00	0.00	0.00	0.00
From Savings	0.00	0.00	0.00	0.00	0.00	0.00
From Vanguard Index	0.00	0.00	0.00	0.00	0.00	0.00
From VISA	0.00	0.00	0.00	0.00	0.00	0.00
Total Inflows	**3,000.00**	**3,000.00**	**3,000.00**	**3,000.00**	**3,000.00**	**3,000.00**
Total Budget Inflows	3,000.00	3,000.00	3,000.00	3,000.00	3,000.00	3,000.00
Total Budget Outflows	0.00	0.00	0.00	0.00	0.00	0.00
Difference	3,000.00	3,000.00	3,000.00	3,000.00	3,000.00	3,000.00

QuickBudget | Fill Row | View by : Month ▼

Figure 3-2:
The Budget window with a $3,000-a-month salary input.

You need to scroll the screen to the right to see months near the middle and end of the year. Unless you're using a really short categories list, you need to scroll down to see categories (usually expense categories) that aren't at the top of the list.

The easiest way to scroll is by using the mouse to click and drag on the scroll bars.

If you don't want to use the mouse or you just need to be different, you can use the old navigation keys, too. To scroll the screen right by moving the selection cursor, just press the Tab key. To scroll the screen back, or left, by moving the selection cursor press Shift+Tab. To scroll the screen up and down, use the PgUp and PgDn keys.

The Category row doesn't scroll when you move the window left and right. Oh, something else. The Total Budget Inflows and Total Budget Outflows rows don't scroll when you move the window up and down. Quicken leaves these elements frozen in the window so that you can tell which column and row is which and how things are going.

Entering budgeted amounts the fast way

It just figures, doesn't it? There's the simple way and there's the fast way, and "never the 'twain shall meet."

If monthly budgeted amounts are the same over the year

Enter the first month's figure (as I described earlier). After you've done this, choose the Fill Row button, which appears at the bottom of the window. (If you can't see the Fill Row button on your screen, resize the Budget window so that you can see the bottom of the screen.

If budgeted amounts are the same as last year

If you used Quicken for record-keeping in the preceding year, you can copy the actual amounts from the previous year and use these as part or all of the current year's budget.

To do so, choose the QuickBudget button. Quicken displays the Automatically Create Budget dialog box, as shown in Figure 3-3. You use it to tell Quicken what it should copy from last year.

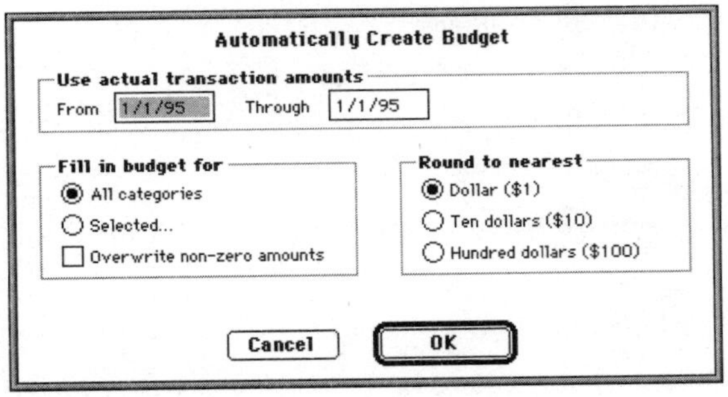

Figure 3-3:
The Auto-
matically
Create
Budget
dialog box.

Automatically Create Budget

Use actual transaction amounts
From `1/1/95` Through `1/1/95`

Fill in budget for
◉ All categories
○ Selected...
☐ Overwrite non-zero amounts

Round to nearest
◉ Dollar ($1)
○ Ten dollars ($10)
○ Hundred dollars ($100)

[Cancel] [**OK**]

Here's how:

1. **Indicate which months you want to copy.**

   Use the From and To text boxes to indicate from which months in the previous year actual category totals should be copied. If you want to copy the entire previous year and it's now 1996, for example, specify these entries as **1/1/95** and **12/31/95**.

2. Indicate whether the actual category totals should be rounded.

Want to round the actual category totals? No problem. Just use the Round To Nearest option buttons to indicate how much rounding you want: to the nearest $1, to the nearest $10, or to the nearest $100.

3. Limit the categories automatically budgeted (optional).

To tell Quicken you want only some of your categories automatically budgeted, mark the Selected option button in the Fill In Budget For option button set. Quicken adds a list of categories to the dialog box (see Figure 3-4). Indicate which categories should be automatically budgeted by clicking them. To mark or unmark a category, click it. As you click, Quicken marks. (Try a click and you'll see what I mean.) To mark all the categories, choose All. To unmark all the categories, choose None. To return to the Automatically Create Budget dialog box, choose OK.

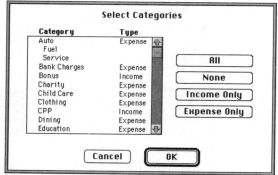

Figure 3-4:
The Select
Categories
dialog box.

4. (Optional) Tell Quicken if you want to wipe out your existing budget.

If you want Quicken's automatic budgeting feature to wipe out, or erase, any budgeting numbers you've already entered, mark the Mark the Overwrite non-zero amounts check box.

5. Choose OK.

Quicken uses the information entered in the Automatically Create Budget dialog box and the preceding year's actual category totals to completely fill in the Budget window.

When you finish entering your budget

After you enter your secret plan, either the simple way or the fast way (if you're the adventurous type), you can just close the Budget window. Quicken saves your work automatically.

I'll talk more about using the budget in later chapters (Chapter 6, for example). If you want to print a hard copy (computerese for paper) of the budget, choose the Print Budget command from the File menu. (If you have a printing question, go to Chapter 6.)

You're not going to use the budget for a while. But don't worry. In Chapter 6, I explain how to print reports, including a report that compares your actual spending with, ugh, your budget. Stay tuned. Same time. Same place. Same Bat channel.

What about the View By list box?

If you look closely at the Budget window, you can see that I haven't described the View By list box that also appears at the bottom of the Budget window.

To use the View By list box, click the button that's just right of the list box name. When you do, Quicken displays a pop-up list that lists three budget viewing options: Month, Quarter and Year. To choose a selection, you just click. Here's the lowdown on the various View by options:

- *Month.* Tells Quicken you want to budget by the month. You don't need to use this option button unless you've used one of the other column's buttons; Quicken budgets by the month unless you tell it to do otherwise.

- *Quarter.* Tells Quicken you want to budget by the quarter.

- *Year.* Tells Quicken you really are a big picture person (or business) and that you'll be budgeting by the year. (If you flip-flop between months, quarters, and years, Quicken automatically converts the budget figures for you.

Part II
The Absolute Basics

The 5th Wave — By Rich Tennant

PORTRAIT OF A CYBERHOLIC

CYBERHOLICS SPEND HOURS BALANCING THEIR CHECKBOOKS ON A COMPUTER, WHEN THEY COULD DO IT IN MINUTES WITH A PEN AND CALCULATOR.

In this part...

OK, you're ready for the show to start. Which is good. This part — "The Absolute Basics" — covers all the nitty gritty details of using Quicken to keep your personal and business financial records.

If you're just starting to use the Quicken program or if you've just come from Part I, you'll find the stuff covered here dang important — dare I say essential — to using Quicken even in the most basic way.

Chapter 4

Checkbook on a Computer

This is it. The big time. You're finally going to do those everyday Quicken things: entering checks, deposits, and transfers. Along the way, you'll also learn about some of the neat tools that Quicken provides for making these tasks easier, more precise, and faster.

Finding Your Checkbook

To enter checkbook transactions, use the register window (see Figure 4-1). If you don't see the register window, choose the Register icon from the iconbar.

If you've set up more than one account — say you've set up both a checking account and a savings account — you may need to tell Quicken which account you want to work with. Geez Louise, how can you tell if Quicken gets confused? Easy. The register window title bar names the wrong account. To correct this problem, just choose the Accounts icon from the iconbar and double-click the right account.

The starting balance you specified as part of setting up the account will be the first account listed. Figure 4-1, for example, shows a starting balance of $4.16. Bummer.

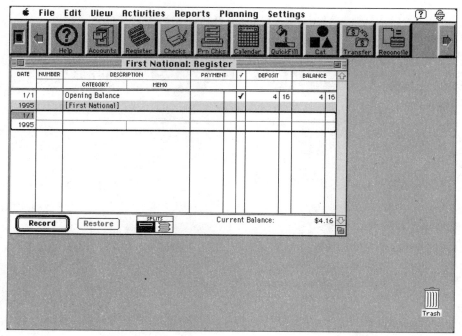

Figure 4-1:
The register
window.

The account name appears at the top of the register window.

As you move the selection cursor through the register window's fields, Quicken may display *Qcards* — little message boxes that tell you what goes where — if you haven't already turned them off. These little reminders are helpful but can get a little tiresome in much the same way a back-seat driver gets tiresome.

I turned them off because I reached my breaking point. When you reach your breaking point, click the close box on the Qcard currently showing. This tells Quicken, "Geez, enough already. Stop nagging me, will ya?"

Recording Checks

First things first: you can enter checks using either the register window (refer to Figure 4-1) or the Write Checks window, described in Chapter 5.

You use the register window for the checks you don't want to print with Quicken; you use the Write Checks window to enter the checks you do want to print using Quicken. (This isn't an *ironclad* rule, but it does make things easier for you, so it's the rule we'll follow.)

Entering a check into the register

OK, back to the chase. Entering a check in the register window is a simple matter of describing who you wrote it to and how much you paid. Let's say, for the sake of illustration, that you paid $25.50 to the cable television company for your monthly cable service. Here's how you enter this check:

1. **Enter the check date.**

   Move the cursor to the Date field in the next empty row of the register (if it isn't already there) and type the date using the MM/DD format. January 1, 1995, for example, gets entered as $^1/1$. You usually won't have to enter the year because Quicken retrieves the current year number from the little clock inside your Macintosh.

    You can adjust the date in a date field using the + and – keys. The + key adds one day to the current date; the – key subtracts one date from the current date.

2. **Enter the check number.**

   Move the cursor (or tab) to the Number field. Type the next check number. You can also press the + key to have Quicken create the check number by adding 1 to the last check number you used. Oh. I should tell you about another little quirk. You can use the + or – key to increase or decrease the check number.

3. **Enter the payee.**

   Move the cursor to the Description field. Enter the name of the person or business you're paying. If the cable company name is "Movies Galore," for example, type **Movies Galore**.

4. **Enter the check amount.**

   Move the cursor to the Payment field and enter the check amount — $25.50 in this example. You don't have to type the dollar sign, but you do have to type the period to indicate the decimal place and cents.

5. **Enter the category.**

   Move the cursor to the Category field. Click the Cat icon to display the Category/Transfer list. You can select one of these categories by double-clicking. Or, if you're the independent type, you can just type the name yourself. A payment to your cable company can be categorized as "Utilities," for example.

   If you go with the typing approach and you're not a super fast typist, Quicken will probably be able to guess which category you're entering before you enter it. If you start typing **Ut**, for example, Quicken will fill in the rest of the category name "ilities" for you ("Ut" + "ilities" = "Utilities"). This is called *QuickFill,* and I'll talk about it later in the chapter in a bit more detail.

6. **Enter a memo description.**

Move the cursor to the Memo field and describe the specific reason you're paying the check. You may identify the cable payment as the January cable bill, for example. Businesses should use this field to identify the invoice paid — usually by entering the actual invoice number you're paying.

7. **Select Record.**

Click the Record button at the bottom of the register window. This option tells Quicken you want to record the transaction into your register. Quicken calculates the new account balance and moves the cursor to the next slot, or row, in the register.

Figure 4-2 shows the cable television check recorded into the register. You can't see it in the figure, but the Balance field after the $25.50 check shows as a negative number. If your Mac has a color monitor, the balance even shows in red. This negative number, this *red ink* indicates that you've overdrawn your account. I don't need to tell you what that means. Overdraft charges.

Fixing Mistakes

What if you need to change a check after you've already entered it? Say, for example, you make a terrible mistake like recording a 52.50 check as 25.20. Can you fix it? Sure. Just use the arrow keys or the mouse to highlight the check transaction you want to change. Use the Tab and Shift+Tab keys to move the cursor to the field you want to change. (You can also click the field with the mouse.) Then make your fix. Choose the Record button when you finish, or press Return.

A kooky (and clever little thing) named QuickFill

Here's kind of a funny quirk about Quicken. If Quicken can guess what you're typing into a field, it will fill in the rest of the field for you. I already mentioned how this works when you type category names. But it gets even better than that.

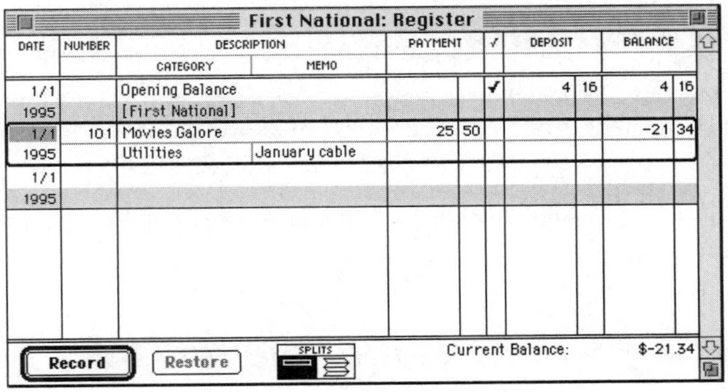

DATE	NUMBER	DESCRIPTION		PAYMENT	√	DEPOSIT		BALANCE	
		CATEGORY	MEMO						
1/1		Opening Balance			√	4	16	4	16
1995		[First National]							
1/1	101	Movies Galore		25	50			-21	34
1995		Utilities	January cable						
1/1									
1995									

First National: Register

Current Balance: $-21.34

Record · Restore · SPLITS

Figure 4-2:
The register
you use to
write the
check to
the cable
company.

The second time you use a payee name in the Description field, for example,
Quicken knows that it's the second time. Quicken also figures that, "hey, there's
probably stuff from the last Movies Galore transaction that'll be the same for
this transaction." So guess what Quicken does if you reuse a payee name? It
uses the last transaction's information to fill in all the current transaction's
fields.

This isn't as dumb as it sounds at first. In fact, it's a real time-saver. Suppose
that you did write a $25.50 check to Movies Galore for your January cable
television bill. When you type **Movies Galore** to record the next month's cable
television check, the amount will probably be the same. The complete payee
name will certainly be the same, and the category will also be the same. So
Quicken fills in all these fields, too.

QuickFill doesn't do everything for you, however. You still need to make sure
that the date and check number are correct. If Quicken "quickfills" a field with
the wrong information, just replace the wrong information with what's right.

If you want to see Quicken's list of QuickFill, or memorized, transactions, click
the QuickFill icon. Or choose the QuickFill Transactions command from the
View menu. Quicken displays a list of transactions in a window. At the bottom
of the window are buttons named Use, Edit and Delete. Click Use to copy a
QuickFill transaction to the selected row of the register or the write checks
window. Click Edit to display a dialog box that lets you change the transaction.
Click Delete to remove the QuickFill transaction from the list.

The QuickFill transactions list is a handy tool. But if you're feeling a little
overwhelmed, don't spin your wheels trying to get up to speed on the feature.
QuickFill will almost always do the job for you because — get this — it automatically grabs transactions from the list for you.

Recording Deposits

You know what? Recording a deposit works almost the exact same way as recording a check. The only difference is that you enter the deposit amount in the Deposit field rather than enter the check amount in the Payment field.

If this all sounds vaguely familiar, it's because you actually set up the account's opening balance by recording a deposit.

Entering a deposit into the register

Suppose that you receive a $100 birthday gift from your elderly Aunt Enid. Here's how you would record this deposit into the register:

1. **Enter the deposit date.**

   Move the cursor to the Date field of the next empty row of the register (if it isn't already there) and type the date. Use the MM/DD format. January 3, 1995, for example, gets entered as ¹/₃. As with check dates, you only have to enter the year if the current year number, which Quicken retrieves from the little clock inside your Macintosh, is wrong.

   You can adjust the date in a Date field in Quicken by using the + and – keys. The + key adds one day to the current date; the – key subtracts one date from the current day. Hey, you know what else. There are some other tricky keys you can use to adjust the date, too. Pressing an "M" or"m" changes the date to the first day in the month, and pressing a "H" or "h" changes the date to the last day in the month. (Get it? M and H are the first and last letters in the word, "month.") Pressing a "Y" or "y" changes the date to the first day in the year, and pressing an "R" or "r" changes the date to the last day in the year. (Yep, that's right. This is because Y and R are the first and last letters in the word, "year.") Finally, pressing "T" or "t" changes the date to today's date according to your Macintosh's internal clock and calendar. You see the pattern now, right? "T." Today. Hmm.

2. **Enter the secret code for deposit, DEP.**

   As soon as you type a D, Quicken will fill in the rest of the secret deposit code for you, DEP.

3. **Enter the name of the person from whom you received the deposit.**

   In this case, move the cursor to the Description field and enter Aunt Enid. (I don't mean to sound presumptuous, but, well, the next time Aunt Enid sends you birthday money, you'll be able to have Quicken QuickFill her name.)

4. Enter the deposit amount.

Move the cursor to the Deposit field and enter 100. Don't type the dollar sign — or any other punctuation. (If Aunt Enid sweats money and sometimes passes out $1,000 gifts, for example, you would record the deposit as 1000 — not 1,000 or $1,000.)

5. Enter the category.

You know how this works by now. Move the cursor to the Category field and type something appropriate. Or type something inappropriate. Aunt Enid's check may be described as "Gift Received." (This is an income category on the standard category list.)

To add a category, remember, all you need to do is display the Categories window. (You can do this by choosing the Cat icon from the iconbar.) Then choose the New button. Refer to Chapter 2 if you have questions about how this works.

6. (Optional) Enter a memo description.

Move the cursor to the Memo field and describe something like the reason for the deposit. Aunt Enid's money may be described as "Birthday Gift." If you're a business depositing a customer's check, though, use this entry to identify the invoice the customer is paying.

7. Select Record.

This command tells Quicken that you want to record the transaction in your register. Quicken beeps in protest but then adds the transaction.

Figure 4-3 shows the check register after you deposit Aunt Enid's thoughtful gift. Your account's no longer overdrawn — so you've got that going for you. Maybe before you go any further, you should call Aunt Enid to thank her.

Figure 4-3:
The check register after you deposit Aunt Enid's gift.

		First National: Register						
DATE	NUMBER	DESCRIPTION		PAYMENT	✓	DEPOSIT	BALANCE	
		CATEGORY	MEMO					
1/1 1995		Opening Balance [First National]			✓	4 16	4 16	
1/1 1995	101	Movies Galore Utilities	January cable	25 50			-21 34	
1/3 1995	DEP	Aunt Enid Gift Received	B-day gift			100 00	78 66	
1/3 1995								

Record   Restore   SPLITS

Current Balance: $-21.34
Ending Balance: $78.66

Changing a deposit you've already entered

Big surprise here, but this works just like changing a check. First, use the arrow keys or the mouse to highlight the deposit. Use the Tab and Shift+Tab keys to move the cursor to the field you want to change. (You can also click the field with the mouse.) Then make your fix and select Record.

Recording Account Transfers

Account transfers occur when you move money from one account — like your savings account — to another account — like your checking account. But, jeepers, why am I telling you this? If you've got one of those combined savings and checking accounts, you probably do this sort of thing all the time.

Oh, now I remember why I brought this up — Quicken makes quick work of account transfers as long as you've already got *both* accounts set up.

If you don't have the second account set up, you'll need to do this first. If you don't know how, flip back to Chapter 2.

Entering an account transfer

Buckle up. I'll speed through the steps for recording an account transfer. For the most part, recording an account transfer works the same way as recording a check or deposit.

Suppose that you want to record the transfer of $50 from your checking account to your savings account. Maybe you want to set aside a little money — little, presumably, being a key adjective — to purchase a gift for generous Aunt Enid.

Here's what you need to do:

1. **Enter the transfer date.**

   Move the cursor to the Date field. Then enter the date that you move the money from one account to another.

2. **(Optional) Flag the transaction as a transfer.**

   Move the cursor to the Number field. Enter something like XFER. (I just made this up as the secret code. You can use some other abbreviation, though.)

3. Enter a description of the transaction.

Use the Description field to describe the transfer — for example, "For Aunt Enid's Next Gift." You know how this works by now, don't you? You just move the cursor to the field. Then you pound away at the keyboard. Bang. Bang. Bang.

4. Enter the transfer amount.

Amounts transferred out of an account get entered in the Payment field. Amounts transferred in to an account get entered in the Deposit field. So move the cursor to the right field ("right" as in "right" and "wrong" not "right and left"); then enter the transfer amount.

5. Indicate the other account.

Enter the category as the name of the account to which or from which money is being transferred. (This is actually the only tricky part.) Move the cursor to the Category field. Enter the account name. If you can't remember, you can display the Categories window by choosing the Categories & Transfers command from the View menu. Then scroll to the very bottom of the list and then select the other account.

6. (Optional) Enter a memo description.

Enter more information about the transaction (if it's needed) in the Memo field. Perhaps a gift idea for Aunt Enid?

7. Select Record.

This command tells Quicken that you want to record the transfer transaction into your register.

Figure 4-4 shows the check register after transferring money from your checking account to your savings account so that you'll have money to purchase something nice for Aunt Enid's next birthday. Maybe that new Def Leppard compact disc.

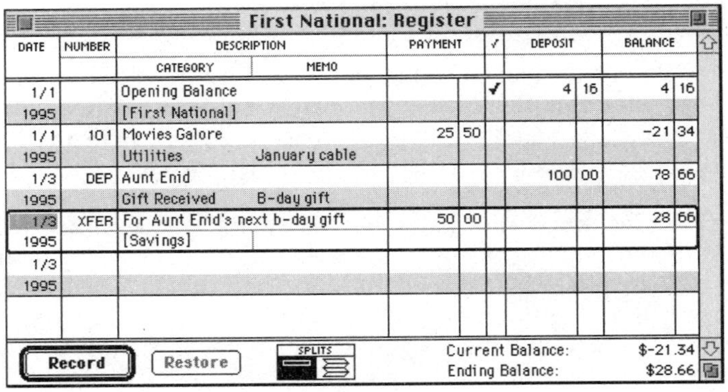

DATE	NUMBER	DESCRIPTION		PAYMENT	√	DEPOSIT	BALANCE	
		CATEGORY	MEMO					
1/1		Opening Balance			√	4 16	4 16	
1995		[First National]						
1/1	101	Movies Galore		25 50			-21 34	
1995		Utilities	January cable					
1/3	DEP	Aunt Enid				100 00	78 66	
1995		Gift Received	B-day gift					
1/3	XFER	For Aunt Enid's next b-day gift		50 00			28 66	
1995		[Savings]						
1/3								
1995								

First National: Register

Record Restore SPLITS Current Balance: $-21.34 Ending Balance: $28.66

Figure 4-4: The transfer transaction.

Take a look at the Category field. Notice that Quicken uses the [and] symbols to identify the Category field entry as an account and not as an income or expense category.

About the other half of the transfer

Here's the cool thing about transfer transactions. Quicken automatically records the other half of the transfer for you. Figure 4-4 shows the $50 reduction in the checking account because of the transfer. Quicken uses this information to record a $50 increase in the savings account. Automatically. Biddabam. Biddaboom.

To see the other half of a transfer transaction, highlight the transfer transaction using the arrow keys or the mouse. Then activate the Activities menu and choose the Go To Transfer command. Quicken displays the other account in a new register window (see Figure 4-5).

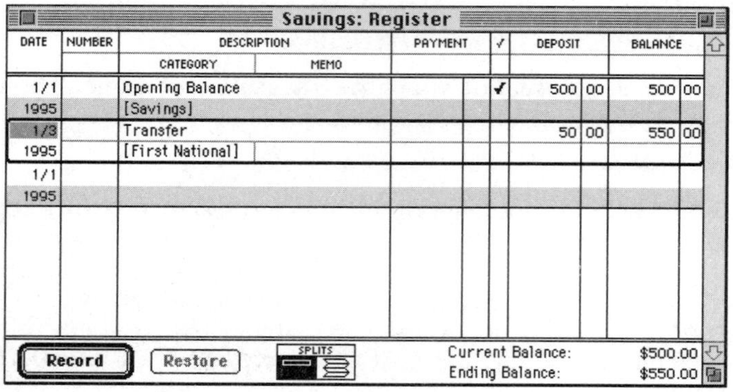

Figure 4-5: The other side of the mountain.

DATE	NUMBER	DESCRIPTION		PAYMENT	✓	DEPOSIT		BALANCE	
		CATEGORY	MEMO						
1/1		Opening Balance			✓	500	00	500	00
1995		[Savings]							
1/3		Transfer				50	00	550	00
1995		[First National]							
1/1									
1995									

Savings: Register

Record   Restore   SPLITS   Current Balance: $500.00   Ending Balance: $550.00

Another way to transfer

I really think that it's easiest to just enter account transfer transactions right into the register. But, there is another way to skin the cat. If you choose the Transfer Money command from the Activities menu, Quicken displays a dialog box, appropriately named Transfer Money, that you can use (see Figure 4-6).

To use the Transfer Money dialog, you enter some clever notation in the Description field. (This will get plugged into the Description field in the register window.) Next you enter the amount of the transaction. Then, as your final task, you specify the account from which you'll be moving money (using the Source drop-down list box) and the account to which you'll be moving money (using the Destination drop-down list box).

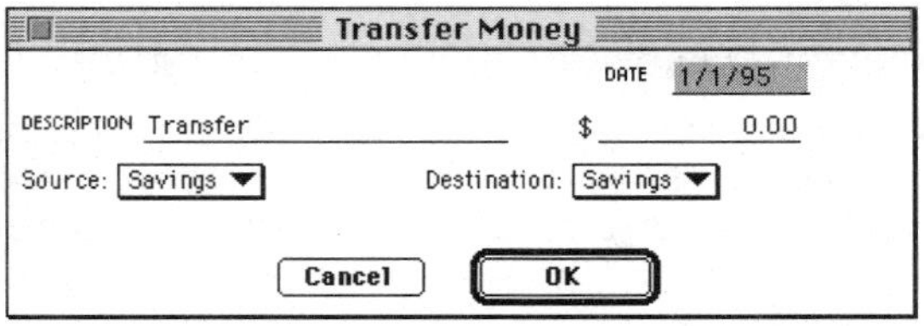

Figure 4-6:
The Transfer Money dialog box.

Changing a transfer you've already entered

Predictably, this works just like changing a check or a deposit. First, you highlight the transfer by using the arrow keys or by clicking the mouse. Then you use the Tab and Shift+Tab keys to move the cursor to the field that you want to change. Make your fix and then select Record and go to lunch.

Splitting Hairs

Here's a sort of Quicken riddle for you. Suppose that you've got a check that pays more than one kind of expense. You trot down to the grocery store, for example, and pick up $10 of junk food and junk beverages (which should be categorized as a "Groceries" expense) and $10 of 10W-40 motor oil (which should be categorized as an "Auto" expense). How do you categorize a transaction like this? Well, I'll tell you. You use a *split category*.

Here's how a split category works. When you're ready to categorize the check, you choose the Splits command buttons, which appear at the bottom of the register window. Quicken expands the register to show split category information for the selected transaction (see Figure 4-7).

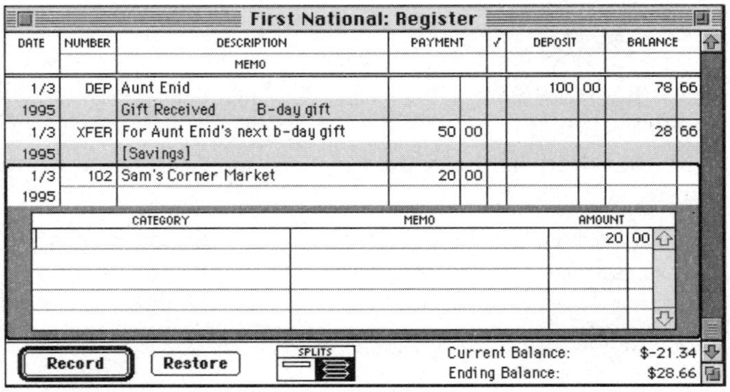

Figure 4-7:
The expanded version of the register shows split category information for the selected transaction.

Steps for splitting a check

If you're a clever sort, you probably already know how the splits category stuff works. Let's go through the steps anyway. Suppose that you want to categorize a $20 check that includes $10 for groceries and $10 for car motor oil.

To categorize a check in the Splits window, do the following:

1. **Enter the first category name in the first Category field.**

   Move the cursor to the Category field and type the category name. If you don't know the category, remember that all you really need to do is type the first part of the name and QuickFill will do the rest. If you're really stumped, remember, too, that you can also open the Categories window (by clicking the Cat icon) and then double-click the category name.

   Despite what a dietitian may say, let's call the pork rinds, beer, and pretzels "Groceries."

2. **Enter a memo description for the first categorized portion of the check.**

   Move the cursor to the first Memo field and then type whatever you want. Maybe a description of the food you bought.

3. **Enter the amount spent for the first category.**

   Move the cursor to the first Amount field and then type, well, the amount. If the first category is what we're calling "Groceries," and you spent $10 on this, you type **10**.

4. **Repeat steps 1, 2, and 3 for each spending category.**

   If you spent another $10 on car motor oil, for example, move the cursor to the second Category field and enter the category you use to summarize spending on "Auto." Move the cursor to the second Memo field and enter a memo description of the expenditure, such as **10W-40 motor oil**. Move the cursor to the second Amount field and enter the amount of the expenditure, such as **10**.

   Figure 4-8 shows the transaction once you've completed the split information. You can have up to 30 pieces of a split transaction. Use the scroll bar and PageUp and PageDown keys to scroll through the list of split amounts.

5. **Verify that there isn't any uncategorized spending shown in the Splits window.**

   If you find "extra" spending, either add the needed category or delete the split transaction line that's uncategorized. To delete a split transaction line, move the cursor to one of the fields in the line, scream "Hi-Ya" loudly and press ⌘+D or choose the Delete Split Line command from the Edit menu. The "Hi-Ya" business is something I learned in tae kwon do. The only other thing I learned, by the way, was that those chest protectors don't really protect middle-aged men during full-contact sparring. So I quit. If you want to insert a new line, move the selection cursor to the line above which you want to make your insertion and then choose the New Split Line command from the Edit menu (or press ⌘+N).

Figure 4-8:
The
completed
splits
window.

6. Choose Record.

After you complete the split category information — that is, you've completely and correctly categorized all the little pieces of the transaction — choose Record. Quicken records the transaction and selects the new empty row of the register so you can enter another transaction. To let you know that the transaction is one that you've split, however, the Category field shows the word Split.

7. (Optional) Hide the Split Information.

If you don't want to enter split transaction information for any more transactions, you can hide the split transaction information by clicking the left Splits button at the bottom of the register window. Quicken, never one to fool around, immediately hides the split transaction information.

Steps for splitting deposits and transfers

Wondering if you can split deposits and transfers? Well, you can. The steps for doing so work just like the steps for splitting categories for a check transaction. The basic trick — if you can call it a trick — is just to use the Split Category fields to list each of the category names and amounts.

Splitting hairs

Quicken assumes that any transaction amount you enter in the register window should agree with the total of the individual split transaction amounts entered in the Splits window.

If you're not sure what the split transaction amounts total is, your best bet is to NOT — I repeat, NOT — enter the amount in the register window. Instead, enter the individual split transaction amounts in the Splits window. When you leave the Splits window, Quicken totals your individual split amounts and then enters the total into either the Payment column or the Deposit column. "How," you're probably wondering, "does Quicken know whether the transaction is a pay-

ment or deposit?" Good question. Quicken looks at whatever you stick into the Number field. If you put a number in the field, Quicken assumes the number is a check number and, therefore, that the transaction is a payment. If you type the secret code for a deposit, "DEP," Quicken assumes the transaction is a deposit.

By the way, Quicken shows any difference between the amount shown in the register window and the individual split transaction amounts. It shows this difference as the last split transaction line. So you'll be able to tell whether the individual splits agree with the payment or deposit amount shown in the register.

One other point I should make here is that you can mix and match categories and transfers. Some of the splits, for example, can be categories and some can be transfer accounts. It would be quite common to do this in a business setting (see Chapter 15, for example).

Deleting and Voiding Transactions

You can delete and void register transactions using the Edit menu's Delete Transaction and Void Transaction commands. If you've looked at the Edit menu, of course, you've probably already guessed as much.

Using either command is a snap. Just highlight the transaction you want to delete or void by using the arrow keys or by clicking the mouse. Then choose the command. And that's that.

Use the Void Transaction command any time you void a check. Quicken leaves voided transactions in the register, but marks them as void and erases the Payment or Deposit amount. So by using the Void Transaction command, you keep a record of voided, or canceled, transactions.

Use the Delete Transaction command if you want to remove the transaction from your register.

The Big Register Phenomenon

If you start entering a bunch of checks, deposits, and transfers into your registers, you'll shortly find yourself with registers that contain hundreds and even thousands of transactions. You can still work with one of these big registers using the tools and techniques I've talked about in the preceding paragraphs. Nevertheless, let me give you some more help for dealing with . . . (drum roll, please) . . . the big register phenomenon.

Moving through a big register

You can use the PageDown and PageUp keys to page up and down through your register, a screenful of transactions at a time. Some people call this *scrolling*. You can call it whatever you want.

You can use the Home key to move to the first transaction in a register. Just press Home.

You can use the End key to move to the last transaction in a register. Bet you can guess how this works. You press End.

Of course, you can use the vertical scroll bar along the right edge of the register window, too. Click the arrows at either end of the vertical scroll bar to select the next or previous transaction. Click either above or below the square scroll bar marker to page back and forth through the register. Or, if you've no qualms about dragging the mouse around, you can drag the scroll bar marker up and down the scroll bar.

Sort of a voiding bug. . .

When you mark a transaction as void, Quicken does three things. It sticks the word Void: at the very start of the Description field, it marks the transaction as cleared, and it erases the amount in the Payment or Deposit field. So far, so good. But if you happen to later fill in the Payment or Deposit field, Quicken will use that payment or deposit amount to adjust the account balance — even though Quicken still shows the transaction as void. I keep thinking the folks at Intuit will fix this, but they haven't — at least not yet. The bottom-line is that you need to make sure that you don't edit transactions after you've voided them. Otherwise, it's all too easy to foul up your account balance. I won't tell you about how I happened to learn this. . . .

Finding that darn transaction

Want to find that one check, deposit, or transfer? No problem. The Find command on the Edit menu provides a handy way for doing just this. Here's what you do:

1. **Choose Find command from the Edit menu.**

    Quicken, with restrained but obvious enthusiasm, displays the Find dialog box (see Figure 4-9). You'll use this dialog box to describe the transaction you want to find in as much detail as possible.

Figure 4-9:
The Find
dialog box.

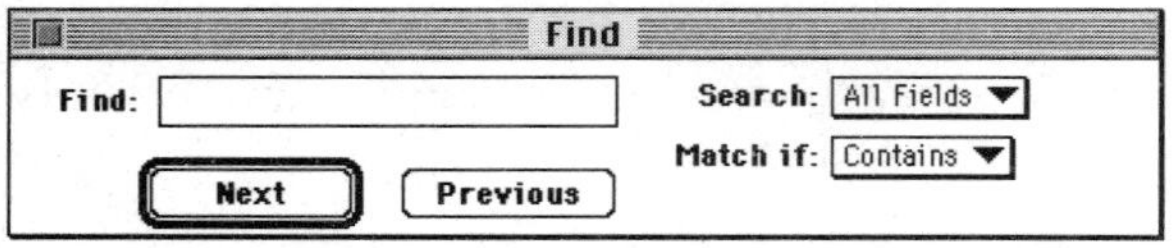

Find
Find: [   ]　Search: [All Fields ▼]
Match if: [Contains ▼]
[Next]　[Previous]

2. **Enter the piece of text or number that identifies the transaction you want to locate.**

    With the cursor positioned in the Find text box, type the text or number. By the way, the case of the text doesn't matter. If you type **aunt**, for example, Quicken will find AUNT or Aunt.

3. **Specify which pieces, or fields, of the register transaction you want Quicken to look at.**

    Move the cursor to the Search drop-down list box, drop down the list box, and then select the field Quicken should look at during the search: Date, Number, Description, Amount, Memo, or Category-Class (whatever is in the Category field). Or get truly crazy and pick the All Fields list entry so that Quicken looks both high and low.

4. **Tell Quicken whether you're using a shotgun or a rifle.**

    You need to specify how closely what you stuck in the Find text box needs to match whatever you selected in the Search drop-down list box. To do this, drop down the Match If drop-down list box. Then select the appropriate matching rule as follows:

    • *Contains.* Select this rule if the field or fields you're searching just need to use a piece of text. If you enter **Aunt** into the Find text box and use this matching rule to search Description fields, Quicken will find transactions that use the following payee names: Aunt Enid, Aunt Enid and Uncle Ob, Uncle Joob and Aunt Edna, and — well, you get the idea.

- *Exact.* Select this rule if the field you're searching needs to exactly match your Find text box entry. If you enter the Find text box entry as **Aunt,** for example, and you're searching Description fields, Quicken looks for transactions where the Description field shows *Aunt* — and nothing more or nothing less.

- *Starts with.* Select this rule if the field you're searching for just needs to start with what you entered in the Find text box. For example, you enter **Aunt** in the Find text box and you're searching the Description fields. Quicken looks for transactions where the Description field starts with the word *Aunt* — such as Aunt Enid or Aunt Enid and Uncle Ob. (Uncle Joob and Aunt Edna wouldn't cut the mustard in this case, though.)

- *Ends with.* Select this rule if the field you're searching for just needs to end with what you entered in the Find text box.

- *Equal.* Select this rule if the amount you're searching for needs to hold a value that equals the number you entered in the Find text box.

- *Greater.* Select this rule if the field you're searching for needs to hold a value that exceeds the number you entered in the Find text box. This makes sense, right?

- *Greater or equal.* Select this rule if the field you're searching for needs to hold a value that either exceeds or equals the number you entered in the Find text box.

- *Less.* Select this rule if the field you're searching for needs to hold a value that is less than the number you entered in the Find text box.

- *Less or equal.* Select this rule if the field you're searching for needs to hold a value that is less than or equal to the number you entered in the Find text box.

5. Let the search begin.

Select the Previous command button in the Find dialog box to begin looking backwards starting with the selected transaction. Or select the Next button to begin looking forward starting with the selected transaction. (The selected transaction is simply the one that is highlighted when you choose Find.)

If Quicken can find a transaction like the one you described, it pages through the register to that transaction and then highlights it. If you want to keep searching, you can click Next or Previous again. Or if you've found what you're looking for in life, you can click the Find dialog box's close box.

Quicken supplies another command that works very similar to Find. The Edit menu's Replace command lets you both locate and modify transactions that look like the one you describe. For example, you might say you want to locate any transaction showing Aunt Enid as the payee so you can replace Description fields showing "Aunt Enid" with "Great Aunt Enid." The Replace command works in a fashion very similar to the Find command except you need to describe what you want to modify in the found transactions. In fact, the Replace dialog box, shown in Figure 4-10, looks almost identical to the Find dialog box, shown in Figure 4-9. The only real difference, not counting the command buttons (which I'll talk about in a minute), is that there's a new text box, called With. It's here that you enter the substitute text or number you want to use to replace stuff. (In our example where you're replacing "Aunt Enid" with "Great Aunt Enid," you enter "Aunt Enid" in the Replace field and you enter "Great Aunt Enid" in the With field.)

Once you complete the initial dialog box that Quicken displays when you choose the command (see Figure 4-10), you click one of the dialog boxes command buttons: Find, Replace, Replace, then Find, and Replace All.

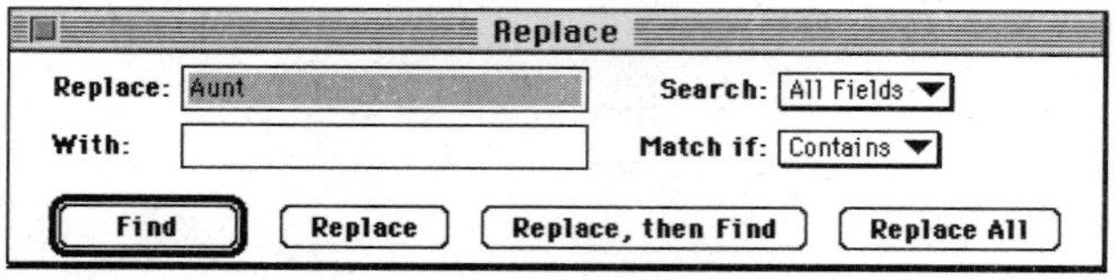

Figure 4-10:
The Replace
dialog box.

Replace	
Replace: Aunt	Search: All Fields ▼
With:	Match if: Contains ▼
Find	Replace	Replace, then Find	Replace All

If you take a few minutes, you can probably figure out on your own what these command buttons do. But let's see if some quick explanation from me can help you save even those minutes. Life is precious, right? OK. I'll start fooling around. The Find button, if clicked, tells Quicken to find a transaction like the one you describe with the Replace, Search, and Match If option. The Replace button tells Quicken to make the substitution ("Great Aunt Enid" for "Aunt Enid," for example) for the selected transaction. In other words, Replace assumes you just clicked Find and that you've found something. The Replace, Then Find button is equivalent to clicking the Replace button and then clicking the Find button. Click-click. Finally, the Replace All button tells Quicken to make the substitution you've described for any transactions in the register.

QuickMath

Can I tell you about one other neat thing you can do with Quicken? Good. The newest version of Quicken has something called QuickMath which is really pretty cool.

Here's what QuickMath does. It lets you create things called QuickCalc keys that automatically adjust the value in a field. This sounds goofy, of course. But it's very handy. For example, if you always need to add sales tax to amounts and sales tax is, say, 8.25%, you can tell Quicken to adjust a value up by 8.25% every time you press a key — such as the letter "T". (This only works when the selection cursor is in a value field — such as the Payment or Deposit column.)

To create a QuickCalc key, you first choose the QuickMath command from the Settings menu. Quicken displays the dialog box shown in Figure 4-11. Unfortunately, this dialog box is rather poorly laid-out, but we'll get through this. Don't worry.

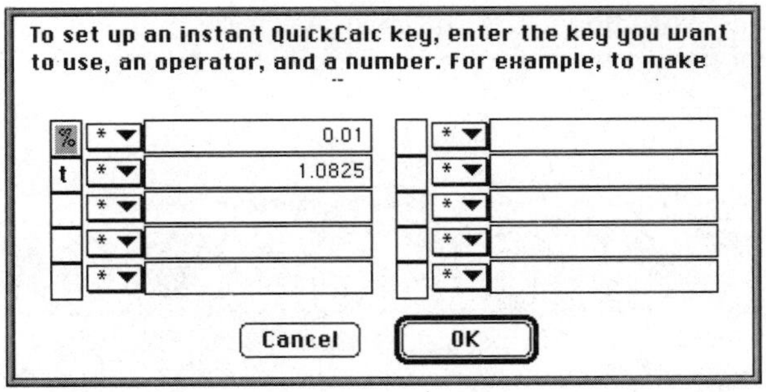

Figure 4-11:
The dialog box you use to set up QuickCalc keys.

> To set up an instant QuickCalc key, enter the key you want to use, an operator, and a number. For example, to make
>
> | % | * ▼ | 0.01 | * ▼ | |
> | t | * ▼ | 1.0825 | * ▼ | |
> | | * ▼ | | * ▼ | |
> | | * ▼ | | * ▼ | |
> | | * ▼ | | * ▼ | |
>
> (Cancel) (OK)

You enter three inputs to create a QuickCalc key: the one-character abbreviation you'll use to represent the QuickCalc key, the mathematical operator the QuickCalc key will perform, and the other value that will be used in the calculation. The first QuickCalc key shown in Figure 4-11 indicates whether you've got the selection cursor positioned in some value field; clicking the % (percent) key tells Quicken to multiply the contents of the field by .01. Does that make sense? Let's look at the next one. It tells Quicken that pressing T (the letter *t*) tells Quicken to multiply the contents of the field by 1.0825.

The mathematical operator is set by selecting an entry from a drop-down list box. You may already know this, but * is the multiplication symbol, / is the division symbol, + is the addition symbol, and – is the subtraction symbol.

The minus sign needs to be pressed twice (if you're starting in a field that contains either no number or a positive number). The first press adds a minus sign, and the second press opens the small calculator.

Remember the Macintosh Calculator!

Geepers. I almost forgot something. The Macintosh calculator. Remember that your Mac comes with a calculator you can use to make quick calculations on the fly. Figure 4-12 shows how I arrange my Mac desktop when I'm working with Quicken. See the calculator on the right half of the screen? I figure that I can use it whenever I need to do a little math.

To start the calculator, just choose the Calculator command from the Apple menu.

Do the calculator keys make sense? Here's how they work. Use the / (slash) key for division. Use the * (asterisk) for multiplication. Use the - (hyphen) and the + (plus) keys for subtraction and addition. Use the . (period) to indicate the decimal point. Use the = (equals sign) to calculate the amount. You can use the C key to clear the amount text box.

If you want to move the number shown on the calculator display to a field in the Quicken register, you can do that too. Here's how. With the value showing on the Calculator display, choose the Edit menu's Copy command. Then, click the Quicken Register field you want to enter the value and choose the Edit menu's Paste command.

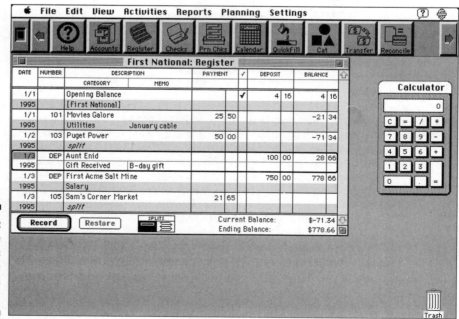

Figure 4-12:
The Macintosh's built-in calculator is often handy.

And the Pop-up Ten Key, too!

And now I really am embarrassed. I guess it wouldn't have been so bad to forget to talk about the Mac's calculator. But, it would have been shameful to have omitted the Quicken pop-up ten-key calculator. (My deepest apologies.)

But let me explain what I'm talking about and you'll understand why my face is beet red and covered with egg. If the cursor is in an amount field, you can press any of the mathematical operator keys: * (for multiplication) + (for addition), − (for subtraction), and / (for division) to open a small calculater (see Figure 4-13). If you're starting in a field that contains either no number or a positive number, press − twice to open the calculator.

The pop-up calculator works like a regular ten-key calculator. (You know what I mean? Those calculators that have paper tape and that you always see on accountant's desks?) For example, to calculate the product 25 times 3, you type **25 * 3.** When you click the calculator's Total button, Quicken plops the total, 75 in this example, into the amount field.

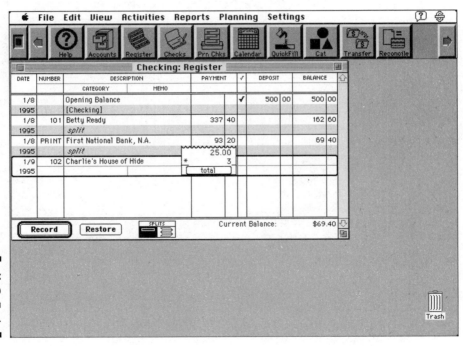

Figure 4-13:
The pop-up Quicken calculator.

The 5th Wave By Rich Tennant

"IT SAYS HERE IF I SUBSCRIBE TO THIS MAGAZINE, THEY'LL SEND ME A FREE DESK-TOP CALCULATOR. DESKTOP CALCULATOR?!! WHOOAA — WHERE HAVE I BEEN?!!"

Chapter 5
Printing 101

● ●

In This Chapter

▶ Collecting the information needed to print a check

▶ Fixing your mistakes before printing the check

▶ Printing a check

▶ Fixing check form alignment problems

▶ Recovering from a mistake after you've printed out the check

▶ Printing a register

● ●

1 bet you can't guess what this chapter describes. Gee, you guessed it — how to print checks and reports.

Printing Checks

Printing checks in Quicken is, well, quick. All you need to do is collect the information you want printed on the check form, press a couple of keys, and enter the number you want Quicken to use to identify the checks. Sounds simple enough, doesn't it? It is, as you'll read in the paragraphs that follow.

Collecting the check information

When you want to write a check, you collect the information needed for the actual check form and the information needed to record the printed check into your register. If you've worked with the Quicken register or read Chapter 4, you'll find this all rather familiar.

Make sure that the active account is the one on which you want to write checks. You can confirm this by looking at the register window's title bar. This title bar identifies both the type of document window (a register, for example) and the account showing in the window. If the account in the register window isn't the one you want, display the Accounts List window by choosing the Accounts icon from the iconbar. Then select the account that you are writing checks from and choose the Open command button or double-click the account. Quicken then displays a register window with this account's information.

One other thing. If you've done this before, you'll have several document windows on the Quicken desktop, or application window. You can close the unneeded windows if you want. To do this, click the window's close boxes. The close box is that small square you see in each window's (and each dialog box's) upper left corner.

To collect the information needed to print a check, follow these steps:

1. **Display the Write Checks window.**

   Choose the Checks icon from the iconbar, or choose the Write Checks command from the Activities menu. Figure 5-1 shows the Write Checks window. Get ready for some excitement.

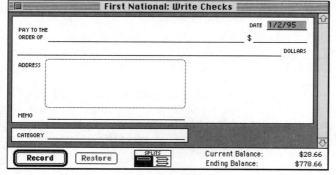

Figure 5-1:
The Write
Checks
window.

2. **Enter the check date.**

   First use the mouse or the Tab key (or Shift+Tab) to move the cursor to the Date field. Then enter the date you'll print the check (probably today's date.) Remember to enter the date in a MM/DD/YY format — April 8, 1995 is entered as 4/8/95. You don't need to enter the year if the year number that Quicken retrieves from your computer's internal system clock is correct. If you want, you can use your new friend, the pop-up calendar. You can also adjust the date by a day using the + and – keys.

3. Enter the name of the person or business you're paying.

Move the cursor to the Pay To The Order Of field and type away. For example, to write a check to me, type **Steve Nelson.** (Feel free to do this, by the way. If you send me a check, I'll even cash it as a sort of public service.) Or if you've written a check to the payee before, type just enough of the name so that Quicken can QuickFill the field. (I described the whole QuickFill business in the last chapter, in you're starting your reading here in this chapter.)

4. Enter the amount of the check.

Move the cursor to the $ text box and type the amount. (If you are sending a check to me, be sure to make the amount nominal — for sure, not more than $10 or $20.) When you move the cursor down to the next field, Quicken writes the amount out in words on the line under the payee name and before Dollars.

5. Enter the payee's address.

If you plan to mail the check in a window envelope, move the cursor to the Address field. Then enter the name and address of the person or business you're paying.

Here's a little address-entry trick: You can copy the payee name from the Pay To The Order Of text box to the first line of the Address field. To do so, press the ' (apostrophe) key either before you type the address or with the cursor to the left of the first line of the address.

6. (Optional) Enter a memo description of the check.

Move the cursor to the Memo field and enter a description for why you are sending your money to this person or business, such as an account number or an invoice number. Or if you're sending someone a check because you didn't have time to go out and buy a real gift, type **Happy Birthday** in the Memo field. It's the little things that make a difference.

7. Enter the category.

Move the cursor to the Category field and type the category name for the expense you're paying with the check. If you don't remember the category name, display the Categories window by clicking the Cat icon on the iconbar, Then pick the category you want to use from the list. Figure 5-2 shows the completed window for a rent check payable to one of the nicer places in the fictional town of Pine Lake, the venerable Marlborough Apartments.

```
┌─────────────────────────────────────────────────────────────┐
│ ▫           First National: Write Checks              ▒ │ ⇧
│                                                          │
│                                          DATE  1/2/95    │
│  PAY TO THE                                              │
│  ORDER OF  Marlborough Apartments _____ $    250.00   │
│  Two hundred fifty and 00/100*************************** DOLLARS │
│  ADDRESS ┌─ Marlborough Apartments ──────────────┐       │
│          │  123 Main Street                      │       │
│          │  Pine Lake, WA 98053                  │       │
│          │                                       │       │
│          └───────────────────────────────────────┘       │
│  MEMO      January rent _____         │
│  CATEGORY  Household _____         │ ⇩
├─────────────────────────────────────────────────────────┤
│ ┌────────┐ ┌─────────┐   SPLITS    Current Balance: $28.66 │
│ │ Record │ │ Restore │   ▭▭         Ending Balance: $778.66 │
│ └────────┘ └─────────┘                                    │
└─────────────────────────────────────────────────────────────┘
```

Figure 5-2:
The rent
is due.

You can assign a check to more than a single category by using the split
Category fields. Using the split Category fields with the Write Checks
window works the same way as using them with the register window. (I
described using the Splits window with the register window in the last
chapter.) OK. So why do I bring this up? You may want to do this when a
check pays more than one type of expense or is transferred to more than
one account. For example, if you're writing a check to pay your mortgage,
with part of the check paying the actual mortgage and part of the check
going into an escrow account for property taxes, you can use the split
Category fields to describe the transaction's individual components. To
split a check amount so that it's assigned to multiple spending categories,
choose the right-hand Splits button at the bottom of the Write Checks
window. Or choose the Edit Splits command from the Edit menu. Either
way, Quicken expands the Write Checks window so it includes a bunch of
fields for entering split transaction information. If you have questions
about how split transactions work, refer to Chapter 4.

8. Choose Record.

Quicken records the check. It displays the current account balance (which
is the today's balance) and the ending account balance (which is the
balance after any post-dated transactions). Shoot, it even scrolls the
completed check off the screen and replaces it with a new, blank check
that you can use to pay your next bill. It doesn't get much better than this,
does it?

What if you make a mistake entering a check?

Don't worry; be happy. It's easy to fix the mistakes you make if you haven't yet printed the check. Use the PageUp or PageDown keys to scroll back and forth through the checks you've entered using the Write Checks window. This way you can display any check that you used the Write Check window to write (but have not yet printed).

When you find the incorrect check, you can fix the mistake in two ways. If you incorrectly entered some bit of check information, move the cursor to the field with the incorrect data and just type over the data.

Or if you're really mad or frustrated, you can delete the entire check by pressing ⌘+D or by choosing the Delete Transaction command from the Edit menu. (Honesty and ethics compel me to say that you should do this now if you actually entered a check to me, for example.)

Don't use this method to delete a check that you've already printed. To *void* a check that you've already printed, you must go into the register window. To display the register window, you can choose the Register icon from the iconbar. Then find the check in the register window, highlight the check, and void it by selecting the Void Transaction command from the Edit menu. You should also write something like **VOID** in large letters across the face of the check using a ball-point pen.

Printing a check you've entered

OK, I'm not going to lie to you. The first couple of times you print a check with Quicken, it'll seem a little complicated. But once you get the hang of it, it's super-easy. *Super*-easy. Here's how check printing works.

If this is the first time you've printed checks, you need to describe how you want Quicken to print the checks. Choose the Check Printing command from the Settings menu. Quicken displays the Check Printing Settings dialog box, shown in Figure 5-3. Use the Check Style drop-down list box to identify the check form you're printing. You can use the Font and Size drop-down list boxes to control the style and size of the type used to print the check. You can use the Partial Page Orientation settings to identify how you will feed partial pages of check forms through your printer. (Click the setting that shows how you'll feed the checks through the printer.) The Check Printing Settings dialog box also provides check boxes you can mark to indicate you're using a check page feeder, that you want category information printed on check vouchers (if your check style provides vouchers), and that you want the check date set to the check printing date.

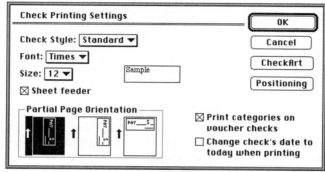

Figure 5-3:
The Check
Printing
Settings
dialog box.

1. Load the checks into your printer.

This process works the same way as when you load any paper into your printer. If you have questions about how this works, refer to your printer documentation. (Sorry, I can't help more on this, but there are a million different printers out there, and I can't guess which one you have.)

2. Choose the Prn Chks icon on the iconbar.

As long as the Write Checks: Checking window is the active window, Quicken displays the Print Checks dialog box, as shown in Figure 5-4. At the top of the dialog box Quicken shows how many checks to print. Quicken should also tell you the total dollar amount of those checks — just like its Windows and DOS cousins do — but it doesn't.

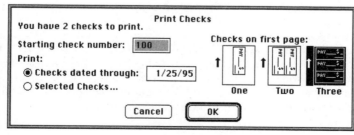

Figure 5-4:
The Print
Checks
dialog box.

3. Enter the first check number.

Move the cursor to the Starting Check Number box and enter the number printed on the first check form you'll print. Figure 5-4 shows 100, for example, so the first check form is numbered 100. To quickly increase or decrease the check numbers, use the + and − keys from the keypad.

4. Tell Quicken if you're printing a partial page.

If you're printing a partial page of forms on a laser printer, indicate the number of check forms on the partial page by using the Checks On First Page option buttons. Mark the Three button if there are three checks, the Two button if there are two checks, and the One button if there is one check.

5. Indicate which checks Quicken should print.

Mark the Checks Dated Through option button under Print if you want to print all the checks through a certain date and then type in that date in the text box. Or if you want to pick and choose which checks to print, mark the Selected Checks option button.

6. If you selected which checks to print by marking the Selected Checks option button, select the checks to print.

If you mark the Select Checks option button, Quicken, with almost noticeable annoyance, displays the Select Checks to Print window, as shown in Figure 5-5. Initially, Quicken marks all the checks dated on or earlier than the current date by placing a check mark next to each one in the Print column. If you don't want to print a check, click the check using the mouse. When only the checks you want to print are check-marked, click the OK button to continue with this crazy little thing called *check printing*. Quicken, happy with your progress, redisplays the Print Checks dialog box (refer to Figure 5-4).

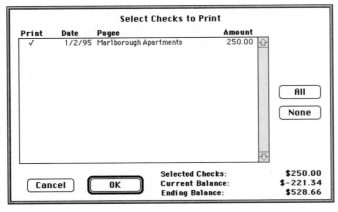

Figure 5-5:
The Select Checks to Print window.

7. Click OK.

This command tells Quicken that you're ready, willing, and able to begin check printing. Quicken displays the standard Macintosh Print dialog box. Figure 5-6 shows how this puppy looks on my Mac, but your Print dialog box may look different. Different printers have different printing options.

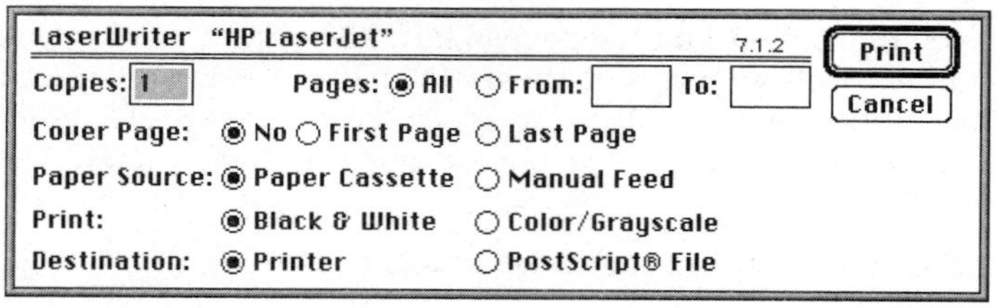

Figure 5-6:
The Print dialog box.

8. Tell Quicken you're ready to print.

Click Print. Quicken prints your check. Then it asks whether it printed the check correctly (see Figure 5-7).

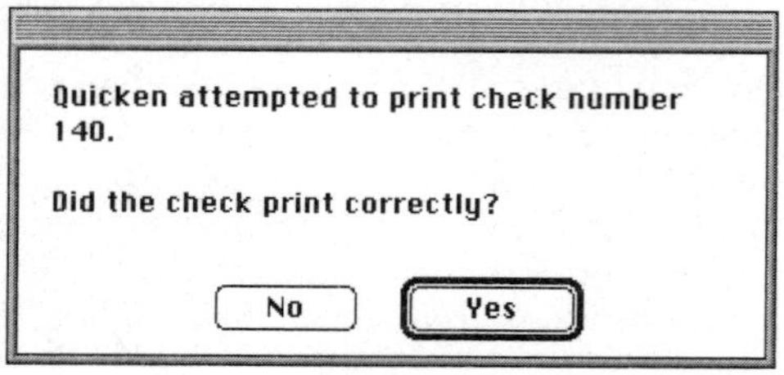

Figure 5-7:
The dialog box Quicken displays to ask about the check printing job.

Figure 5-8 shows an example check made payable to Marlborough Apartments. At last, you get that landlord off your back. Basically, it's just like one you would fill out manually. The only difference is that your computer has written the check for you.

9. Review the check or checks Quicken printed.

If it printed the checks correctly, answer the Did Checks Print OK? message box by clicking Yes. (In this case, Quicken, apparently thinking you'll now want to do nothing but print checks, redisplays the Write Checks window.) If Quicken didn't print a check correctly, answer the message by clicking No. You can fix whatever is wrong and then reprint the checks in the same way you printed them before.

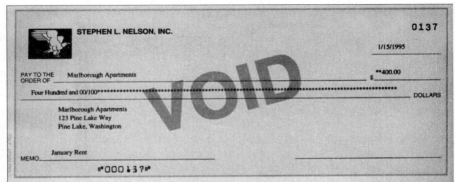

STEPHEN L. NELSON, INC.   0137

                                                                1/15/1995

PAY TO THE   Marlborough Apartments   **400.00
ORDER OF _____ $

Four Hundred and 00/100*** DOLLARS

        Marlborough Apartments
        123 Pine Lake Way
        Pine Lake, Washington

MEMO____January Rent

        ⑆000137⑆

VOID

Figure 5-8:
A printed
check.

10. **Sign the printed checks.**

> Then — and I guess you probably don't need my help here — put the
> checks in the mail.

A few words about check printing

Check printing is kind of complicated, isn't it?

For the record, I'm with you on this one. I really wish it wasn't so much work.
But you'll find that printing checks does get easier after the first few times.

Pretty soon, you'll be running instead of walking through the steps. Pretty soon,
you'll just skate around things like check-form alignment problems. Pretty soon,
in fact, you'll know all this stuff and never have to read "pretty soon" again.

What if I discover a mistake after I've printed the check?

This problem isn't as big as you might think.

If you've already mailed the check, there's not a whole lot you can do. You can
try to get the check back (if the person you paid hasn't cashed it) and replace it
with one that's correct. (Good luck on this one.)

If the person has cashed the check, there's no way to get the check back. If you overpaid the person by writing the check for more than you should have, you need to get the person to pay you the overpayment amount. If you underpaid the person, you need to write another check for the amount of the underpayment.

If you printed the check but haven't mailed it, void the printed check. This operation is in two-parts. First, write the word VOID in large letters across the face of the check form. (Use a ball point if you're using multipart forms so that the second and third parts also show as VOID.) Second, display the register, highlight the check, and then choose the Void Transaction command from the Edit menu. (This option marks the check as one that's been voided in the system so Quicken does not use it in calculating your account balance.)

Printing a Check Register

You can print a check register or a register for any other account, too. Select the Register icon from the iconbar to display the register window; then choose the Print Register command from the File menu.

When you do this, Quicken displays the Print Register dialog box, as shown in Figure 5-9. To print a register, you follow these magic steps:

Oh where, oh where, do the unprinted checks go?

Unprinted checks — those you've entered using the Write Checks window but haven't yet printed — are stored in the register. To identify them as unprinted checks, Quicken sets their check numbers as PRINT. What's more, when you tell Quicken to print the unprinted checks, what it really does is print the checks in your register that have Print in the Check Number text box. All this is of little practical value in most instances, but it results in several interesting possibilities. For example, you can enter the checks you want to print directly into the register — all you need to do is enter the check number as PRINT. (Note that you can't enter an address anywhere in the register, so this process isn't practical if you want addresses printed on your checks.) Another thing you can do is cause a check you've printed once to print again by changing its check number from, say 007, to PRINT. There aren't many good reasons you would want to do this. The only one I can think of is that you accidentally printed a check on plain paper and want to reprint it on a real check form.

```
                          Print Register
Print transactions from:   1/1/95      ☐ Sort by check number
                                        ☐ Print one line per transaction
             through:       1/3/95      ☐ Show split detail

                   Cancel        OK
```

Figure 5-9:
The Print
Register
dialog box.

1. **(Optional) Limit the range of dates.**

   To print a register of something other than the current year-to-date transactions, use the Print Transactions From and Through text boxes. This is pretty dang obvious, isn't it? You just move the cursor to one and then the other text boxes and enter the range of months the register should include.

2. **Tell Quicken to print transactions in check number order.**

   To print check and deposit transactions in check number order instead of transaction date order, move the cursor to the Sort by number check box. Then click the check box to mark it. (If you do this, your deposits will probably be listed before your checks because deposits usually don't have numbers.)

3. **(Optional) Tell Quicken to use a single line per transaction.**

   To print each check and deposit transaction on a single line, move the pointer to the Print one line per transaction check box. Then press the spacebar or click the check box to mark it.

4. **(Optional) Tell Quicken to print split transaction information.**

   To print the Split Transaction information — categories, memos, and amounts — move the cursor to the Show split detail check box. Then press the spacebar or click the check box to mark it.

5. **Choose OK.**

   Quicken displays the regular Macintosh Print dialog box. (See Figure 5-10.) You don't have to fool around with this dialog box. If you want to print a register, pronto, just choose Print. Then again, if you're the sort of person who likes to fool around with this kind of stuff, carry on with the rest of these steps.

   If you want to see the effect the different register-printing text boxes and check boxes have, just experiment. You can't hurt anything or anybody.

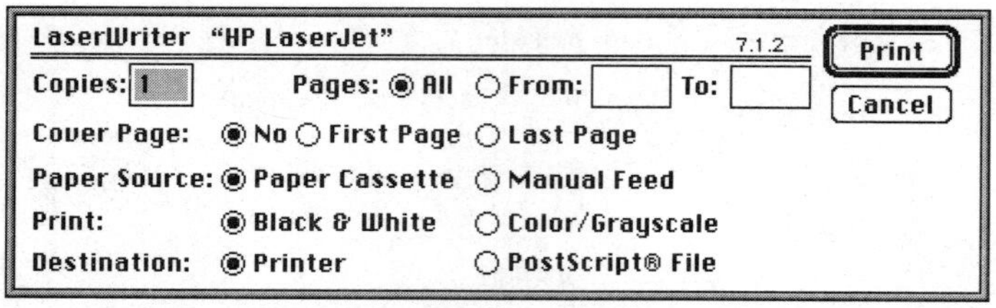

Figure 5-10:
The regular
Macintosh
Print dialog
box.

LaserWriter "HP LaserJet"		7.1.2	Print
Copies: 1	Pages: ⦿ All ◯ From: [ ] To: [ ]		Cancel
Cover Page:	⦿ No ◯ First Page ◯ Last Page		
Paper Source:	⦿ Paper Cassette ◯ Manual Feed		
Print:	⦿ Black & White ◯ Color/Grayscale		
Destination:	⦿ Printer ◯ PostScript® File		

6. (Optional) Color your world.

If you've got a color printer and want your register printed in color, mark the Print Color/Grayscale option button on the Print Report dialog box. You can do this by clicking.

7. (Optional) Tell Quicken which pages to print.

Use the Pages option buttons and text boxes to limit the pages Quicken prints. How? Mark the Pages From option button; then enter the range of page numbers you want printed. That's simple enough, right?

8. Choose Print.

Now choose Print one last time. Quicken finally prints the register. If you're still with me, take a look at Figure 5-11. It shows a printed check register.

Figure 5-11:
The printed
check
register.

```
                              Check Register
Checking                                                        Page 1
5/19/1995
Date   Num              Transaction        Payment  C  Deposit   Balance
 1/1          Opening Balance                         x    4.16      4.16
 1995  memo:
       cat:   [Checking]
 1/1   101    Movies Galore                 25.50                  -21.34
 1995  memo:  February
       cat:   Utilities
 1/3   DEP    Aunt Enid                              100.00        78.66
 1995  memo:  birthday gift
       cat:   Gift Received
 1/5   TXFR   For Aunt Enid's next gift     50.00                  28.66
 1995  memo:  Def Leppard CD?
       cat:   [Savings]
 1/15  137    Marlborough Apartments        400.00             -371.34
 1995  memo:  January Rent
       cat:   Rent Paid
 1/15  Print  Junebug's Antiques            75.00              -446.34
 1995  memo:
       cat:   Household
 1/15  Print  Puget Power                   24.89              -471.23
 1995  memo:
       cat:   Utilities
 2/1   DEP    Salt Mine, Ltd                        1,000.00   528.77
 1995  memo:
       cat:   Salary
```

Chapter 6

Reports, Charts, and Other Cool Tools

. . . .

In This Chapter

▶ Printing Quicken reports

▶ Using the Reports menu commands

▶ QuickZooming report totals

▶ Sharing information with a spreadsheet

▶ Editing and rearranging report information

▶ Creating a chart

. . . .

*Q*uicken lets you summarize, slice, and dice register and account information in a variety of ways. This chapter describes how to use reports and produce graphs easily. This stuff is much easier to understand if you know how to print a register first. I describe this trick at the end of Chapter 5.

Creating and Printing Reports

After you learn how to print checks and registers, all other printing in Quicken is easy, easy, easy.

Just the facts (of printing), ma'am

The transactions you enter in the register window and the checks you enter in the Write Checks window determine the information in a report. To print a report, then, just choose the Reports menu and tell Quicken which kind of report you want to print (see Figure 6-1).

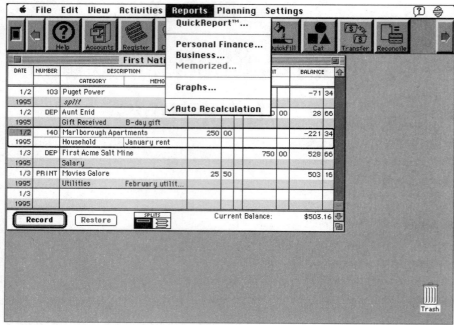

Figure 6-1:
The
activated
Reports
menu.

Though I tried and tried, I really couldn't think of some super clever way to organize a discussion of how you produce and use these reports. So, I'll just talk about them in the same order as they appear on the menu, OK?

The QuickReport trick

QuickReports let you summarize the transactions with a particular payee or the transactions assigned to a given category. When you choose the QuickReport command from the Reports menu, Quicken displays the QuickReport dialog box, as shown in Figure 6-2.

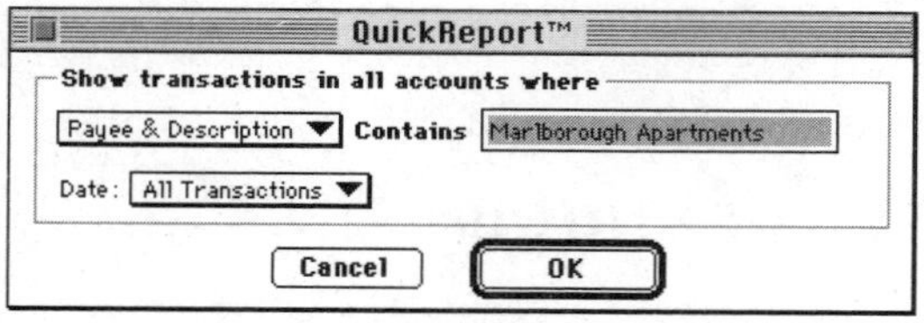

Figure 6-2:
The
QuickReport
dialog box.

Here's the neat and, I guess, unique thing about QuickReports. Quicken fills out the QuickReport dialog box so that your report will summarize transactions using the contents of the selected field. OK. This sounds complicated. But it's not. If you had just clicked a check written to Marlborough Apartments, for example, and the selection cursor was in the Description field which shows Marlborough Apartments, Quicken fills in the QuickReports dialog box so that your report will summarize all the transactions that use Marlborough Apartments as the Description. If you did want to see a report summarizing all the Marlborough Apartments transactions, you would just click OK. Quicken would then produce a report like that shown in Figure 6-3.

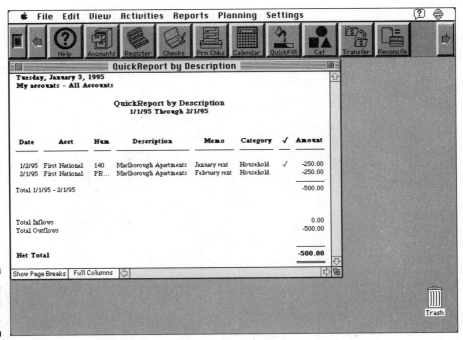

Figure 6-3:
The actual QuickReport.

This makes for some pretty easy reports. Want to know how much you've spent on utilities, for example? Just click a transaction's category field that shows utilities, choose the QuickReport command from the Reports menu, and click OK.

You can also use the QuickReports drop-down list boxes and the Contains text box to describe the thing you want to summarize. The first drop-down list box lets you pick the field you want to tally: Payee or Description, Category, Class, Memo, and so on. The second, or Date, drop-down list box lets you specify a time interval: All transactions, Year-to-date, Last Quarter, Last Month, and so on. Finally, the Contains text box lets you specify what it is you want to summarize. If you were summarizing transactions with the Payee and Description or Category field set to Marlborough Apartments, you would enter **Marlborough Apartments** into the Contains text box.

Personal Finance and Business reports

Quicken produces a bunch of different reports for use at home or in a business. To make sense of what might otherwise become mass confusion, Quicken arranges all of its personal and business reports into two groups: Personal Finance reports and Business reports. (These sort of sound like PBS documentaries, don't they? "Tonight, Joob Taylor explores starting a business with somebody else's money in, the *Business Report*.")

To see the reports in one of these groups, select the report group from the Reports menu.

Figure 6-4 shows the Personal Finance group of reports. Pretty exciting stuff so far, don't you think?

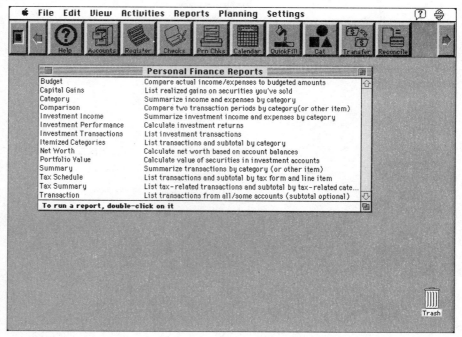

Figure 6-4:
The
Personal
Finance
Reports
window.

To print a Personal Finance report (or any other report, for that matter), double-click the report. For example, to print the Personal Finance Category report, select the Personal Finance command from the Reports menu and then double-click the Category report. (It's the third report listed on the window.)

Quicken displays the Create Category Report dialog box. (The precise name of this report will vary depending on the report you select.) This dialog box lets you give the report a name using the Title text box and asks you to identify the range of dates the report should cover, as shown in Figure 6-5. You don't have to specify either piece of information.

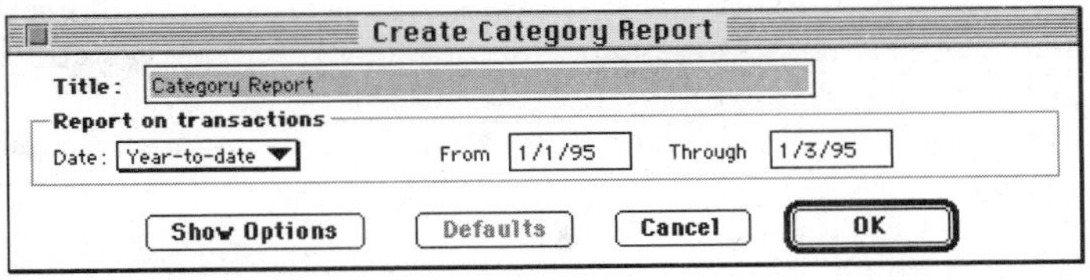

Figure 6-5:
The Create
Category
Report
dialog box.

```
┌──────────────── Create Category Report ────────────────┐
│  Title :  Category Report                               │
│  ┌─ Report on transactions ──────────────────────────┐  │
│  │ Date :  Year-to-date ▼     From  1/1/95   Through  1/3/95 │
│  └───────────────────────────────────────────────────┘  │
│        ( Show Options )  ( Defaults )  ( Cancel )  ( OK )│
└─────────────────────────────────────────────────────────┘
```

If you don't enter a new range of dates, Quicken assumes that you want to
include transactions from the start of the current calendar year through the
present date.

Note that a report that shows account balances — such as the Personal Finance
Net Worth report, the Business Balance sheet, or the Investment Portfolio
report — doesn't need a range of dates because these reports show account
balances as of a specific date. In these cases, if you don't enter a date, Quicken
assumes that you want account balances for the current system date from your
computer's internal clock.

When the stuff shown in the Create Category Report dialog box looks right,
click OK. Quicken then copies an on-screen version of the report to a new
document window. Figure 6-6 shows an on-screen version of the Personal
Finance Category report. (The information shown in this report, by the way, is
based on the transactions collected in Chapters 4 and 5.)

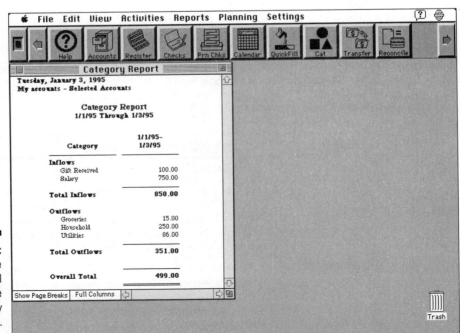

Figure 6-6:
The
Personal
Finance
Category
report.

You can't see the entire on-screen version of a report unless your report is very small (or your screen is monstrously large). Use the PageUp and PageDown keys to scroll up and down and the Tab and Shift+Tab keys to move left and right. Or, if you're a mouse lover, you can click and drag various pieces of the scroll bars.

To print your report, choose the Print Report command from the File menu.

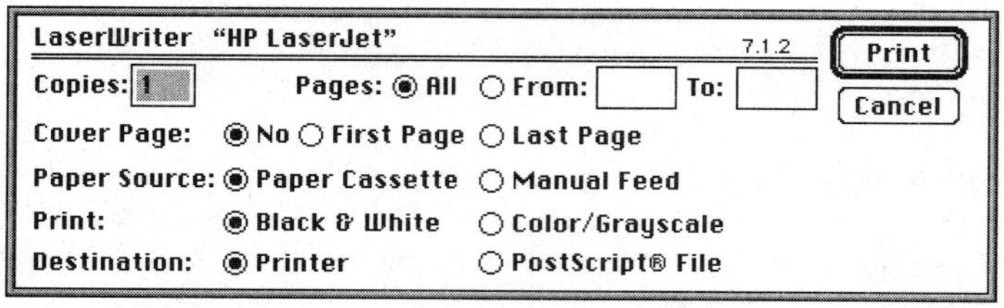

Figure 6-7:
The regular, old Macintosh Print dialog box.

```
┌──────────────────────────────────────────────────────────────────┐
│ LaserWriter  "HP LaserJet"                        7.1.2   ( Print )│
│ Copies: 1            Pages: ◉ All  ○ From:      To:       (Cancel) │
│ Cover Page:   ◉ No ○ First Page  ○ Last Page                      │
│ Paper Source: ◉ Paper Cassette  ○ Manual Feed                     │
│ Print:         ◉ Black & White  ○ Color/Grayscale                 │
│ Destination:   ◉ Printer        ○ PostScript® File                │
└──────────────────────────────────────────────────────────────────┘
```

Quicken displays the regular, old Macintosh Print dialog box (see Figure 6-7).

To accept the given specifications — which will almost always be fine — just click the Print button. You'll never guess what happens next. Quicken prints the report!

When you're ready — but not before — remove the on-screen version of the report by clicking the report document window's Close button.

Reviewing standard reports

Tables 6-1 and 6-2 describe Quicken's Personal Finance and Business reports. Some of these babies won't make sense unless you understand how to collect the information that goes into the report, as described in Chapters 12, 13, and Part IV.

Table 6-1	Quicken's Personal Finance Reports
Report	*Description*
Budget	Summarizes income and expense categories and compares actual category totals to budgeted category amounts. This report only includes transactions recorded in your bank, cash, and credit card accounts. (For this report to make any sense, of course, you need to have a budget set up.)
Capital Gains	Lists all the unrealized gains on individual investments you hold. *Unrealized* means that the investment is worth more than what you paid for it, but because you still own the investment, your gain is unrealized. When you sell the investment, you realize the gain.

Report	Description
Category	Summarizes the money that flows into and out of an account by income and expense categories and by transfers.
Comparison	Lets you compare category totals from two periods. You can use this report to compare January's activity with February's activity, for example. Remember: because you are comparing two periods, you need to enter two transaction date ranges.
Investment Income	Summarizes income and expense categories for transactions recorded in your investment accounts.
Investment	A power-user report. This report calculates the internal rates of Performance delivered by each of the individual investments in your portfolio.
Investment Transactions	Lists transactions recorded for all your investment accounts.
Itemized Categories	Summarizes income and expense category totals. This report includes transactions from all of your accounts.
Net Worth	Lists all accounts, their balances, and the difference between the sum of the asset accounts and the sum of the liabilities accounts, which the report identifies as your net worth.
Portfolio Value	Lists the current value of all securities in your investment accounts.
Summary	Summarizes transactions by category or some other bit of transaction data: payee or description, class, and so on.
Tax Schedule	Summarizes income and expense category totals for those categories marked as tax related and assigned to specific tax schedule lines. This report includes transactions from all accounts. (If you export Quicken information to a tax preparation package like TurboTax, this report gets passed on to the package.)
Tax Summary	Summarizes income and expense category totals for those categories marked as tax related. Like the Itemized Categories report, this report includes transactions from all of your accounts.
Transaction	Lists transactions from one of your accounts or a whole bunch of your accounts.

Table 6-2	Quicken's Business Reports
Report	**Description**
A/P by Vendor	Summarizes unprinted checks by payee for all your bank accounts. (*A/P* stands for *accounts payable.*)
A/R by Customer	Summarizes uncleared transactions for all other assets accounts. (*A/R* stands for *accounts receivable.*)

(continued)

Table 6-2 *(continued)*

Report	Description
Balance Sheet	Lists all accounts, their balances, and the difference between the sum of your asset accounts and the sum of your liabilities accounts, which the report identifies as your equity. Almost identical to the Home Net Worth report.
Budget	Like its Personal Finance report cousin, summarizes income and expense categories and compares actual category totals to budgeted category amounts. This report only includes transactions recorded in your bank, cash, and credit card accounts and requires you to have first set up a budget.
Cash Flow	Summarizes the money received by and paid out of an account by income and expense categories and by transfers. This report only includes transactions recorded in your bank, cash, and credit card accounts.
Comparison	Lets you compare category totals from two periods. You can use this report to compare January's activity with February's activity, for example. (Because you are comparing two periods, you must enter two transaction date ranges.) Identical to the Home Comparison report.
Income Statement	Summarizes income and expense category totals. This report includes transactions from all your accounts. It also helps you answer the business question, "Am I getting fairly compensated for the hassle and the risk?"
Itemized Categories	Summarizes income and expense category totals. This report includes transactions from all of your accounts.
Job/Project	Summarizes income and expense category totals with each class's information displayed in a separate column. You must be using an advanced Quicken feature called *classes* for this report to make any sense.
Payroll	Summarizes income and expense categories which begin with the word *payroll.* If you've done things right, you can use this report to prepare quarterly and annual payroll tax reports. (See Chapter 15 for the rest of the story.)
Reconciliation	Lists and summarizes both your cleared transactions and your uncleared transactions. Sometimes, after you reconcile an account, you'll want one of these babies as a momento.
Summary	Summarizes transactions by category or some other bit of transaction data: payee or description, class, and so on.
Transaction	Lists transactions from one of your accounts or a whole bunch of your accounts.

Customizing Reports

If you're an attentive type, you may have noticed the Show Options button in Figure 6-5. (Go ahead, if you really aren't all that attentive, and take another peek at Figure 6-5.)

This little button, if clicked, tells Quicken you want to have it your way — that you're someone who wants a custom-tailored report. When you click the button, Quicken expands the Create Report dialog box so that it holds a whole bunch of other boxes and buttons. Figure 6-8 shows the expanded version of the Create Summary Report dialog box, which Quicken displays whenever you say you want to produce a Personal Finance or Business Summary report.

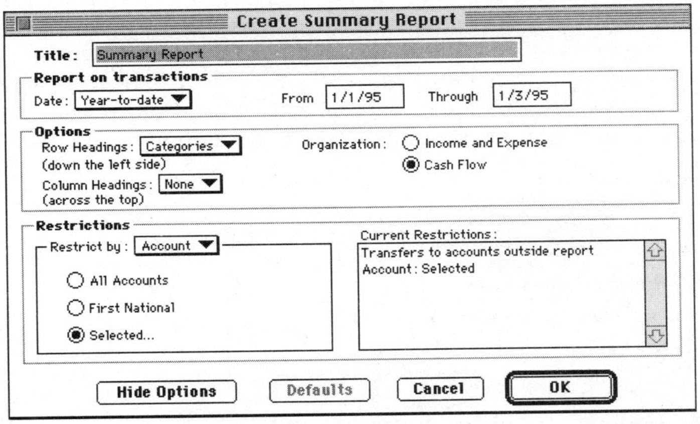

Figure 6-8: The expanded Create Summary report dialog box. For people who absolutely have to have it their way.

```
============== Create Summary Report ==============

  Title :  [ Summary Report                          ]
 ┌─Report on transactions ──────────────────────────────┐
 │ Date : [Year-to-date ▼]    From [1/1/95]  Through [1/3/95] │
 └───────────────────────────────────────────────────────┘
 ┌─Options ──────────────────────────────────────────────┐
 │ Row Headings : [Categories ▼]   Organization : ○ Income and Expense │
 │ (down the left side)                          ◉ Cash Flow │
 │ Column Headings : [None ▼]                              │
 │ (across the top)                                        │
 └───────────────────────────────────────────────────────┘
 ┌─Restrictions ─────────────────────────────────────────┐
 │ ┌Restrict by : [Account ▼]┐   Current Restrictions :   │
 │ │                          │  Transfers to accounts outside report │
 │ │  ○ All Accounts          │  Account : Selected        │
 │ │  ○ First National        │                            │
 │ │  ◉ Selected...           │                            │
 └───────────────────────────────────────────────────────┘

   ( Hide Options )   ( Defaults )   ( Cancel )   (( OK ))
```

I'm not going to spend tons of time and lots of ink explaining how these options work. The best way for you to get the report you want is by experimenting with the different options. (You'll get the report you want sooner, with more fun, and without having to read additional drivel from me, your hard-working but still imperfect writer.)

All that said, however, let me share the highlights with you. The Options drop-down list boxes and buttons let you specify how Quicken organizes your report into rows and columns and which accounts it uses. The rows and columns stuff is pretty self-explanatory.

Those Organization buttons, though, can be a little confusing. So, I'll fill you in. If you mark the Income and Expense option button, Quicken uses transactions from all your accounts. If you mark the Cash Flow option button, Quicken only uses transactions from your bank, cash, and credit card accounts.

The Restrictions buttons and list box at the bottom of the dialog box lets you tell Quicken that there's some stuff you don't want to see. No way, man. You use the drop-down list box in the Restrictions half of the dialog box to specify what it is you want to restrict: the accounts included on a report, the payee or description of transactions summarized, the categories reported, and so on. Once you indicate this, you use the option buttons to indicate whether you want all of the accounts, payees, categories, or whatever — or just a subset of them.

If you want to un-expand the Create Report dialog box, you click Hide Options.

Memorized Reports

If you do play around with these items, you can save any custom report specifications that you create. To do so, choose the Memorize command from the Edit menu. Quicken displays a dialog box that asks you to supply a name for your customized report. (See Figure 6-9.) You can also provide a default report date range. After you name the customized report, Quicken lists it whenever you choose the Memorized command from the Reports menu (see Figure 6-10).

Figure 6-9: The Memorize dialog box.

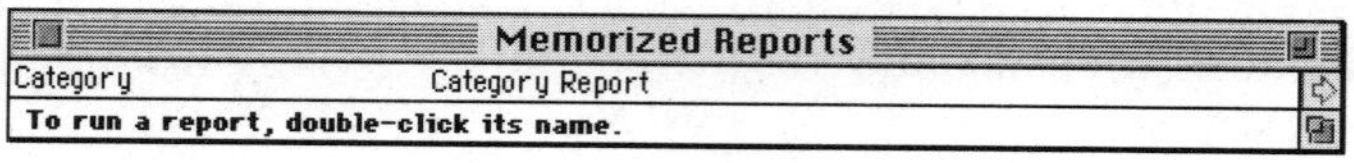

```
═════ Memorize Report Template ═════
Name:          Category
Description:  Category Report
☒ Preview template before running report
☒ Use current Date
     [ Cancel ]    [   OK   ]
```

Figure 6-10: The Memorized Reports dialog box.

```
▢═══════════ Memorized Reports ═══════════▢
Category              Category Report
To run a report, double-click its name.
```

At the printing dog-and-pony show

There are some neat things you can do with the reports you've created. I won't spend a bunch of time talking about these things, but I do want to give you a quick rundown of some of the most valuable tricks.

Got a question about a number? Just zoom it

If you don't understand where a number in a report came from, point to it with the mouse. As you point to numbers, Quicken changes the mouse pointer to a magnifying glass. Double-click a number and Quicken displays a list of all the transactions that make up that number.

This feature, called *QuickZoom,* is extremely handy for understanding the figures that appear on your reports. If you double-click the Gift Received number in the report (see Figure 6-6), for example, Quicken displays the QuickZoom report shown in Figure 6-11.

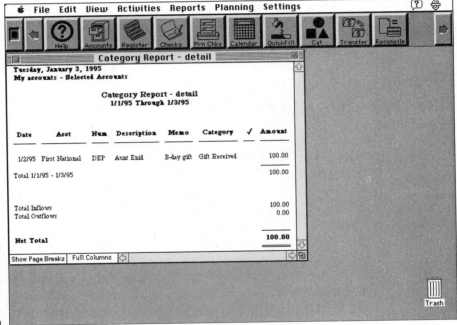

Figure 6-11:
A
QuickZoom
report.

Ah, yes. You remember Aunt Enid's thoughtful gift. You have to send her that thank-you note.

Sharing report data with spreadsheets

If you use a Windows spreadsheet like Microsoft Excel, you can copy the stuff that shows in a report document window to a file and then import, or use, the file in Excel. To do this, just choose the File menu's Export Report command. Then, when Quicken displays the dialog box shown in Figure 6-12, give the file a name and indicate whether the file should be an Excel (SYLK) file or a regular old text file.

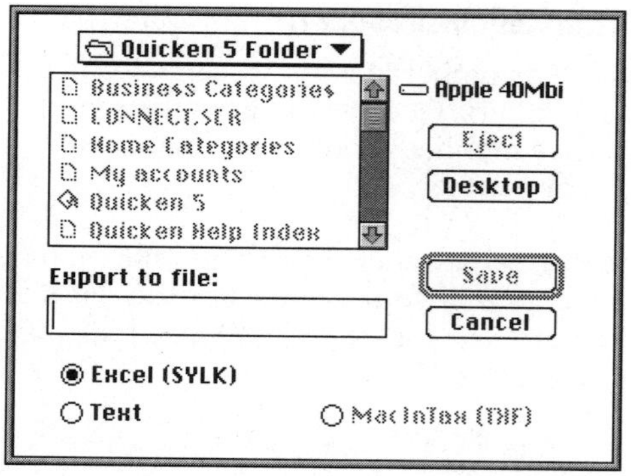

Figure 6-12:
The dialog box you use to export a report to a spreadsheet.

This process really isn't very hard, so go ahead and try it. You might want to do this if you want to analyze the report data with a spreadsheet.

Charts Only Look Tricky

I love charts. I know that sounds goofy. But data graphics — as the snobs and academics call it — opens up wonderful opportunities for communicating. And Quicken's charts are really easy to use.

To produce a Quicken chart, choose the Graphs command from the Reports menu. Quicken displays the Create Graphs dialog box in which you specify how you want the chart to look (see Figure 6-13).

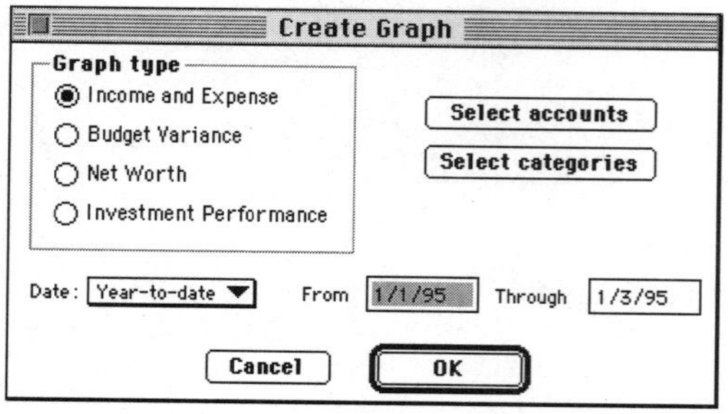

Figure 6-13:
The Create Graphs dialog box.

Use the Graph Type option buttons to pick the type of graph you want. The graph type titles are all pretty self-explanatory, so I won't waste your time by being redundant. If you have questions in spite of the titles, just experiment. You can't hurt anything.

Use the Date drop-down list box and the From and Through text boxes to tell Quicken which days or months of account information you want summarized in the graph.

Finally, use the Select Accounts and Select Categories command buttons to tell Quicken that you want to pick and choose which accounts and categories you want included in the graph. If you choose a button, Quicken displays another dialog box that lists the things you pick and choose.

When you're ready to produce the graph, just command Quicken to do so. You can try saying "Quicken, I command thee to produce a graph." Unfortunately, this command doesn't work. So your best bet is to click the OK button.

Figure 6-14 shows a picture of a bar graph of monthly income and expense figures and a pie chart that breaks down your spending. They're kind of cool, but you'll have much more fun looking at your own data in a picture. By the way, you can use QuickZoom on a chart to see a report that describes the data being plotted.

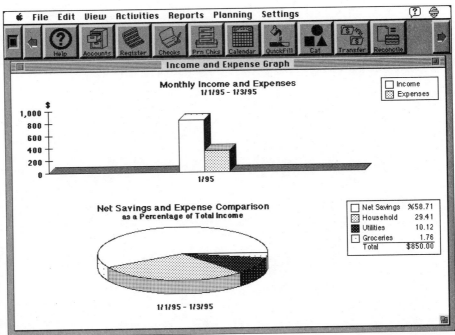

Figure 6-14:
The Quicken Income and Expense graph.

The other graph types work basically the same way. The Budget Variance graph depicts your actual and planned spending and income in bar charts. The Net Worth graph shows your total assets, total liabilities, and net worth by month in a bar graph. The Investment Performance graph displays a bar graph showing total portfolio and individual securities values by month. (If you're not working with Quicken's investments, of course, this last description sounds like gibberish. So you'll want to peruse Chapters 12 and 13 first.)

Chapter 7
A Matter of Balance

I want to start this chapter with an important point: balancing a bank account in Quicken is easy and quick.

I'm not just trying to get you pumped up about an otherwise painfully boring topic. I don't think balancing a bank account is any more exciting than you do. (At the Nelson house, we never answer the "What should we do tonight?" question by saying, "Hey, let's balance an account.")

My point is this: because bank account balancing can be tedious and boring, use Quicken to speed up the drudgery.

Selecting the Account You Want to Balance

This step is easy. And you probably already know how to do it, too.

Choose the Accounts icon from the iconbar or choose the Accounts command from the View menu. Quicken displays the My Accounts window (see Figure 7-1).

Figure 7-1:
The My
Accounts
window.

Next, select the account that you want to balance by double-clicking it. Quicken displays the register window, which lists information about the account.

Balancing a Bank Account

Like I said, balancing a bank account is remarkably easy. In fact, I'll go so far as to say that if you have any problems, they'll stem from . . . well, sloppy record-keeping that preceded your use of Quicken.

Enough of this blather; let's get started.

Telling Quicken, Hey, man, I want to balance this account

To tell Quicken that you want to *balance,* or *reconcile,* your account records with the bank's records, choose the Reconcile icon from the iconbar or choose the Reconcile command from the Activities menu. Quicken displays the Reconcile Startup dialog box, as shown in Figure 7-2.

Figure 7-2:
The
Reconcile
Startup
dialog box.

Giving Quicken the banks information

As you probably know, in a reconciliation you compare your records of a bank account with the bank's records of the same account. You should be able to explain any difference between the two accounts — usually by pointing to checks that you've written but that haven't cleared. (Sometimes deposits fall into the same category; you've recorded a deposit and mailed it, but the bank hasn't yet credited your account.)

The first step, then, is to supply Quicken with the bank's account information. You get this information from your monthly statement. Supply Quicken with the figures it needs as follows:

1. **Verify the bank statement opening balance.**

   Quicken displays a figure in the Previous Balance text box. If this figure isn't correct, replace it with the correct figure. To do so, move the cursor to the text box and type over the given figure. (If this is the first time you've reconciled, Quicken gets this opening balance figure from your starting account balance. If you've reconciled before, Quicken uses the New Balance that you specified the last time you reconciled as the Previous Balance.)

2. **Enter the bank statement ending balance.**

   Move the cursor to the New Balance text box and enter the ending, or closing, balance shown on your bank statement.

3. **Enter the bank's service charge.**

   If your bank statement shows a service charge and you haven't already entered it, move the cursor to the Service Charge text box and enter the amount (for example, enter $4.56 as **4.56**).

4. **Enter a transaction date for the service charge transaction.**

   Quicken supplies the current system date from your computer's internal clock as the default service charge date. If this date isn't correct, enter the correct one.

   Remember that you can adjust a date one day at a time by using the + and − keys.

5. **Assign the bank's service charge to a category.**

   Enter the expense category to which you assign bank service charges in the first Category text box — the one in the Service Charge text box. If you're using standard home categories, this category is Bank Charge. Remember that your special friend, QuickFill, is just itching to help. So, all you've really got to do is type enough of the category name for QuickFill to recognize.

6. Enter the account's interest income.

If the account earned interest for the month and you haven't already entered this figure, enter an amount in the Interest Earned text box (for example, enter $.17 as **.17**).

7. Enter a transaction date for the interest income transaction.

You already know how to enter dates. I won't bore you by explaining it again (but see step 4 if you're having trouble).

8. Assign the interest to a category.

Enter the category to which the account's interest should be assigned in the second Category text box. If you're using the standard category list, this category is probably Interest Earned.

9. Tell Quicken that the bank statement information is complete.

To do so, just choose OK.

Explaining the difference between your records and the bank's

Next, Quicken compares your register's account balance with the bank statement's ending account balance. Then it builds a list of checks and deposits that your register shows but that haven't yet *cleared* (been recorded by the bank). Figure 7-3 shows the window Quicken displays to provide you with this information.

As Figure 7-3 shows, the Reconcile window is basically just two lists — one of account withdrawals and one of account deposits. The window also displays some extra information at the bottom of the screen: the number and the dollar amount of checks and deposits that you or Quicken have marked as cleared, and the difference between the bank statement balance and the cleared balance.

If you don't like the order in which withdrawals and deposits are arranged, you can change it. Mark the Sort by Date option button, and Quicken reorders the transactions by date. Mark the Sort by Type/Number option button, and Quicken reorders the transactions by number.

Marking cleared checks and deposits

You need to tell Quicken which deposits and checks have cleared at the bank. (Refer to your bank statement for this information.)

1. Identify the first deposit that has cleared.

You know how to do so, I'm sure. Just leaf through the bank statement and find the first deposit listed.

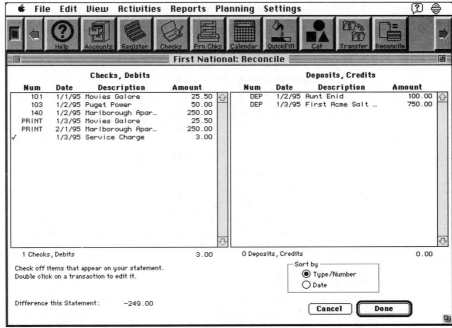

Figure 7-3:
The
Reconcile
window.

2. Mark the first cleared deposit as cleared.

Scroll through the transactions listed in the Reconcile window, find the deposit, and then click it. Quicken places a check mark in front of the deposit to mark it as cleared and updates the cleared statement balance.

3. Record any cleared but missing deposits.

If you can't find a deposit, you haven't entered it into the Quicken register yet. I can only guess why you haven't entered it. Maybe you just forgot, for example. In any event, return to the Quicken register by clicking the Register icon and then enter the deposit in the register in the usual way — but enter an asterisk in the cleared column. (The cleared column is the one showing a check mark.) This mark identifies the deposit as one that's already cleared at the bank. When you're done, return to the Reconcile window by clicking the Reconcile icon.

4. Repeat steps 1, 2, and 3 for all deposits listed on the bank statement.

5. Identify the first check that has cleared.

No sweat, right? Just find the first check or withdrawal listed on the bank statement.

6. Mark the first cleared check as cleared.

Scroll through the transactions listed in the Reconcile window, find the first check, and then click it. Quicken inserts a check mark to label this transaction as cleared and updates the cleared statement balance.

7. Record any missing but cleared checks.

If you can't find a check or withdrawal — guess what? — you haven't entered it in the Quicken register yet. Display the Quicken register by clicking the Register icon. Then enter the check or withdrawal in the register. Be sure to enter an asterisk in the cleared column to identify this check or withdrawal as one that's already cleared at the bank. Return to the Reconcile window by clicking the Reconcile icon.

8. Repeat steps 5, 6, and 7 for each withdrawal listed on the bank statement.

By the way, these steps don't take very long. It takes me about two minutes to reconcile my account each month. And I'm not joking or exaggerating. By two minutes, I really mean two minutes.

Does the difference equal zero?

After you mark all the cleared checks and deposits, the difference between the cleared balance for the account and the bank statement's ending balance should equal zero. Notice that I said "should," not "will." Figure 7-4 shows a Reconcile window in which everything is hunky-dory and life is grand.

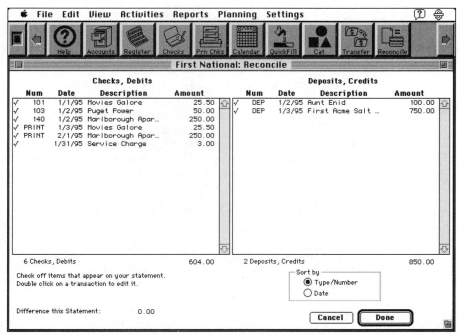

Figure 7-4:
The Reconcile window after you've reconciled.

If the difference does equal zero, you're done. Just click the Done button to tell Quicken that you're finished. Quicken displays a congratulations message saying how proud it is of you (see Figure 7-5).

Figure 7-5:
The "Your
mother and
I are very
proud of
you"
message.

Congratulations! Your account is balanced. The items you have marked have been cleared in your register.

OK

If you want, you can print a reconciliation report by using the Reconciliation command on the Reports menu. I described how you print reports in Chapter 6 in case you need more information than that.

By the way, unless you're a business bookkeeper or accountant reconciling a bank account for someone else — your employer or a client, for example — you don't need to print the Reconciliation report. All printing does is prove that you reconciled the account. (Basically, this proof is the reason you should print the report if you *are* a bookkeeper or an accountant — the person for whom you're reconciling the account will know that you did your job and has a piece of paper to come back to later if there are questions.)

If the difference doesn't equal zero, you've got a problem. If you choose Done, Quicken provides some cursory explanations as to why your account doesn't balance via a dialog box like that shown in Figure 7-6. This box tells you that you can force the two amounts to agree by clicking the Adjust Balance button.

Figure 7-6:
The
"There's a
problem,
Hal"
message
box.

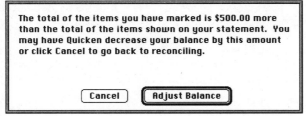

The total of the items you have marked is $500.00 more than the total of the items shown on your statement. You may have Quicken decrease your balance by this amount or click Cancel to go back to reconciling.

Cancel   Adjust Balance

Forcing the two amounts to agree isn't a very good idea. To do so, Quicken adds a cleared transaction equal to the difference. (I'll talk about this transaction a little later in the chapter.)

If you just click Cancel because you're distraught and can't get the account to reconcile, Quicken re-displays the Reconcile Startup dialog box (see Figure 7-2.) If you click this dialog box's Cancel button, Quicken closes the dialog box, throws away almost all of the reconciliation information you've entered or collected, and returns you to the register. (Quicken will leave any cleared transactions you marked on the Reconciliation window as cleared.)

Ten Things You Should Do If Your Account Doesn't Balance

Let me give you some suggestions for reconciling an account when you're having problems. If you're sitting in front of your computer wringing your hands, try the following tips.

Are you working with the right account?

Sounds dumb, doesn't it? If you have a bunch of different bank accounts, however, it's darn easy to end up in the wrong account. So go ahead and confirm, for example, that you're trying to reconcile your checking account at Mammoth International Bank using the Mammoth International checking account statement.

Look for transactions that the bank has recorded but you haven't

Go through your bank statement and make sure that you have recorded every transaction that your bank has recorded. Cash machine withdrawals, special fees or service charges (such as for checks or your safety deposit box), automatic withdrawals, direct deposits, and so on are easily overlooked.

If the difference is positive — that is, the bank thinks you have less money than you think you should — you may be missing a withdrawal transaction. If the difference is negative, you may be missing a deposit transaction.

Look for reversed transactions

Here's a tricky one. If you accidentally enter a transaction backwards — a deposit as a withdrawal or a withdrawal as a deposit — your account won't balance. And the error can be difficult to find. The Reconcile window dialog box shows all the correct transactions, but a transaction amount appears positive when it should be negative or negative when it should be positive. (In other words, it'll just appear on the wrong half of the window.) The check you wrote to Mrs. Travis for your son's piano lessons appears as a deposit (or on the deposit side of the window) instead of as a check (or on the check side of the window).

Look for a transaction that's equal to half the difference

One handy way to find the transaction that you entered backwards — *if* there's only one — is to look for a transaction that's equal to half the irreconcilable difference. For example, if the difference is $200, you may have entered a $100 deposit as a withdrawal or a $100 withdrawal as a check.

I don't want to beat a dead horse, but the sign (that is, positive or negative) of the difference should help you find the problem. If the difference is positive — the bank thinks you have less money than your register indicates — you may have mistakenly entered a withdrawal as a deposit. If the difference is negative — the bank thinks you have more money than your register says — you may be missing a deposit transaction.

Look for a transaction that's equal to the difference

While I'm on the subject of explaining the difference by looking at individual transactions, let me make an obvious point. If the difference between the bank's records and yours equals one of the transactions listed in your register, you may have incorrectly marked the transaction as cleared or incorrectly left the transaction marked as uncleared.

I don't know. Maybe that was too obvious.

Check for transposed numbers

Transposed numbers occur when you flip-flop two digits in a number. For example, you enter $45.89 as $48.59.

These turkeys always cause accountants and bookkeepers headaches. If you look at the numbers, it's often difficult to detect an error because the digits are the same. For example, when comparing a check amount of $45.89 in your register with a check for $48.59 shown on your bank statement, both check amounts show the same digits: 4, 5, 8, and 9. They just show them in different orders.

Transposed numbers are tough to find, but here's a trick you can try. Divide the difference shown on the Reconcile window by nine. If the result is an even number of dollars or cents, there's a good chance that there's a transposed number somewhere.

Have someone else look over your work

This idea may seem pretty obvious, but it amazes me how often a second pair of eyes can find something that you've been overlooking.

If you're using Quicken at home, ask your spouse. If you're using Quicken at work, ask the owner or one of your coworkers (preferably that one person who always seems to have way too much free time).

Be on the lookout for multiple errors

By the way, if you find an error using this laundry list and there's still a difference, it's a good idea to start checking at the top of the list again. You may, for example, discover after you find a transposed number that you entered another transaction backwards or incorrectly cleared or uncleared a transaction.

Try again next month (and maybe the month after that)

If the difference isn't huge in relation to the size of your bank account, you may want to wait until next month and attempt to reconcile your account again.

Before my carefree attitude puts you in a panic, consider the following example. You reconcile your account in January and the difference is $24.02. Then you reconcile the account in February and the difference is $24.02. Then you reconcile the account in March and, surprise, surprise, the difference is still $24.02.

What's going on here? Well, your starting account balance was probably off by $24.02. (The more months you try to reconcile your account and find that you're always mysteriously $24.02 off, the more likely it is that this type of error is to blame.)

After the second or third month, I think it's pretty reasonable to tell Quicken that it should enter an adjusting transaction for $24.02 so that your account balances. (In my opinion, this is the only circumstance that merits your adjusting an account to match the bank's figure.)

By the way, if you've successfully reconciled your account with Quicken before, your work may not be at fault. The mistake could be (drum roll, please) the bank's! And in this case, there's something else you should do. . . .

Get in your car, drive to the bank, and beg for help

As an alternative to the preceding idea — which supposes that the bank's statement is correct and that your records are incorrect — I propose this idea: Ask the bank to help you reconcile the account. Hint that you think the mistake is probably theirs. Smile a lot. And one other thing — be sure to ask about whatever product they're currently advertising in the lobby. (This will encourage them to think that you're interested in that 180-month certificate of deposit, and they'll be extra nice to you.)

In general, the bank's record-keeping is usually pretty darn good. I've never had a problem as a business banking client or as an individual. (I've also been lucky enough to deal with big, well-run banks.)

Nevertheless, it's quite possible that your bank has made a mistake, so ask them to help you. Be sure to have them explain any transactions that you've learned about only by seeing them on your bank statement.

Chapter 8
Housekeeping for Quicken

. . . .

In This Chapter
▶ Backing up your Quicken data

▶ Knowing when and how often to back up your data

▶ Knowing what to do if you lose your Quicken data

▶ Creating and working with more than one set of Quicken data

▶ Setting up a new file password

▶ Changing a file password

. . . .

*O*K, chasing dust bunnies isn't something you need to worry about in Quicken, but you do have little housekeeping tasks to take care of. This chapter describes these chores and how to get them done right with minimal hassle.

Backing Up Is Hard to Do

You should back up the files that Quicken uses to store your financial records. But you need to know how to back up before you can back up. Got it? So let's get to it.

Backing up the quick and dirty way

You're busy. You don't have time to fool around. You just want to do a passable job of backing up. Sound like your situation? Then follow these steps:

1. **Insert a blank, formatted floppy disk into your floppy drive.**

   You've done this before, presumably. But if you haven't, just gently slide a floppy disk into the floppy drive so the side with the metal sleeve goes in first. If you still have questions, ask someone to show you how.

2. **Display the Quicken folder.**

   You may already know how to do this, but if you don't, click the disk icon to display a window that lists its folders. Then, click the folder that's named something like "Quicken 5 folder." Figure 8-1 shows the Quicken 5 Folder window.

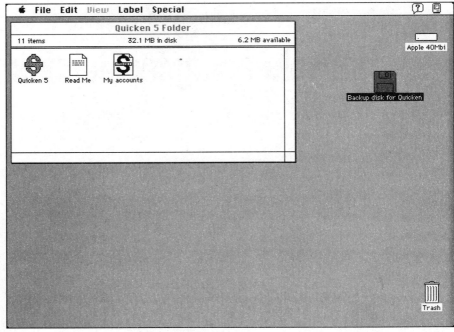

Figure 8-1:
The
Quicken 5
Folder
window.

3. Start the backup operation.

Drag the My Accounts icon, which represents your Quicken file, to the Floppy Disk icon. In Figure 8-1, I labeled the floppy disk, "Backup disk for Quicken." As your Macintosh backs up the My Accounts file, it displays a message that says something like, "Copying My Accounts."

Just as a point of interest, I'll mention that what you've just accomplished in three easy steps (backing up) takes seven rather complicated steps on an IBM compatible. Another example of how your Mac is easier to use than an IBM compatible.

So when should you back up?

Sure, I can give you some tricky, technical examples of fancy backup strategies, but they have no point here. You want to know the basics, right? So here's what I do to back up my files. I back up every month after I reconcile. Then I stick the floppy disk in my briefcase, so if something terrible happens at home, I don't lose both my computer and the backup disk with the data.

I admit that there are a few problems with my strategy, however. For example, because I'm only backing up monthly, I may have to reenter as much as a month's worth of data if the computer crashes toward the end of the month. In my case, I wouldn't lose all that much work. However, if you're someone with real heavy transaction volumes — if you write hundreds of checks a month, for example — you may want to back up more frequently than this, such as once a week.

A second problem with my strategy is only remotely possible but is still worth mentioning. If something bad does happen to the Quicken files stored on my computer's hard disk and the files stored on the backup floppy disk, I'll be up the proverbial creek without a paddle. I should also note that a floppy disk is far more likely to fail than a hard drive. If this worse case scenario actually occurs, I'll need to start over from scratch from the beginning of the year. To prevent this scenario from happening, some people — who are religiously careful — make backups of their backups to reduce the chance of this mishap.

Losing your Quicken data after you've backed up

What happens if you lose all your Quicken data? First of all, I encourage you to feel smug. Get a cup of coffee. Lean back in your chair. Gloat for a couple of minutes. You, my friend, will have no problem. You have followed instructions.

After you've sufficiently gloated, carefully do the following to reinstate your Quicken data on the computer:

1. **Quit Quicken (if you're using it).**

   To do this, just choose the Quit command from the File menu.

2. **Get your backup floppy disk.**

   Find the backup disk you created and carefully insert it into one of your disk drives. (If you can't find the backup disk, forget what I said about feeling smug — stop gloating and skip to the next section.)

3. **Stick the backup floppy disk into the floppy drive.**

4. **Open the floppy disk folder and the Quicken 5 folder.**

   You want both folders open so that they appear on-screen, as shown in Figure 8-2. You can open a folder for a disk — a hard disk or a floppy disk — by clicking it.

5. **Start the restore operation.**

   Drag the My Accounts icon shown in the folder for your backup disk to the regular Quicken 5 folder on your hard disk, which represents your Quicken file, to the Floppy Disk icon. As your Macintosh restores the My Accounts file, it displays a message that says something like, "Copying My Accounts."

   One warning. When you restore a file, you replace the current, on-your-hard-disk version of the file with the backup version stored on the floppy disk. Don't restore a file for fun. Don't restore a file for entertainment.

Restore a file only if the current version is trashed and you want to start over by using the version stored on the backup floppy disk.

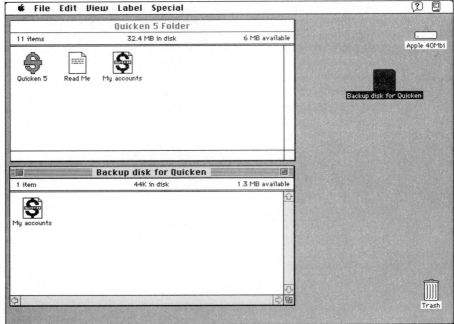

Figure 8-2:
How your Mac screen should look if you open both the hard disk and the backup disk folders.

6. Update the accounts' registers as necessary.

Using the register windows for each of the accounts in a file, reenter each of the transactions you recorded since you created the backup. Be sure that you update your accounts because you've almost certainly entered transactions since the last time you backed up.

I should mention that the restoration process sort of trashes some of the index headers Quicken's files use for internal organization. So, the next time you start Quicken, you'll see a message that says something about "Reconstructing Index Headers." Pay no attention to the message.

Just to be on the safe side, you should back up the file after you complete this process. I have heard that lightning never strikes the same place twice, but I'm not sure that the old saying is true. If you have hard disk problems or another recurring problem, whatever fouled up your file this time may rear its ugly head again — and soon.

Losing your Quicken data when you haven't backed up

What do you do if you haven't backed up your files in a while and you lose all the data in your Quicken files? OK. Stay calm.

All you have to do is reenter all the transactions for the entire year. Yeah. I know. It's a bummer. This method isn't quick and it isn't pretty, but it works.

If you have copies of the registers, of course, you can use these as your information source to reenter the information in your files. If you don't have copies of the registers, you need to use your bank statements and any of the other paper financial records you have.

Files, Files, and More Files

As part of setting up Quicken, you create what Quicken calls a file, a place where all your accounts get stored (bank accounts, credit card accounts, investment accounts, and so on).

You can have more than one Quicken file at any time. In today's world, for example, it is wise to keep personal financial records separate from business financial records. You can use Quicken to create two files: a personal accounts file and a business accounts file. (In the old days, Quicken referred to these files as *account groups*. I mention this fact for the benefit of those readers who are history buffs and, therefore, love to fill their heads with irrelevant bits of technology trivia.)

Using multiple files does have a little drawback, however. You can't easily record, in one fell swoop, account transfer transactions between accounts in different files. You need to record the transaction twice — once in the source account, which will be in the file where the transaction originates, and again in the destination account, which will be in the file where the transaction is being transferred to.

If the two accounts involved in a transfer are in the same file, all you have to do is enter the account name in the Category text box. Quicken then records the transfer in the other account for you.

Setting up a new file

To set up a new file so that you can create accounts in it, just follow these steps:

1. **Choose the New File command from the File menu.**

   Quicken displays the Creating New File dialog box, as shown in Figure 8-3. (This screen may look familiar because you filled it in when you installed Quicken.)

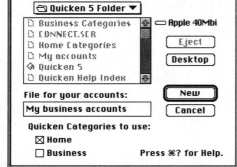

Figure 8-3:
The dialog box you fill out to create a new Quicken file.

2. **Enter a name for the Quicken file.**

   With the cursor positioned on the File For Your Accounts text box, type something meaningful. If this is your business accounts file, for example, you might type "My business accounts."

3. **Use the default file location.**

   Accept Quicken's suggestion to store the file in the regular Quicken 5 folder because there is no good reason to put it in some other file location.

4. **Indicate which categories list you want.**

   Mark the Home check box if you'll use Quicken to track home finances. Mark the Business check box if you'll use Quicken to track business finances. If you'll use Quicken for both purposes, mark both check boxes.

5. **Choose New.**

   Quicken displays the Set Up Account Type dialog box, as shown in Figure 8-4.

6. **Mark the appropriate account-type option button.**

   You need to set up at least one account for the new file, so mark the appropriate account-type option button.

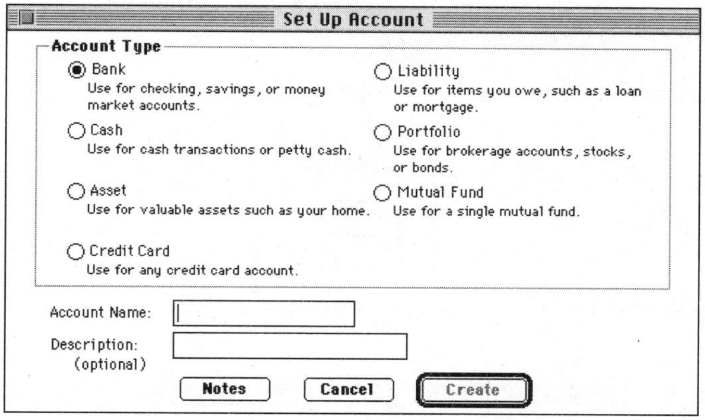

Figure 8-4:
The Set Up
Account
dialog box.

7. **Name and Describe the Account.**

   Fill out the text boxes to collect the name and, optionally, the description for the new account. Because I have described how to fill out this dialog box in previous chapters, I won't go into detail here. If you need help in filling it out, refer to Chapter 2.

8. **Click Create.**

   Quicken will display a register window for the new account. To enter the starting balance, you'll need to enter a deposit again. Again, I described how to do this in Chapter 2, so I won't go into detail here. If you need help in filling it out, refer to Chapter 2.

Flip-flopping between files

You can only work with one file at a time. So, after you create a second file, you need to know how to flip-flop between your files. If you're recording business stuff, for example, you want to be using the business file. However, a transaction comes in that clearly is meant for your personal file, and you want to enter it there immediately. Flip-flopping allows you to get from one file to another in no time.

Flip-flopping is easy: just choose the Open File command from the File menu. Quicken displays the Open a Quicken data file dialog box. (see Figure 8-5). Use its list boxes to select the file location and name. Then select Open. Zap! You are in the new file.

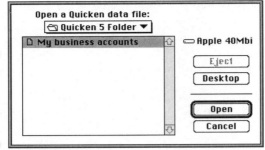

Figure 8-5:
The Open a
Quicken
Data File
dialog box.

When files get too big for their own good

If your file starts to get unwieldy, you can create a new file that has only the
transactions you most need. For example, you can create a file that has only the
current year's or the last two years' transactions in it.

This means you have a copy of the big file you won't use anymore, and a
smaller, shrunken file with just the current year's transactions. This may sound
like much ado about nothing, but it means you end up working with a smaller
file. So, that probably means Quicken will run faster. And smaller files should
make backing up easier because you will probably be able to keep your files
small enough to fit on a single double-density floppy disk.

To shrink a Quicken file, follow these steps:

1. Choose the Save a Copy command from the File menu.

Quicken displays a portrait of Barry Nelson, the first actor to portray
James Bond. No, not really — I just wanted to see if you were awake.
Actually, Quicken displays the dialog box shown in Figure 8-6.

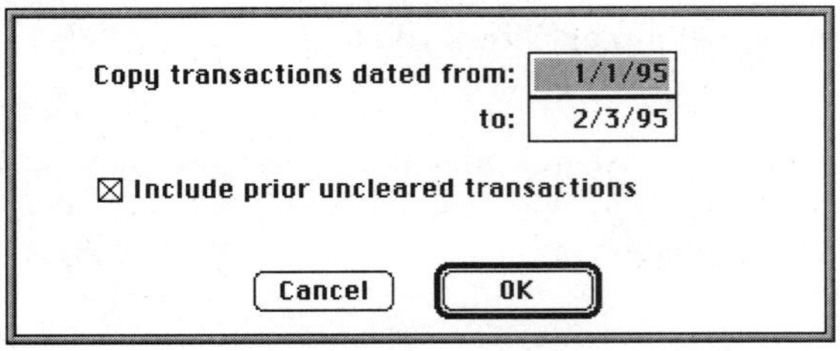

Figure 8-6:
The dialog
box Quicken
displays
when you
choose the
File menu's
Save a Copy
command.

Copy transactions dated from: | 1/1/95

to: | 2/3/95

⊠ Include prior uncleared transactions

Cancel | OK

2. Specify the transaction date range for the new file.

Using the Copy Transactions Dated From and To text boxes, you specify the range of dates you want included in the new file. Typically, this date range starts at the beginning of the current year (or the beginning of the preceding year) and ends at the current date.

3. Make sure that the Include Prior Uncleared Transactions check box is marked.

You need to have old uncleared transactions in the register so that you can reconcile the accounts.

4. Choose OK.

Quicken displays the dialog box shown in Figure 8-7.

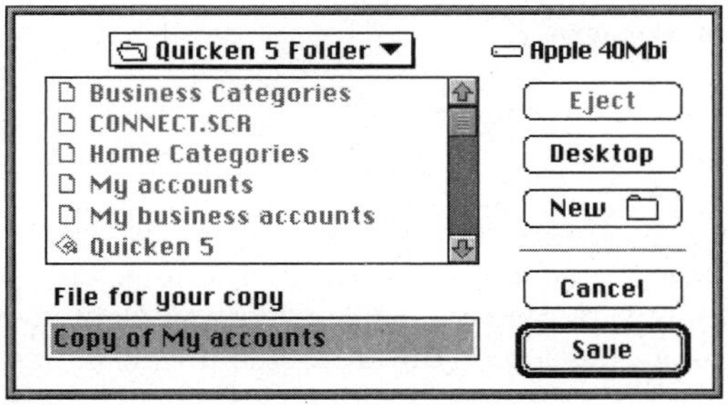

Figure 8-7:
The dialog box you use to name the new, shrunken file.

```
┌─────────────────────────────────────────────────┐
│   ⬚ Quicken 5 Folder ▼        ⊂⊃ Apple 40Mbi     │
│   ☐ Business Categories   ⬆   ┌──────────┐       │
│   ☐ CONNECT.SCR               │  Eject   │       │
│   ☐ Home Categories           └──────────┘       │
│   ☐ My accounts               ┌──────────┐       │
│   ☐ My business accounts      │ Desktop  │       │
│   ⬚ Quicken 5            ⬇   └──────────┘       │
│                               ┌──────────┐       │
│   File for your copy          │ New  ☐   │       │
│   ┌───────────────────────┐   ┌──────────┐       │
│   │ Copy of My accounts   │   │  Cancel  │       │
│   └───────────────────────┘   ┌──────────┐       │
│                               │  Save    │       │
│                               └──────────┘       │
└─────────────────────────────────────────────────┘
```

5. Enter a name in the File For Your Copy text box.

Give a name to the new file. Quicken suggests something along the lines of "Copy of" followed by the original account name. I also think you can use a name that identifies the year. For example, you might name a file containing 1995 financial records as, well, "1995's Financial Records."

6. Choose Save.

Quicken saves the new file.

7. Open the new file if it's the one you now want to use.

To do this step, choose the Open File command from the File menu. Then use its list boxes to identify the file's folder and its name. (I already described how the Open File command works in this chapter, so flip back if you have questions.)

What's the Password?

I have mixed feelings about passwords. Theoretically, they let you lock up your Quicken data so that your rebellious teenagers (if you're using Quicken at home) or the night janitors (if you're using Quicken in a business) can't come in, print checks, process automatic payments, and just generally mess things up.

Using passwords sounds pretty good, of course. But before you set up a password and then start relying on it to protect your information, let me remind you that a Quicken password only prevents someone from accessing your data with Quicken. Using a password does not prevent someone from fooling around with your computer itself. If the night janitors — or, heaven forbid, your teenagers — are the nefarious types, they can erase your files with Finder or scramble them with another program, such as a spreadsheet or word processor. And it's possible that they even can get in and manipulate the data with another checkbook or accounting program.

There's one other last little annoying problem with passwords, too. Darn it, you have to remember them.

For these reasons, I think that passwords are best left to computer systems that use them on a global basis to control access to all programs and to computer systems that can track all users (you, your teenagers, the night janitors, and anyone else) by name. Your Macintosh doesn't fall in this category.

Setting up a file password

You still want a password? OK, with much trepidation, I give you the following steps for setting up a password for a Quicken file:

1. **Select the file you want to protect with a password.**

   If the file you want to password-protect is not the active file, select it by using the Open File command on the File menu.

2. **Select the Passwords command from the Settings menu.**

   Quicken displays the — you guessed it — Password menu, which lists two commands: Open File and Modify Transactions.

3. **Choose the Open File command**

   Quicken displays the Open File Password dialog box, as shown in Figure 8-8.

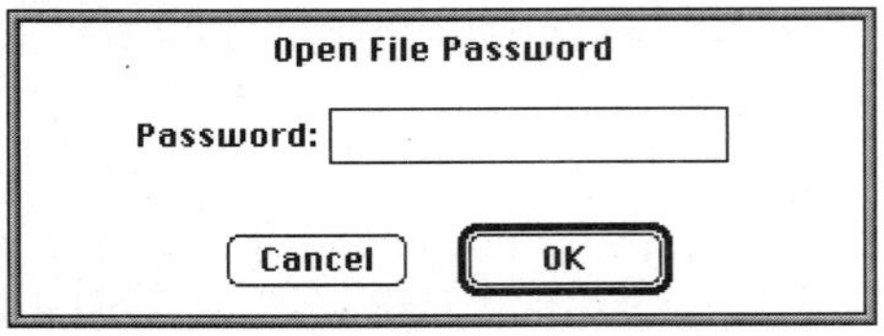

Figure 8-8:
The Open
File
Password
dialog box.

```
          Open File Password

Password: [                    ]

       ( Cancel )  (   OK   )
```

4. Enter the password you want to use.

You can use up to 16 characters. Quicken doesn't differentiate between lowercase and uppercase characters, by the way, so Washington, wASHINGTON, and WASHINGTON are all the same from its point of view. Quicken doesn't display the actual characters you type; it displays asterisks instead. If you type Dog, for example, it displays ***. (Passwords require strict secrecy, you see.)

5. Choose OK.

Quicken, still displaying the Open File Password dialog box, asks you to retype the password. (Quicken does this to confirm that you do indeed know what you typed.)

6. Enter the password you want to use again and choose OK.

Congratulations! You're done.

Assigning a password to a file does not prevent you from doing anything with the file that you would normally do. However, the next time you try to use this file — after you start Quicken or when you try to select the file by using the File menu's Open File command — Quicken will ask you for the file's password. You need to supply the password to gain access to the file.

This brings up an interesting and maybe obvious point. You assign an open file password to a file. So, if you have created multiple files and you want to protect all your files, you need to assign an open file password to each file. You can use the same password for all the files, or you can use a different password for each file.

Changing a file password

After you set up a file password, you're not stuck with it forever. You either can change the password or remove it by using the Passwords Open File command on the Settings menu.

If you've already set up a password, however, Quicken doesn't display the Open File Password dialog box shown in Figure 8-8. Instead, Quicken displays the Enter Old File Password dialog box that asks for the current password you're now using. If you can correctly enter the current password, Quicken displays the Open File Password dialog box — the same one shown in Figure 8-8 — so that you can enter the new password you want to use in the future. From now on, you need to use the new password to gain access to the file. If you don't want to use a password anymore, just leave the Password text box in this dialog box blank.

If you've waded your way through eight chapters of this book, you should be feeling very good by now about using Quicken. Congratulations! You've covered a lot of ground.

Given your progress, it may be time to take a break. Sure, you can read the next chapter (how to use Quicken's calculators and financial planners) or experiment with sophisticated programs like investment record-keeping or payroll preparation. But I think that you deserve a little break.

So what are modify transactions passwords?

After you choose the Passwords command from the Settings menu, Quicken asks whether you want to create an open file password or a modify transactions password. In general, you will be using an open file password to protect the access into a Quicken file.

A modify transactions password works like a file password except that it requires the user to enter the modify transactions password if the date of the transaction the user is trying to enter is before a specified date. You specify the date, called cutoff date, when you set up the modify transactions password.

Maybe it's just me, but modify transactions passwords don't make a lot of sense. I guess the logic is that you use a modify transactions password to prevent some idiot from fouling up last year's or last month's transactions. It seems to me, though, that there are a couple of easier approaches. One is that you can create and safely store backup copies of the Quicken file for last year or last month. Another is to not have idiots fooling around with your Quicken files. Jeepers, if somebody can't understand an instruction like, "Use the current date," do you really want them mucking about in your books?

Chapter 9

Compound Interest Magic and Other Mysteries

*T*he folks at Intuit have added several nifty little calculators (most are dialog boxes called Planners) to recent versions of Quicken. I strongly encourage you to use these tools. At the very least, the calculators should make your work easier. And if you invest a little time, you should gain some enormously valuable perspectives on your financial affairs.

Noodling Around with Your Investments

My favorite Quicken calculator is the Investment & Savings Planner. I guess I just like to forecast portfolio future values and other similar stuff.

Using the Investment Savings Planner

Let's say that you want to know how much you'll accumulate if you save $2,000 a year for 35 years, using a stock mutual fund you anticipate will earn 10 percent annually. Use the Investment Savings Planner to estimate how much you should ultimately accumulate:

1. **Display the Investment Savings Planner.**

   Choose the Investment & Savings Planner from the Planning menu. Quicken displays the Investment Planner dialog box (see Figure 9-1).

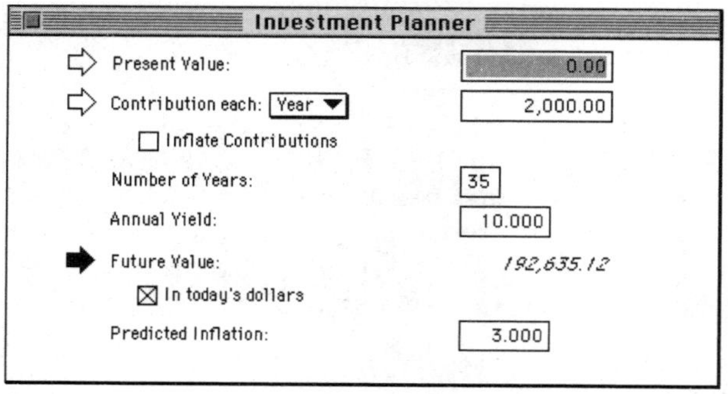

Figure 9-1:
The
Investment
Planner
dialog box
with some
sample
data.

2. Enter what you've already accumulated — your current savings — as the Present Value.

Move the cursor to the Present Value text box; then enter the amount of your current investments. If this amount is zero, for example, enter **0**.

3. Enter the amount you plan to add to your investments every period.

Move the cursor to the Contribution each drop-down list box and indicate how often you plan to add to the savings. Then move the cursor to the Contribution each text box and enter the amount you plan to add. (Figure 9-1 shows how to plan a $2,000 annual contribution.)

4. Indicate whether you plan to increase your annual contribution as a result of inflation.

Mark the Inflate Contributions check box if you plan to annually increase — by the annual inflation rate — the amount you add to your investment portfolio. Don't mark the check box if you don't want to inflate the payments.

5. Indicate how long you plan to let your investments earn income.

Move the cursor to the Number Of Years text box and indicate how long (enter the number of years) you will add to your savings and let the interest compound. (By compound, I just mean you save the interest, too, so it starts earning interest.)

6. Enter the annual yield that you expect your investments to earn.

Move the cursor to the Annual Yield text box and type the percent. If you plan to invest in the stock market and expect your savings to match the market's usual return of about 10 percent, for example, type **10** (don't type .10).

7. Enter the anticipated inflation rate.

Move the cursor to the Predicted Inflation text box and enter the inflation rate. By the way, from 1926 to 1992, the inflation rate has averaged just over 3 percent (refer to Figure 9-1).

After you enter all the information, the Future Value field shows how much you'll accumulate in present-day, uninflated dollars: $192,635.12. Hmmm. Nice.

If you want to know the amount you'll accumulate in future-day, inflated dollars, unmark the In Today's Dollars check box.

To create a permanent copy of the stuff you've entered into and calculated with the Investment Planner, select the Print Investment Planner command from the File menu. When Quicken displays the standard Print dialog box, choose Print. Quicken whips up a quick little report showing the same information as the Investment Planner dialog box. Try it. You may like it.

How to become a millionaire

So you want to be a millionaire some day.

To learn how to realize this childhood dream, use the arrow option buttons that appear to the left of the Present Value, Contribution each, and Future Value boxes. With these arrow buttons, you mark which financial variable you want to calculate. You can tell which variable is marked because its arrow appears black while the others appear white. For example, to determine the annual amount you need to contribute to your investment so that your portfolio reaches $1,000,000, here's what you do:

1. **Mark the Contribution each arrow button.**

2. **Mark the Inflate Contributions check box.**

3. **Unmark the In Today's Dollars check box.**

4. **Enter all the other input variables. Remember to set the Future Value text box to 1000000 (the Future Value field becomes a text box after you mark the Contribution Each arrow button).**

5. **Press Return.**

The Investment Savings Planner computes how much you need to save annually to hit your $1,000,000 target.

Starting from scratch, it'll take 35 years of roughly $2,800-a-year payments to reach $1,000,000.00 (see Figure 9-2). All those zeros look nice, don't they? Note that this calculation assumes a 10 percent annual yield.

A timing assumption you should know

The Investment Savings Planner assumes that you will add to your portfolio at the end of the period—what financial planners call an *ordinary annuity.*

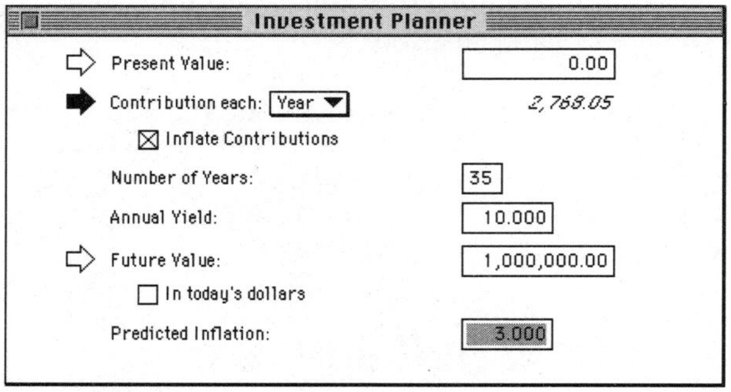

Figure 9-2:
You will
become rich
slowly by
saving
substantial
amounts
over long
periods of
time.

```
┌─────────────────────────────────────────────┐
│ ▣ ▒▒▒▒▒▒▒    Investment Planner    ▒▒▒▒▒▒▒▒  │
│  ⇨  Present Value:              ┌──────────┐ │
│                                │     0.00 │ │
│                                └──────────┘ │
│  ➡  Contribution each: [Year ▼]   2,768.05 │
│        ☒ Inflate Contributions              │
│     Number of Years:          ┌────┐        │
│                               │ 35 │        │
│                               └────┘        │
│     Annual Yield:             ┌──────┐      │
│                               │10.000│      │
│                               └──────┘      │
│  ⇨  Future Value:         ┌──────────────┐  │
│                           │ 1,000,000.00 │  │
│                           └──────────────┘  │
│        ☐ In today's dollars                 │
│     Predicted Inflation:     ▓▓3.000▓▓      │
└─────────────────────────────────────────────┘
```

"Jeepers, creepers," you say. "This seems too darn good to be true, Steve."

Well, unfortunately, the calculation is a little misleading. With 3 percent inflation, your million bucks will *only* be worth $355,383 in current day dollars. To confirm this present value calculation, click the Future Value arrow button and mark the In Today's Dollars check box.

The Often Unbearable Burden of Debt

To help you better manage your debts, Quicken provides a neat Loan Planner, which computes loan payments and balances.

Using the Loan Planner to calculate payments

Let's say that one afternoon, you're wondering what the mortgage payment is on one of those monstrous houses: tens of thousands of square feet, acres of grounds, cottages for the domestic help, and so on. You get the picture — something that's a really vulgar display of wealth.

To learn what you would pay on a 30-year, $9,999,999 mortgage if the money costs 7.5 percent, use the Loan Planner: ($9,999,999 is the biggest mortgage you can calculate a payment for, by the way.)

1. **Display the Loan Planner.**

   Choose the Loan Planner command from the Planning menu. Quicken displays the Loan Planner dialog box. Figure 9-3 shows a picture of this handy tool.

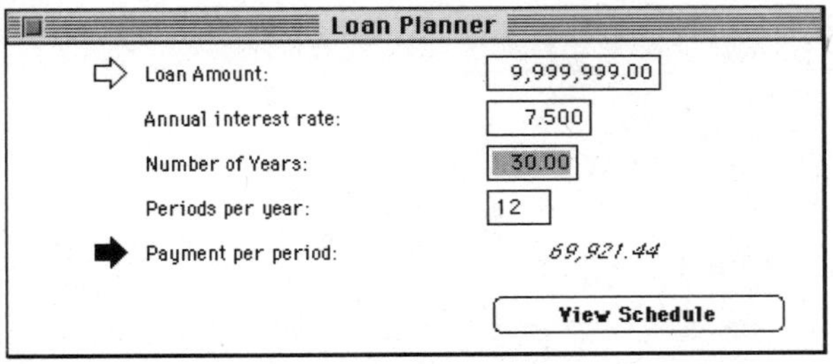

Figure 9-3:
The Loan
Planner
dialog box.

```
┌──────────────────── Loan Planner ────────────────────┐
│  ▭                                                     │
│  ▷  Loan Amount:           ┌──────────────┐          │
│                            │ 9,999,999.00 │          │
│     Annual interest rate:  ┌──────────────┐          │
│                            │    7.500     │          │
│     Number of Years:       ┌──────────────┐          │
│                            │    30.00     │          │
│     Periods per year:      ┌────┐                     │
│                            │ 12 │                     │
│  ➡  Payment per period:          69,921.44           │
│                                                       │
│                            ┌───────────────────┐     │
│                            │   View Schedule   │     │
│                            └───────────────────┘     │
└───────────────────────────────────────────────────────┘
```

2. Enter the loan amount.

Move the cursor to the Loan Amount text box and enter the amount of the loan. (If you're checking the lifestyle of the ostentatious and vulgar, enter **9,999,999.**)

3. Enter the annual interest rate.

Move the cursor to the Annual Interest Rate text box and enter the interest rate percent. If a loan charges 7.5 percent interest, for example, enter **7.5**.

4. Enter the number of years you want to take to repay the loan.

Move the cursor to the Number of Years text box and enter the number of years you'll make payments.

5. Indicate how many loan payments you plan to make a year.

Move the cursor to the Periods Per Year text box and enter the number of loan payments you'll make in a year. If you want to make monthly payments, for example, enter **12**.

Quicken calculates the loan payment and displays the amount in the Payment Per Period field. Yikes! $69,921.44 a month.

I guess if you have to ask how much the mortgage payment is, you really can't afford it.

To create a permanent copy of the stuff you've entered into and calculated with the Loan Planner, select the Print Loan Planner command from the File menu. When Quicken displays the standard Print dialog box, choose Print. Quicken whips up a quick little report showing the same information as the Loan Planner dialog box.

To get more information on the loan payments, interest and principal portions of payments, and outstanding loan balances, select the View Schedule button, which appears on the face of the Loan Planner dialog box. Quicken whips up a quick loan amortization schedule showing all this stuff (see Figure 9-4).

Payment Schedule				
Pmt	Principal	Interest	Balance	Total Interest
		7.500%	9,999,999.00	
1	7,421.45	62,499.99	9,992,577.55	62,499.99
2	7,467.83	62,453.61	9,985,109.72	124,953.60
3	7,514.50	62,406.94	9,977,595.22	187,360.54
4	7,561.47	62,359.97	9,970,033.75	249,720.51
5	7,608.73	62,312.71	9,962,425.02	312,033.22
6	7,656.28	62,265.16	9,954,768.74	374,298.38
7	7,704.14	62,217.30	9,947,064.60	436,515.68
8	7,752.29	62,169.15	9,939,312.31	498,684.83
9	7,800.74	62,120.70	9,931,511.57	560,805.53
10	7,849.49	62,071.95	9,923,662.08	622,877.48
11	7,898.55	62,022.89	9,915,763.53	684,900.37

Figure 9-4:
An amortization schedule.

You can print the amortization schedule by selecting the Print Payment Schedule command from the File menu.

Calculating loan balances

To calculate the loan principal amount, click the Loan Amount arrow button. Then enter all the other variables.

For example, those $70,000-a-month payments for the monster mansion seem a little ridiculous. So calculate how much you can borrow if you make $1,000-a-month payments over 30 years and the annual interest rate is 7.5 percent:

1. **Mark the Loan Amount arrow button.**

2. **Enter 7.5 in the Annual interest rate text box.**

3. **Enter 30 in the Number of years text box.**

4. **Enter 12 in the Periods per year text box.**

5. **Enter 1000 in the Payment per period text box.**

6. **Press Return.**

The Loan Planner computes a Loan Amount of $143,017.63.

Why You Won't Read About the Refinance Planner Here

You won't read about the Refinance Planner here — but not because I'm lazy. (Believe it or not, I enjoy writing about things that help you make better financial decisions.) The Refinance Planner merely calculates the difference in mortgage payments if you make lower payments; then it tells you how long it would take with these lower payments to pay back the refinancing costs you incur.

For example, if you save $50 a month because you refinance and it costs $500 to refinance, the Refinance Planner tells you that it would take ten months of $50-a-month savings to recoup your $500.

You know what? Although you may want to know how long it would take to recoup the refinance costs, that information doesn't tell you whether it's a good idea to refinance.

Deciding whether to refinance is very, very complicated. You can't just look at your next few payments, like the Refinance Planner does. You also need to look at the total interest you would pay with the old mortgage and the new mortgage. And you need to factor in the time value of money.

I don't think there's any good reason to use the Refinance Planner; it just doesn't do what it purports to do.

So that I don't leave you hanging; however, let me give you two rules of thumb to help you make smarter refinancing decisions.

First, if you want to save interest costs, don't use refinancing as a way to stretch out your borrowing. That is, if you refinance, make sure that you make payments large enough to pay off the new mortgage by the same time you would have paid off the old mortgage. In other words, if you have 23 years left on your old mortgage, don't go out and get a 30-year mortgage. Find a lender who will let you pay off the new mortgage in 23 years.

Here's a second trick, if you can find a willing lender. Ask the lender to calculate the annual percentage rate (APR) on the new mortgage, assuming you'll pay off the mortgage by the same time you would have paid off the old mortgage. (An APR includes all the loan's costs — interest, points, miscellaneous fees, and so on — and calculates an implicit interest rate.) If the APR on the new loan is lower than the current loan's interest rate, you would probably save money by refinancing.

Let me issue one caveat. When you base your refinancing decision on the comparison between the new loan's APR and the current loan's interest rate, you're saying that you'll live in your current house until the mortgage is paid.

I hope this information helps. Like I said, mortgage refinancing decisions are tough if you truly want to save money.

Using the Retirement Planner

I think this is the book's most important section. No joke. Your financial future is much too consequential to go for easy laughs or cheap shots.

The dilemma in a nutshell

By the time the 30-something and 40-something crowd reaches retirement, Social Security coverage probably will be scaled back. As you may know, the current recipients are getting everything they paid in as well as much of what we pay in.

If you currently receive Social Security, please don't feel defensive or betrayed. Your generation overcame challenges far more important (World War I, the Great Depression, World War II, the Cold War, the end of segregation, and so on) than the problem of inadequate Social Security funding we younguns face.

I know this sentiment sounds corny, but I think you've left the world a better place. I hope my generation does the same.

And the problem isn't just Social Security. More and more often, employer-provided pension plans are defined contribution plans, which add specific amounts to your pension (like 2 percent of your salary), rather than defined benefit plans, which promise specific pension amounts (like $1,000 a month). As a result, although you know that someone will throw a few grand into your account every so often, you don't know how much you'll have when you retire.

I urge you to think ahead about your financial requirements. Fortunately, Quicken's Retirement Planner can help you.

I'll get off my soapbox now. Thank you.

Making retirement planning calculations

Imagine that you've decided to jump into your employer's 401K thing (a type of deferred compensation system), which will allow you to plop about $3,000 into a retirement account that you think will earn about 9 percent annually.

Fortunately, you don't need to be a rocket scientist to figure this stuff out. You just use the Retirement Planner:

1. **Display the Retirement Planner.**

   Choose the Retirement Planner command from the Planning menu. Quicken displays the Retirement Planner dialog box shown in Figure 9-5.

2. **Enter what you've already saved as your Current Savings.**

   Move the cursor to the Current Savings text box and enter your current retirement savings (for example, if you have some individual retirement account money or you've accumulated a balance in an employer-sponsored 401K account). Don't worry if you don't have anything saved — most people don't.

Figure 9-5:
The
Retirement
Planner
dialog box.

3. **Enter the annual yield that you expect your retirement savings to earn.**

   Move the cursor to the Annual Yield text box and type the percent. In the little example shown in Figure 9-5, I say the annual yield is 10 percent.

4. **Enter your current marginal tax rate, if needed.**

   If you're investing in taxable stuff, move the cursor to the Current Tax Rate text box. Then enter the combined federal and state income tax rate that you pay on your last dollars of income.

5. **Indicate whether you plan to save retirement money in a tax sheltered investment.**

   Mark the Tax-sheltered check box if your retirement savings earns untaxed money. Tax sheltered investments are things like individual retirement accounts, annuities, and employer-sponsored 401Ks and 403Bs (a 403B is kind of a profit-sharing plan for a non-profit agency). As a practical matter, tax sheltered investments are the only way to ride. By deferring income taxes on your earnings, you earn interest on the money you otherwise would have paid as income taxes.

6. **Enter the annual amount added to your retirement savings.**

   Move the cursor to the Contribution each year text box and enter the amount that you or your employer will add to your retirement savings at the end of each year. In the example, I say that I plan to add $3,000 (refer to Figure 9-5).

7. **Enter the anticipated inflation rate.**

   Move the cursor to the Predicted Inflation text box and enter the inflation rate. By the way, from 1926 to 1992, the inflation rate has averaged just above 3 percent (refer to Figure 9-5).

8. **Indicate whether the annual additions will increase.**

   Mark the Inflate Contributions check box if the additions will increase annually by the inflation rate. (Because your salary and 401K contributions will presumably inflate if there's inflation, Figure 9-5 shows the Inflate Contributions check box marked.)

9. **Enter your current age.**

Move the cursor to the Current Age text box and enter a number. You're on your own here, but let me suggest that this is a time to be honest.

10. **Enter your retirement.**

Move the cursor to the Retirement Age text box and enter a number. Again, purely a personal matter. Figure 9-5 shows this age as 65, but you should retire when you want.

11. **Enter the age to which you want to continue withdrawals.**

Move the cursor to the Withdraw until age field and enter a number. Let's not beat around the bush here. This number is how old you think you'll be when you die. I don't like the idea any better than you do. Let me say, though, that ideally you want to run out of steam — there, that's a safe metaphor — before you run out of money. So go ahead and make this age something pretty old — like 95 (sorry, Grandma).

12. **Mark the In Today's Dollars check box.**

This tells Quicken to calculate your retirement income in current-day, uninflated dollars.

13. **(Optional) Mark the After-tax check box and enter your anticipated retirement tax rate.**

Click the After-tax check box. Then move the cursor to the Retirement Tax Rate text box, then . . . No, wait a minute. Who knows what the rates will be next year, let alone when you're retired. I think you should enter **0,** but remember that the Retirement Income figure is really your pretax income (just like your current salary is really your pretax income).

14. **Press Return.**

After you enter all the information, take a peek at the Retirement Income field Figure 9-5, for example, shows $19,443.98. Not bad. Not bad at all.

To create a permanent copy of the stuff you've entered into and calculated with the Retirement Planner, select the Print Retirement Planner command from the File menu. Quicken whips up a quick little report showing the same information as the Retirement Planner dialog box.

More about timing

The Retirement Planner assumes that you or your employer will add to your retirement savings at the end of the year — what financial planners call an *ordinary annuity.* If you or your employer adds to your retirement savings at the beginning of the year, you earn an extra year of interest. As a result, your aftertax income will be more than Quicken shows.

If you're now bummed out about retirement

First, don't feel depressed. At least you know *now* if your golden years seem a little tarnished. After all, you acquired Quicken to help you sort out your finances. Now you can use Quicken and your newly gained knowledge to help improve your financial lot.

Basically, retirement planning depends on just three things:

- The number of years that the retirement savings will accrue interest
- The real yield (that is, adjusted for inflation) you earn — in other words, the annual yield minus the predicted inflation
- The yearly payments

Anything you do to increase one of these variables will increase your retirement income.

If you invest, for example, in something that delivers higher real yields, such as the stock market, you should see a big difference (of course, you usually bear more risk). Or if you wait an extra year or two to retire, you wind up making more annual payments and earning more interest. Finally, if you boost the yearly payments (for example, by participating in an employer-sponsored 401K or 403B plan, where your employer matches a portion of your contribution), you'll see a huge change.

Noodle around with the variables. See what happens. You may be surprised.

Playing retirement roulette

Use the arrow buttons to determine a retirement income variable. You can calculate current savings, contribution each year, or, as described earlier, the retirement income.

To calculate the yearly payment required to produce a specific level of retirement income, for example, mark the Contribution Each Year arrow button. Then enter all the other variables — including the desired retirement income. The Retirement Planner calculates how much you need to save to hit your target retirement income.

Planning for the Cost of College

Ouch. I have a couple of daughters, so I know how you feel. Man, oh man, do I know how you feel.

Using the College Planner

Let's say that you have a daughter who may attend college in 16 years. And you haven't started to save yet. If the local university costs $9,500 a year and you can earn 9 percent annually, how much should you save?

The College Planner works like the Retirement Planner:

1. **Display the College Planner.**

   Choose the College Planner command from the Planning menu. Quicken displays the College Planner dialog box shown in Figure 9-6.

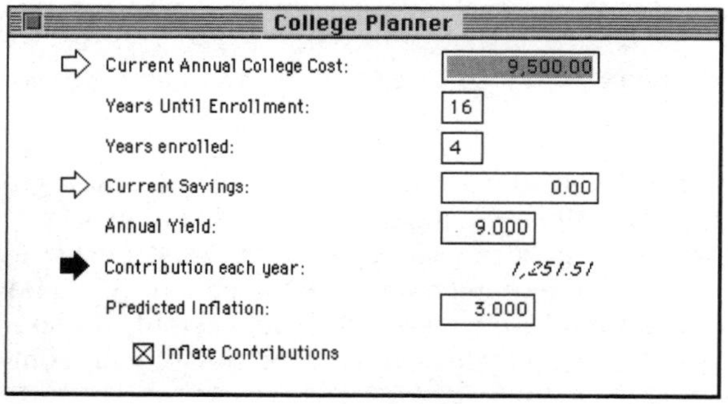

Figure 9-6:
The College
Planner
dialog box.

College Planner	
⇨ Current Annual College Cost:	9,500.00
Years Until Enrollment:	16
Years enrolled:	4
⇨ Current Savings:	0.00
Annual Yield:	9.000
➡ Contribution each year:	*1,251.51*
Predicted Inflation:	3.000
☒ Inflate Contributions	

2. **Enter the annual college costs.**

   Move the cursor to the Current Annual College Cost text box. Then enter the current annual costs at a school Junior may attend. Figure 9-6 shows this amount as $9,500.

3. **Enter the number of years until enrollment.**

   Move the cursor to the Years Until Enrollment text box and enter a number. For example, if Junior will start college in 16 years, enter **16**.

4. **Enter the number of years enrolled.**

   Move the cursor to the Years Enrolled text box and enter a number. Assuming Junior doesn't fool around, enter **4** or **5**.

5. **Enter the amount of the current college savings.**

   Move the cursor to the Current Savings text box and enter an amount. Figure 9-6 shows this amount as $0.00.

6. **Enter the annual yield that you expect the college savings to earn.**

   Move the cursor to the Annual Yield text box and type the percent. Figure 9-6 shows the yield as 9 percent.

7. **Enter the inflation rate anticipated in college tuition.**

   Move the cursor to the Predicted Inflation text box and enter the inflation rate percent. Figure 9-6 shows this rate as 3 percent.

8. **Indicate whether you plan to increase your annual contribution as a result of inflation.**

   Mark the Inflate Contributions check box if you plan to annually increase — by the annual inflation rate — the amount you save. Figure 9-6 shows this check box marked.

After you enter all the information, the Contribution Each Year field shows how much you need to save each year until the child graduates from college.

Just to beat this thing to death, Figure 9-6 shows that the lucky student will attend four years at a college that currently costs $9,500 a year and that you expect to earn 9 percent annually and anticipate 3 percent annual inflation. Given these cold hard facts, you need to ante up $1,251.51 every year.

If you're now bummed out about college costs

Look at the positive side: you now understand the size of the problem and the solution.

College planning depends on four things:

- College costs
- The number of years that the savings will earn interest
- The real yield (that is, adjusted for inflation) you earn — in other words, the annual yield minus the predicted inflation
- The yearly payments

I don't mean to sound like a simpleton, but there are three basic ways to successfully save for a college education:

- Reduce the costs (find a less expensive school)
- Invest in things that deliver higher real yields
- Boost the yearly payments

Use the arrow buttons to compute a specific financial variable. Mark which variable you want to calculate; then input the other values. The College Planner computes the flagged variable.

Estimating Your Income Tax Expenses

The folks at Quicken added a very cool calculator to the most recent release of Quicken, a Tax Estimator. Okay — you two guys in the back row. Stop sniggering. I'm serious. I think it's really neat. Not because I like income tax planning and preparation. No, I think it's neat because this tool makes it possible to estimate with a fair degree of accuracy one of the most complicated expenses of our little lives: federal income taxes.

Using the Tax Planner Calculator

The Tax Planner works pretty much like the other financial planning calculators. Here's the straight scoop:

1. **Display the Tax Planner.**

   Select Tax Planner command from the Planning menu. Quicken displays the Quicken Tax Planner dialog box shown in Figure 9-7.

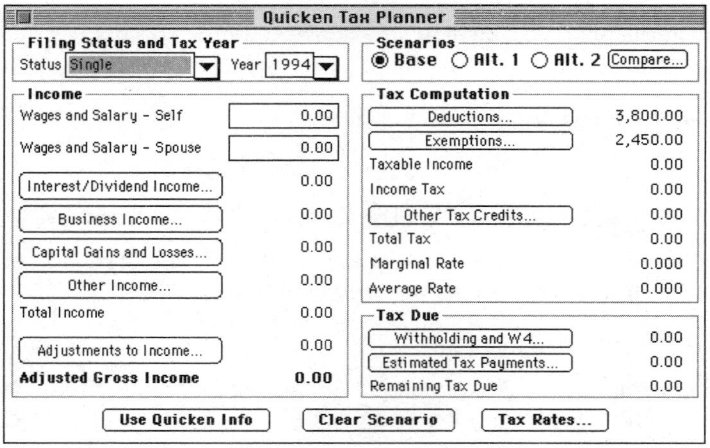

Figure 9-7:
The Tax
Planner
calculator. It
doesn't get
much better
than this!

```
▤▤▤▤▤▤▤▤▤▤▤▤▤  Quicken Tax Planner  ▤▤▤▤▤▤▤▤▤▤▤▤▤
┌─Filing Status and Tax Year─┐  ┌─Scenarios─────────────────┐
│ Status│Single      ▼│ Year│1994│▼│  ● Base ○ Alt. 1 ○ Alt. 2 [Compare...]│
┌─Income──────────────────┐  ┌─Tax Computation───────────┐
│ Wages and Salary – Self    │    0.00 │  │   Deductions...    │  3,800.00│
│ Wages and Salary – Spouse  │    0.00 │  │   Exemptions...    │  2,450.00│
│ [ Interest/Dividend Income... ]  0.00 │  Taxable Income         0.00│
│ [ Business Income... ]           0.00 │  Income Tax             0.00│
│ [ Capital Gains and Losses... ]  0.00 │  │ Other Tax Credits... │  0.00│
│ [ Other Income... ]              0.00 │  Total Tax              0.00│
│ Total Income                     0.00 │  Marginal Rate         0.000│
│ [ Adjustments to Income... ]     0.00 │  Average Rate          0.000│
│ Adjusted Gross Income            0.00 │  ┌─Tax Due──────────────┐
│                                       │  │ [ Withholding and W4... ]  0.00│
│                                       │  │ [ Estimated Tax Payments... ] 0.00│
│                                       │  │ Remaining Tax Due         0.00│
│   [ Use Quicken Info ]  [ Clear Scenario ]  [ Tax Rates... ]   │
```

2. **Indicate your filing status.**

   Activate the Status drop-down list box. Then, when Quicken displays a list of possible filing statuses, pick the one you think you'll use this year: single, married filing separate, married filing jointly, and so on.

3. **Indicate the tax year.**

   Activate the Year drop-down list box. Then, pick the right tax year: either 1994 or 1995.

4. Enter the wages and salaries you and your lovely or handsome spouse expect.

Move the cursor to the Wages and Salaries-Self text box and type what you think you'll make this year. Then, move the cursor to the Wages & Salaries-Spouse field and type what you think your spouse will make this year.

5. Indicate approximately how much other taxable income you'll have.

Quick as you can, click the Interest/Dividend Income, Business Income, Capital Gains/Losses, and Other Income buttons and fill in the dialog boxes that Quicken displays. (In each case, Quicken's pop-up worksheets prompt you for a handful of inputs.) If some income thingamajig doesn't apply, just leave it blank. Figure 9-8 shows the Interest/Dividend Income pop-up worksheet. This makes sense, right? You enter your taxable interest income into the first input field. You enter your taxable dividend income into the second field. When you're done, click OK. Quicken calculates the total and then plugs this value back into the Tax Planner calculator.

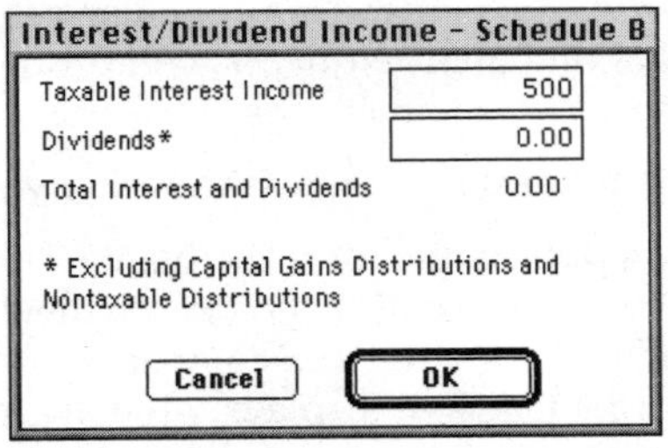

Figure 9-8:
The
Interest/
Dividend
Income
pop-up
worksheet.

Interest/Dividend Income – Schedule B	
Taxable Interest Income	500
Dividends*	0.00
Total Interest and Dividends	0.00

* Excluding Capital Gains Distributions and Nontaxable Distributions

[Cancel] [OK]

6. Indicate whether you'll have any adjustments to your gross income.

This sounds too technical, I know. But there are really only a handful of these adjustments: IRA, SEP/IRA, and Keogh deductions; alimony; moving expenses; a couple of adjustments for self-employed types (half their self-employment tax and a chunk of their health insurance premiums); and any penalty on early withdrawals of savings. If you have one or more of these, click the Adjustments to Income button and fill in the appropriate blanks on the dialog box Quicken displays. When you're done, click OK.

7. Estimate your itemized deductions.

Click the Deductions button and then describe any itemized deductions you have by filling in the blanks on the dialog box Quicken displays. You'll also need to answer a handful of questions including, "Is taxpayer a dependent?" and "Are you or your spouse blind or over age 65?" You answer these questions by marking or unmarking check boxes. Once you enter all this information, click OK. Quicken calculates your standard deduction and then uses whatever is larger for your return: your standard deduction or your total itemized deductions.

For most people, there are only three itemized deductions that actually matter: Mortgage interest, property taxes, and charitable deductions.

8. Indicate the number of personal exemptions you'll claim.

You know the drill by now, right? Click the Exemptions button and then use the dialog box that Quicken displays to indicate the number of personal exemptions you get. The basic rule is that you get one exemption for everybody in your family (you, your spouse if you're filing jointly, and each of your dependents) as long as they live at your house. I should mention, however, that things get tricky if you've got shirt-tail relatives living at your house, your kids live away from home or are married, or some of the kids in the house have divorced parents. If you have questions because one of these situations sounds vaguely familiar, get the IRS return preparation instructions and read the part about who is and is not dependent.

9. Indicate whether you owe any other taxes or have tax credits you can use to reduce your taxes.

Click the Other Tax Credits button and fill in the blanks on the dialog box that Quicken displays. By the way, if you and your spouse get all your income from salaries and a handful of investments, you probably don't need to worry about this "other taxes and credits" business.

10. Enter any estimated taxes or federal income withholding you've paid.

Click the Withholding and W-4 button and fill in the blanks on the dialog box that Quicken displays. If you make estimated tax payments — and you'll know if you do — click the Estimated Tax Payments button and fill in the blanks on the dialog box that Quicken displays. All you are doing here is indicating how much you and your spouse have already had withheld and how much you'll have withheld from your future pay checks.

When you complete these ten steps, you'll be able to see not only what your total income taxes are, but also whether you'll need to increase your payments. (Look at the Remaining Tax Due field in the lower right corner of the screen to see whether it looks like you're coming up short.)

If you want to print the tax planner information, select the Print Tax Planner command from the File menu. If you want to erase all your inputs and start over, click the Clear Scenario button. When you're done using the calculator, click the close box.

Some More Tax Planner Tricks

I think the way I've described in the preceding paragraphs makes the most sense for the average Quicken user. There are a couple of other tricks the Tax Planner lets you try. First, rather than enter the data into text boxes (as I described here), you can tell the Tax Planner to grab taxable income and tax deduction information from your registers. This is pretty straightforward as long as you're diligently using tax-related categories to track these income and expense amounts and — this is important — you've indicated the tax schedule line on which category totals should be reported.

You can update the tax rates and tax brackets by clicking the Rates button and then filling a worksheet that Quicken provides. (If you're still using Quicken 5 in 1996, for example, you'll either need to do this or get new tax rate information from Quicken to use the Tax Planner calculator.) This worksheet pretty much mirrors the tax schedules provided by the Internal Revenue Service, so if you're familiar with these, updating the tax rates should be a breeze.

This chapter wraps up the Quicken for the Macintosh basics. If you plan to use Quicken mostly at home, Part III talks about Quicken's record-keeping tools for loans and investments. If you use Quicken at your business, skip ahead to Part IV.

Part III
Home Finances

In this part...

Are you going to be using Quicken for personal financial stuff? If so, you should know that there's more to the program than just the checkbook-on-a-computer business described in the preceding part. Quicken can help you manage and monitor things like credit cards, home mortgages, and investments. If this stuff sounds interesting, keep reading.

Chapter 10

Credit Cards (and Debit Cards, Too)

You can use Quicken to track your credit cards in much the same way you use Quicken to keep a checkbook. The process works very much the same, but with a few wrinkles.

First, I'll discuss whether you should even bother.

To Bother or Not to Bother...

I don't use Quicken to track my credit card purchases because I always pay my credit card balance in full every month. (Don't feel bad if you don't do this — it's like a natural law that CPAs must do this.) Therefore, I don't have an open credit card balance to track. What's more, when I pay the monthly credit card bill, I easily can use the Splits fields to describe my spending categories: $3.53 on food for lunch, $52.64 for a car repair, and $217.54 for books (a personal weakness.)

If you're in the same boat — meaning you use a credit card but you don't carry a balance — you don't need anything special to track your credit card purchases and, of course, you don't need to use Quicken to tell you your account balance because it's always zeroed out at the end of the month.

Of course, if you do carry a credit card balance — and most people do — you can set up a Quicken credit card account and use it for tracking credit card purchases. If you just need to keep track of how much you've charged during the month (even if you are going to pay the balance in full), you must also set up a credit card account and use it.

I should make one other point: in order to track not just what you charged by using spending categories, but also *where* you charged it by using the Payee field, you must set up a credit card account and use it.

My father-in-law uses a Quicken credit card account for this purpose. Although he says doesn't carry a balance, he does like to know how much he spends at International House of Pancakes, K Mart, and the truck stop. He could use the Splits fields to record spending on things like breakfast, clothing, and gasoline when he pays his credit card balance at the end of the month. But, there isn't a splits field to record where he said, "Charge it."

Setting Up a Credit Card Account

If you want to track credit card spending and balances with Quicken, you must set up a special credit card account. (In comparison, you use bank accounts to track things like the money that flows into and out of a checking account).

Adding a credit card account

To set up a credit card account, you follow roughly the same steps as you do for a bank account. Here's what you do:

1. **Choose the Accounts icon from the iconbar.**

   Quicken displays the My Accounts window, as shown in Figure 10-1.

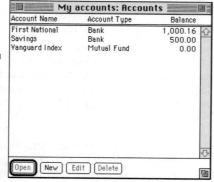

Figure 10-1:
The My Accounts window lists all your Quicken accounts.

2. Select the New button on the My Accounts window.

Quicken displays the Set Up Account dialog box, as shown in Figure 10-2.

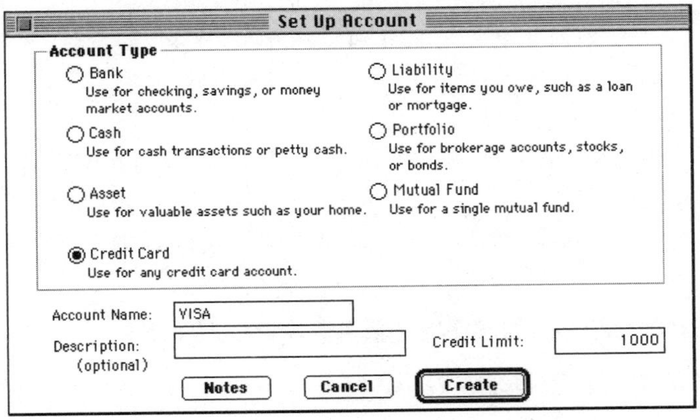

Set Up Account

Account Type

○ Bank
   Use for checking, savings, or money
   market accounts.

○ Liability
   Use for items you owe, such as a loan
   or mortgage.

○ Cash
   Use for cash transactions or petty cash.

○ Portfolio
   Use for brokerage accounts, stocks,
   or bonds.

○ Asset
   Use for valuable assets such as your home.

○ Mutual Fund
   Use for a single mutual fund.

● Credit Card
   Use for any credit card account.

Account Name: VISA

Description: _____ Credit Limit: 1000
(optional)

[Notes]   [Cancel]   [Create]

Figure 10-2:
The Set Up
Account
dialog box.

3. Mark the Credit Card option button.

This option tells Quicken you want to set up a credit card account. This last bit of data, I'm sure, is a big surprise. By the way, when you do mark the Credit Card option button, Quicken adds another text box to the Set Up Account dialog box for entering your Credit Limit.

4. Give a name to the account.

Shoot, I don't know. How about VISA, Master Charge, or AmEx.

5. (Optional) Describe the account.

Hmmm. Maybe you could provide the account number.

6. Type in the amount of your credit limit (optional).

If you want, indicate the amount of your credit card limit by moving the cursor to the Credit Limit text box and then type in whatever number the credit card company has arbitrarily decided is a reasonable balance for you to shoulder.

7. Select Create.

Quicken — always sensitive to your feelings — displays the register window with your new account. Because I'm sensitive to your feelings too, I've included this dialog box as Figure 10-3.

8. Enter the balance you owed on your credit card billing period after making your payment.

Using the Charge column, enter a transaction that records the balance as of the last statement. If you only want to enter "Opening Balance" as the description and the balance in the Charge field, leaving some of the other fields blank, that's OK with me and it's OK with Quicken.

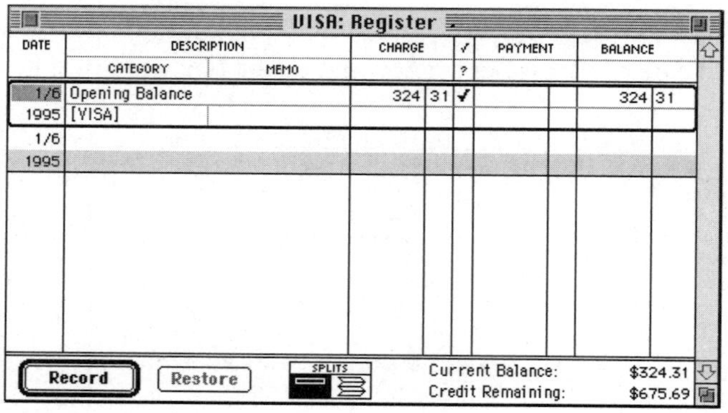

Figure 10-3: The credit card register with a new transaction.

Selecting a credit card account so that you can use it

To tell Quicken you want to work with an account that isn't already shown on the Quicken desktop, you use the My Accounts window — the same window you saw in Figure 10-1. Go figure!

Choose the Accounts icon from the iconbar to display the window. After you display the window, select the account you want to use. You know how this works. You highlight the account you want by using the arrow keys or by clicking the account name with that long-tailed plastic rodent that sits on your desk. Then you select the Open button or press Enter. Quicken selects the account and displays the register window so that you can begin recording transactions.

Entering Credit Card Transactions

After you select a credit card account, Quicken displays a special version of the register window, as shown in Figure 10-3.

A whirlwind tour of the Credit Card register

The Credit Card register works like the regular register window you use for a bank account. You enter transactions into the rows of the register. When you record a charge, Quicken updates the credit card balance and the remaining credit limit (if you entered the optional credit limit info when you set up the account).

You can use the same icons and commands as you do for your regular ol' bank account register. I talked about these in earlier chapters, so I won't regurgitate them here. Old news is no news.

Recording a credit card charge

Recording a credit card charge is similar to recording a check or bank account withdrawal. For the sake of illustration, suppose that you charged $30.47 for dinner at your favorite Mexican restaurant. Here's how you record this charge:

1. **Enter the charge date.**

   Move the cursor to the Date field (if it isn't already there) and type the date using the MM/DD format. For example, enter July 4, 1995 as **7/5**. You usually don't have to type the year because Quicken retrieves the current year number from the little clock inside your computer.

2. **Record the name of the business you paid with a credit card.**

   Move the cursor to the Description field and enter the name of the person or business you paid. If the restaurant is "Mommasita's Cantina," for example, type **Mommasita's Cantina** into the Description field.

3. **Enter the charge amount.**

   Move the cursor to the Charge field and enter the total charge amount — **30.47** in this example. Don't type a dollar sign, but do type the period to indicate the decimal place and cents.

4. **Enter the category.**

   Move the cursor to the Category drop-down list box and enter the appropriate category. A restaurant charge might be categorized as "Entertainment," for example. If you don't know the category, you can display the Categories List by selecting the Categories & Transfers command from the View menu and double-click the category. Or here's another trick. Just type enough of the category name for Quicken to identify and Quicken will fill in the rest of the category name for you.

5. **(Optional) Enter a memo description.**

   Move the cursor to the Memo field and type the specific reason you're charging the item, such as a special date with your spouse or an important business meeting.

6. **Record the charge.**

   Select Record or press Return with the cursor on the Memo text box, for example. Either way, tell Quicken you want to record the charge. Quicken calculates both the new credit card balance and the remaining credit limit. Quicken then moves the cursor to the next slot in the register.

Figure 10-4 shows the charge at Mommasita's Cantina.

DATE	DESCRIPTION		CHARGE		√	PAYMENT		BALANCE	
	CATEGORY	MEMO			?				
1/6 1995	Opening Balance		324	31	√			324	31
	[VISA]								
1/6 1995	Mommasita's Cantina		30	47					354	78
	Entertainment	Lunch							
1/6 1995									

VISA: Register

Record   Restore   SPLITS   Current Balance: $354.78
Credit Remaining: $645.22

Changing charges you've already entered

Use the mouse to highlight the field that contains the misinformation you want to fix, fix the entry, and then record the transaction. That's easy enough, isn't it?

Paying credit card bills

If you're tracking the credit card account balance with a credit card account like I'm describing here, Quicken provides two ways for you to pay a credit card bill.

If you're not using a credit card account, you record the check you sent to pay a credit card bill in the same way you record any other check.

A most bodacious way to pay a credit card bill

This is pretty simple, so don't blink your eyes because you may miss the action.

Look at your credit card statement. Decide how much you want to pay. Select the bank account on which you'll write the check. Then write the check and record it in the bank account register — but as a transfer to the credit card account.

You're done. If you have questions, take a peek at the highlighted check transaction shown in Figure 10-5. It pays $100 of the credit card balance. The only trick — if you want to call it that — is that the credit card account is specified as the account to which the money is transferred.

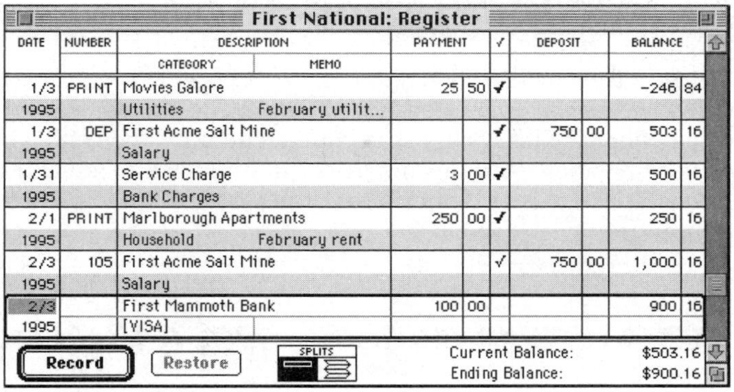

Figure 10-5:
To record a
credit card
payment,
just record
a transfer
from your
bank
account to
the credit
card
account.

First National: Register									
DATE	NUMBER	DESCRIPTION		PAYMENT		√	DEPOSIT		BALANCE	
		CATEGORY	MEMO							
1/3 1995	PRINT	Movies Galore		25	50	√			−246	84
		Utilities	February utilit...							
1/3 1995	DEP	First Acme Salt Mine				√	750	00	503	16
		Salary								
1/31 1995		Service Charge		3	00	√			500	16
		Bank Charges								
2/1 1995	PRINT	Marlborough Apartments		250	00	√			250	16
		Household	February rent							
2/3 1995	105	First Acme Salt Mine				√	750	00	1,000	16
		Salary								
2/3 1995		First Mammoth Bank		100	00				900	16
		[VISA]								

Record   Restore   SPLITS

Current Balance: $503.16
Ending Balance: $900.16

You can see the other account by selecting the Go To Transfer command from the Activities menu. If you look at the credit card account register now, you see that this check reduces the credit card balance by $100 (see Figure 10-6).

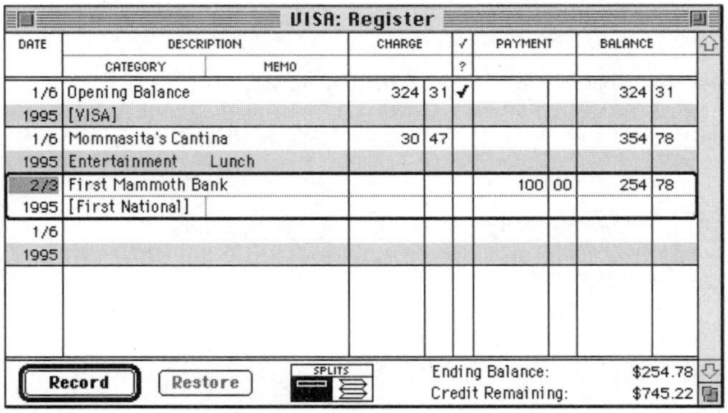

VISA: Register							
DATE	DESCRIPTION		CHARGE		√	PAYMENT		BALANCE	
	CATEGORY	MEMO			?				
1/6 1995	Opening Balance		324	31	√			324	31
	[VISA]								
1/6 1995	Mommasita's Cantina		30	47				354	78
	Entertainment	Lunch							
2/3 1995	First Mammoth Bank					100	00	254	78
	[First National]								
1/6 1995									

Figure 10-6:
The credit
card
register
shows the
transfer,
too.

Record   Restore   SPLITS

Ending Balance: $254.78
Credit Remaining: $745.22

A less bodacious way to pay a credit card bill

You can also tell Quicken that you want to pay some portion of the credit card bill as part of reconciling the credit card's account balance.

I think this method is slightly more difficult, but if you want to reconcile your credit card account, think about using this second method. If you are reconciling a credit card statement and paying some portion of the credit balance at the same time, you may find this method more convenient. Who knows?

I describe how to reconcile a credit card account in the very next section.

That Crazy Reconciliation Trick

You know that trick where you compare your checking account records with your bank's records of your checking account? The one where you calculate the difference between what you think is your account balance and what the bank thinks is your balance? And this difference is supposed to equal the total of the transactions floating around out there in the system? You can do this same trick on your credit card account.

The actual reconciliation, neat and straight-up

To reconcile a credit card account, first get your credit card statement. Next, display the credit card account in a register window. (You can do this by clicking the Accounts icon so the My Accounts window is displayed and then double-clicking the credit card account.)

What the nasty credit card company says

To tell Quicken what that nasty credit card company says, follow these steps, and put on some music if you can't seem to get the rhythm thing right.

1. **Choose the Reconcile icon from the iconbar.**

   Quicken displays the Reconcile Startup dialog box, as shown in Figure 10-7.

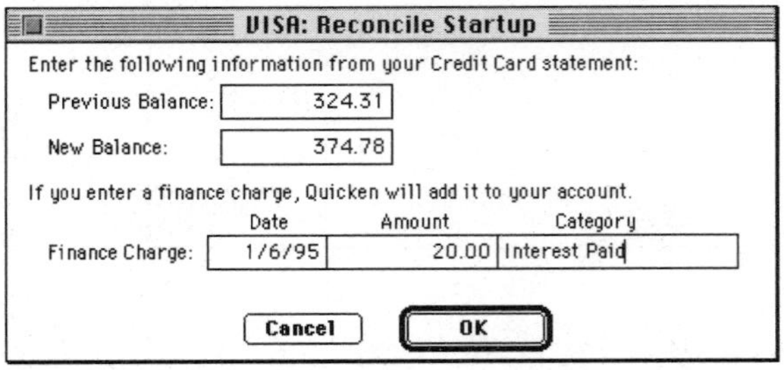

Figure 10-7:
The Reconcile Startup dialog box.

```
═══════════ VISA: Reconcile Startup ═══════════
Enter the following information from your Credit Card statement:

Previous Balance:   [    324.31    ]

New Balance:        [    374.78    ]

If you enter a finance charge, Quicken will add it to your account.
                     Date        Amount      Category
Finance Charge:   [ 1/6/95 ]   [  20.00 ]  [ Interest Paid ]

                    [ Cancel ]    [   OK   ]
```

2. **Enter the previous balance your credit card statement shows.**

   You know the drill: Move the cursor and type the number, tap your foot and swing your partner, do-si-do.

3. **Enter the new balance shown on the credit card statement.**

   Now I bet this is an eye-opener. Go ahead and enter the figure — even if you just can't believe you charged that much.

4. **Enter the monthly interest charged using the Finance Charges text box.**

   Pause for a moment of silence here if this is a sad, sad topic for you.

5. **Assign the monthly interest to the appropriate spending category, such as "Interest Paid"**

Move the cursor to the Category text box and type the category name. (This is getting boring, isn't it? Move and type. . . . Move and type. . . . That's all I ever seem to say.)

6. **Choose OK.**

Quicken displays the Reconcile window (see Figure 10-8). You use it to tell Quicken which credit card charges and payments appear on your statement. (This step is akin to looking at a bank statement and noting which checks and deposits have cleared the bank.)

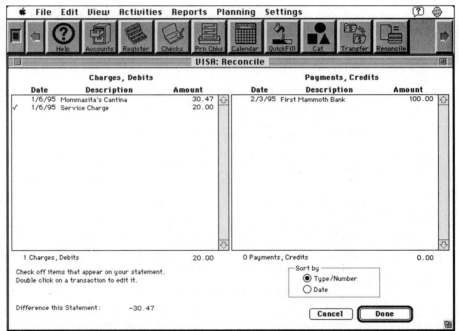

Figure 10-8:
The
Reconcile
window

Ouch! Did I really spend that much?

After you give Quicken an overview of your credit card situation, you can note which charges have cleared and which charges haven't cleared.

If you're comfortable whipping through a bank reconciliation, you can probably do this with your eyes closed. If you need some help, leave your eyes open so that you can read these steps:

1. **Find the first charge listed on the credit card statement.**

2. **Mark the charge as cleared.**

   Scroll through the transactions listed in the Reconcile window until you find the charge and then click the charge. Quicken adds the check mark symbol (✔) in front of the list entry to mark this charge as cleared and then updates the cleared statement balance.

3. **Enter any missing charges.**

   If you can't find a charge, you probably did not enter it in the Quicken register yet. Activate the credit card account register — such as by clicking the Register icon — and then enter the charge into the register in the usual way — except click the Cleared column (which is marked with a check mark) to identify the transactions as cleared. This identifies the charge as one that's already cleared. When you finish, return to the Reconcile window.

   To quickly go to the Credit Card register, you can also click it with the mouse.

4. **Repeat steps 1, 2, and 3 for charges listed on the credit card statement.**

   Or until you're blue in the face.

5. **Find the first payment or credit listed on the credit card statement.**

   The payments and credit appear in the right list box. There's only one of these in Figure 10-8. It's the $100 payment to the credit card company, Mammoth Bank.

6. **Mark the payment or credit as cleared.**

   Scroll through the transactions listed on the Reconcile window until you find the first payment or credit and then click it. Quicken adds the check mark symbol in front of the list entry to mark the payment or credit as cleared and then updates the cleared statement balance.

7. **Enter any missing payments or credits.**

   If you can't find the payment or credit — and you probably know this — it means you haven't entered them into the Quicken register yet. Activate the Credit Card Account register — such as by clicking the Register icon — and then enter the payment or credit into the register in the usual way, except put a ✔ in the check mark column. Return to the Reconcile window when you finish — such as by clicking it.

8. **Repeat steps 5, 6, and 7 for payments or credits listed on the credit card statement.**

If you record a transaction wrong, do this

As you're looking through the credit card statement, you may discover that you incorrectly recorded a transaction. If this happens, just display the credit card register window and make the needed fixes.

Oh, that explains things

After you mark all the cleared charges and payments, the difference between the cleared balance for the credit card and the statement's ending balance should equal zero.

Figure 10-9 shows how this looks. By the way, it's darned easy to reconcile with fictitious data.

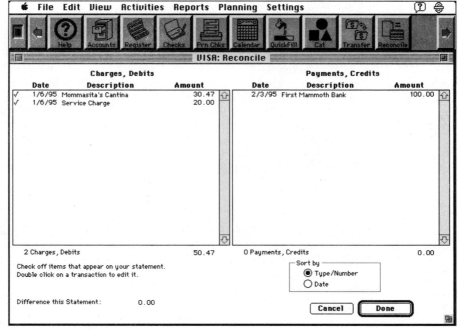

Figure 10-9:
A credit card account I've reconciled.

Finishing the reconciliation

If the difference does equal zero, you're cool. You're golden. You're done. (This sort of makes you sound like chicken, doesn't it?)

All you need to do is select Done to tell Quicken you're finished. Quicken displays a congratulations message telling you how proud it is of you and then asks if you want to pay your credit card bill now.

If the difference doesn't equal zero, you've got a problem. If you select Done in spite of the problem, Quicken will provide some cursory explanation as to why your account doesn't balance via a message. This message also tells you that you can force the two amounts to agree by selecting the Adjust Balance command button.

You know what, though? Forcing the two amounts to agree isn't a very good idea. To do this, Quicken adds a cleared transaction equal to the difference. (Quicken will ask for a category if you choose the adjustment route.)

Despite the ease of making adjustments, a much better way is to fix the reason for the difference.

Chapter 7 provides some ideas for trying to figure out why a bank account that should balance won't. You can apply the same list of ten tips to credit card reconciliations if you're in a bad way.

Postponing the inevitable

You can postpone reconciling the account by selecting the Cancel button. In this case, Quicken basically leaves your reconciliation work half done. Transactions that you marked as cleared still show as cleared with a check in the check mark column. You'll still have an inexplicable difference between the credit card statement and your register. Even so, postponing a reconciliation is usually better than forcing the cleared balance to equal the credit card statement balance. By postponing a reconciliation, you can hopefully find the problem or problems. You can fix them. Then you can restart the reconciliation and finish your work. (You restart a reconciliation the same way you originally start one.)

Paying the bill as part of the reconciliation

When you finish the reconciliation, Quicken politely asks if you want to pay the bill. Figure 10-10 shows the Pay Credit Card Bill dialog box, which is the tool Quicken uses to collect the necessary data.

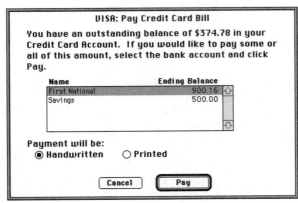

Figure 10-10:
The Pay Credit Card Bill dialog box.

VISA: Pay Credit Card Bill

You have an outstanding balance of $374.78 in your Credit Card Account. If you would like to pay some or all of this amount, select the bank account and click Pay.

Name	Ending Balance
First National	900.16
Savings	500.00

Payment will be:
◉ Handwritten   ○ Printed

[Cancel] [Pay]

You can probably figure out how to use this baby yourself, but hey, I'm on a roll, so here are the steps:

1. **Select the bank account on which you'll write the check.**

   Just grab your mouse and click the account. Notice that the screen tells you what your register shows as the credit card balance, not what your credit card statement shows. I thought this was a nice touch.

2. **Indicate whether you'll print a check with Quicken or write one by hand.**

   Mark the Payment will be Printed option button if you want to print a check with Quicken. Mark the Payment will be Hand Written if you'll write a check by hand.

3. **Choose Pay.**

   If you told Quicken that you want to print a check, Quicken displays the Write Checks window so that you can tell Quicken to print a check. (See Chapter 5 for information on how to do this.) If you told Quicken that you want to hand-write a check, Quicken displays the register window in which you can add the missing information to complete the transaction. (See Chapter 4 for information on this.) Quicken assumes that you want to pay the entire credit card balance.

4. **Enter the check into the Write Checks or register window.**

   Describe the check as one that you will either print with Quicken or write by hand.

As I said earlier in this chapter, this usually isn't the easiest way to pay a credit card bill. But, hey, you're an adult. You make your own choices.

So What About Debit Cards?

Debit cards, when you get right down to it, aren't really credit cards at all. They're more like bank accounts. Rather than withdrawing money by writing a check, however, you withdraw money by using a debit charge.

While a debit card looks (at least to your friends and the merchants you shop with) like a credit card, you should treat it like a bank account.

In a nutshell, here's what you need to do:

✔ Set up a bank account with the starting balance equal to the deposit you make with the debit card company.

✔ When you charge something using your debit card, record the transaction just as you would record a regular check.

> ✔ When you replenish the debit balance by sending more money to the debit card company, record the transaction just as you would record a regular deposit.

If all this sounds pretty simple, it is. In fact, I'd go so far as to say that if you've been plugging along, doing just fine with a bank account, you'll find keeping track of a debit card as easy as eating an entire bag of potato chips.

The IntelliCharge Hoopla

IntelliCharge refers to a special credit card account — specifically provided for people who have the Quicken Visa credit card.

The big hoopla concerning this account is that you don't have to enter the credit card transactions into a register. Rather, you retrieve them from a floppy disk (which the Quicken credit card people send you) or by using a modem.

Is IntelliCharge something you should look into? Does it really save you time? Is it a good deal? Inquiring minds want to know, so I'll tell you what I think. (I should point out that what I'm about to say next is just my humble opinion.)

Although there isn't an annual fee for the credit card and the interest rate is competitive, IntelliCharge, at least as I'm writing this, still isn't all that cheap. The monthly delivery fee for the floppy disk is $4.50. Then the monthly modem charge is $3, so you're looking at $40 to $50 bucks a year.

For this, of course, you save some data-entry time, so maybe it is worth it. (If you're a heavy hitter running $20,000 or $30,000 a month in charges through your account, your time savings will be substantial.)

One thing that bothers me about the whole deal, however, is that you're really just receiving an electronic version of your statement. Reconciling your bank statement against, well, your bank statement isn't going to make a whole heck of a lot of sense. (Golly gee, Batman, the charge to Mulva's Pet School appears on both statements, too!)

Another thing is that you do have some extra fiddling to do. Now there's nothing particularly complicated about grabbing credit card charges off a floppy disk. Nor are there any special magic tricks you need to know to use a modem. (There is a secret handshake your computer and the Quicken credit card computer do every time they want to talk, but you'll get the scoop on this once you join the club.) Nevertheless, the fiddling takes some time.

IntelliCharge is kind of a cool idea, but it has some drawbacks. It won't eliminate the record keeping you have to do. And hey, it's not free.

Chapter 11

Other People's Money

A popular financial self-help writer thinks that one of the secrets to financial success is using other people's money: the bank's, the mortgage company's, the credit people's, your brother-in-law's. . . . You get the idea.

Me? I'm not so sure that other people's money is the key to financial success. I do know that borrowing other people's money can turn into a nightmare.

Quicken can help you out here. No, the folks at Intuit won't make your loan payments for you. But in a way, they do something even better. They provide you with a tool to monitor the money you owe other people and the costs of your debts.

Should You Bother to Track Your Debts?

I think it's a good idea to track your debts — car loans, mortgages, student loans, and so on — when lenders fail to tell you the amount you're paying in annual interest or the amount you owe after each and every payment.

If your lenders are doing a good job at keeping you informed, I don't think there's much sense in using Quicken for this purpose. Heck, it's their money. They can do the work.

Let me make one more observation. If lenders have half a clue, they send you a 1098 tax form at the end of every year. The number shown on that form equals your tax deduction if the interest stems from a mortgage, business, or investment loan. Note that personal interest expenses aren't deductible anymore, so there's little reason to track them unless you really want to be mean to yourself.

How Do I Get Started?

To track other peoples' money with Quicken, you must set up a liability account. Liability is big word — which is why bankers love it. (Say liability really slowly and you realize what a silly-sounding word it is. Lie-a-bill-it-tee.)

But it's easy to set up one of these babies. Just remember that you must set up a liability account for every loan or debt: your mortgage, your car loan, your student loan, and so on, ad nauseam.

Setting up a liability account for an amortizing loan

An *amortized* loan is one on which you make regular, equal-sized payments. Over time, the principal portion of each payment pays off, or amortizes, the loan principal. If you borrowed money to purchase a house, a car, a Winnebago, or anything else that's really expensive and lasts for several years, chances are that your loan is of the amortizing variety.

Here's the recipe for setting up a liability account:

1. **Choose the Loans command from the View menu.**

   Quicken, now well-accustomed to your sure-footed direction, displays the Loans window (see Figure 11-1.)

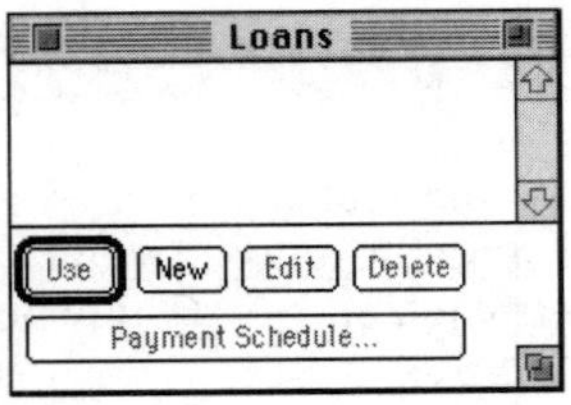

Figure 11-1:
The Loans window.

```
┌─────────────────────────────┐
│ ▣▣    Loans          ▣  │
│                          ⬆ │
│                            │
│                          ⬇ │
│ [ Use ] [ New ] [ Edit ] [ Delete ] │
│   [ Payment Schedule... ]  │
│                         ▣ │
└─────────────────────────────┘
```

2. Choose the New button in the Loans window.

Quicken, with little or no complaint, displays the Set Up Loan dialog box (see Figure 11-2).

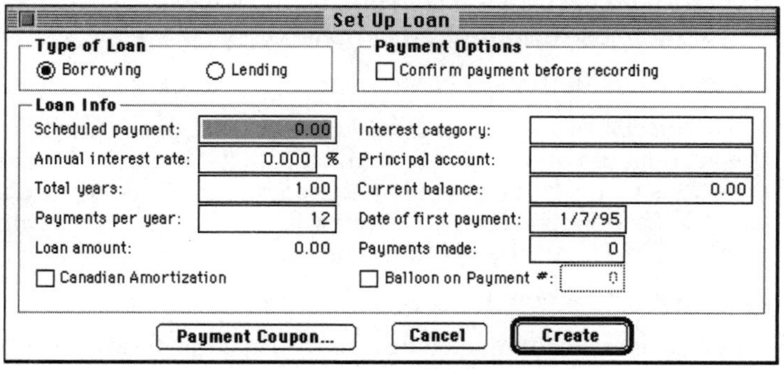

Figure 11-2:
The Set Up
Loan dialog
box.

3. Indicate whether you're the borrower or the lender.

Use the Type of Loan option buttons to indicate whether you're borrowing money or loaning money. Most of the time — unless you're running a loan sharking business on the side or have a pawn shop — you'll mark the Borrowing option button. To date, I've not heard of any banks that use Quicken to track their loans.

4. Enter the loan payment amount in the Scheduled payment text box.

You should be able to get this amount from the loan agreement. Just make sure that what you enter here is the interest and principal portion of the payment — and not any of the other amounts the loan agreement calls for. Escrow stuff. Private mortgage insurance. Late fees.

5. Enter the interest rate in the Annual Interest Rate text box.

Be sure to enter the rate as a decimal value. If a loan charges $8^7/_8$ percent interest, for example, enter **8.875**.

6. Enter the loan term in years in the Total Years text box.

If you set up a 30-year mortgage, for example, enter 30. There's one tiny trick to entering this figure: if you set up a loan that includes a balloon payment, enter the number of years over which the loan will be fully amortized. For example, loan payments might be calculated based on a 30-year term, but the loan might require a balloon payment at the end of 7 years. In this case, enter 30 in the Total Years text box.

7. Enter the number of loan payments you're required to make in a year in the Periods per year text box.

If you make monthly payments, for example, enter **12**.

8. **(Optional) Mark the Canadian Amortization check box if your loan uses semiannual compounding.**

9. **Enter the name of the interest expense category you'll use in the Interest category text box.**

   If you're working with the standard Quicken category list, for example, you may want to use the Interest Paid category.

10. **Enter a name for the account.**

    Move the cursor to the Principal Account text box and enter a name for the account. If you've already set up a liability, great. You can enter that account's name. If you haven't, enter some new name. Quicken will tell you that the account has a zero balance which you need to fix. Don't worry, though. We'll take care of that in the next step.

11. **Enter the loan amount.**

    Enter the loan account balance into the Current Balance text box.

12. **Enter the date of your first payment in the Date of First Payment text box.**

    Enter the date in MM/DD/YY fashion. (For example, type **05/31/95** for May 31, 1995.)

13. **Indicate how many payments you've made.**

    Move the cursor to the Payments made box. Then, enter the number of payments you've already made on the loan. If you haven't yet started making payments, enter a zero.

14. **(Optional) Record any balloon payment provisions.**

    If a loan includes a balloon payment provision, mark the Balloon on Payment # check box. Then, enter the number of the payment that you'll need to include the balloon. If a balloon payment is due after 7 years of monthly payments — or 84 payments — enter **84** (even though the loan is amortized over 30 years).

    At this point, you've recorded most of what Quicken needs to know about the loan itself. But you still need to describe any additional amounts that need to be paid with the regular, interest-and-principal portion of the loan payment.

15. **Choose the Payment Coupon command button.**

    Quicken will check the information you've entered.

16. **Indicate you do want an account set up.**

    If Quicken finds that your principal, or liability, account doesn't yet exist, it displays a message that tells you this and asks if you want Quicken to create the account. If you see that message, click Yes. Quicken displays the Payment Coupon dialog box (see Figure 11-3.)

Figure 11-3:
The
Payment
Coupon
dialog box.

17. Enter the name of the loan or mortgage company.

Select the Payee field and enter the lender's name.

18. (Optional) Indicate any amounts you pay besides principal and interest.

To do this, enter the total loan payment amount including any additional amounts the lender requires you to pay into the amount field that's just right of the payee field. In the case of a mortgage, for example, you might be required to pay $100 per month of property taxes and private mortgage insurance. Then, use the next line of split transaction fields to describe the additional amount. Figure 11-4 shows the Payment Coupon after adding $100 to the loan payment amount to cover $50 a month of property taxes and $50 a month of private mortgage insurance.

Figure 11-4:
The
Payment
Coupon
dialog box
after you
add a bit
more money
for property
taxes and
private
mortgage
insurance.

```
┌──────────────────────────────────────────────────────────┐
│ ▪◫▪▪▪▪▪▪▪▪▪▪▪▪▪▪  Payment Coupon  ▪▪▪▪▪▪▪▪▪▪▪▪▪▪▪▪▪▪▪▪▪▪▪ │
│                                                            │
│  Payee   First National                   $      895.60    │
│                                   ┌─Transaction Type────┐  │
│                                   │  ● Handwritten       │  │
│                                   │  ○ Printed           │  │
│                                   │                      │  │
│  Memo   _____  └──────────────────────┘ │
│                                                            │
│        CATEGORY              MEMO                  AMOUNT   │
│  Interest Paid         interest                  739 58 ⇧  │
│  [Mortgage]            principal                  56 02    │
│  Taxes                 property taxes             50 00    │
│  Insurance             private mortgage insurance 50 00 ⇩  │
│           ┌─ Cancel ─┐        ┌═══ OK ═══┐                 │
└──────────────────────────────────────────────────────────┘
```

19. Indicate how you make payments.

Select one of the payment transaction types listed in the Transaction Type box: Handwritten or Printed.

20. (Optional) Provide an address

If you indicate that you will print checks by using Quicken, Quicken adds a box of address fields to the Payment Coupon dialog box. You can fill these out the same way you fill out the address fields on the Write Checks window.

21. (Optional) Enter a memo description.

Does the lender always get mixed up when you send the check? Stick the loan account number in the check's Memo field. I suggest that you refrain from using this field to comment on the fairness of the bank's interest rate or to mock the intelligence of the loan payment processors.

22. Choose OK.

23. Indicate whether you want Quicken to tell you when it records your payment.

Quicken will automatically record your loan payments. If you want to know when Quicken is about to do this — just so you can give the final OK — mark the Confirm Payment Before Recording check box.

24. Click Create.

Quicken redisplays the Loans window (refer to Figure 11-1.) It'll look different now, though, because it'll list a new loan account.

Fixing loan stuff

Nobody's perfect, right? It's possible that you made a tiny little mistake in setting up either the loan or the loan payment. It doesn't need to be a major financial or personal crisis, however. First, display the Loans window by choosing the Loans command from the View window. Then, select the loan you want to fix and click the Edit button. Quicken displays the Edit Loan dialog box, which looks almost identical to the Set Up Loan dialog box. You just make your changes and choose Change.

Displaying a Payment Schedule

If you've looked closely at the Loans window shown in Figure 11-1, you may have noticed the Payment Schedule button. (If you didn't look all that closely, why not choose the Loans command from the View menu right now.) If you select a loan and then click Payment Schedule, Quicken produces a handy loan amortization schedule that shows the interest and principal portions of your payments and the remaining loan balance after each payment (see Figure 11-5).

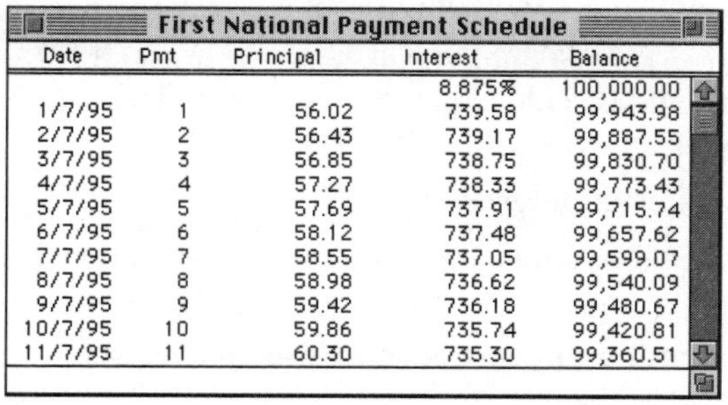

Figure 11-5:
The
Payment
Schedule
window
showing an
amortization
schedule for
your loan.

First National Payment Schedule				
Date	Pmt	Principal	Interest	Balance
			8.875%	100,000.00
1/7/95	1	56.02	739.58	99,943.98
2/7/95	2	56.43	739.17	99,887.55
3/7/95	3	56.85	738.75	99,830.70
4/7/95	4	57.27	738.33	99,773.43
5/7/95	5	57.69	737.91	99,715.74
6/7/95	6	58.12	737.48	99,657.62
7/7/95	7	58.55	737.05	99,599.07
8/7/95	8	58.98	736.62	99,540.09
9/7/95	9	59.42	736.18	99,480.67
10/7/95	10	59.86	735.74	99,420.81
11/7/95	11	60.30	735.30	99,360.51

Working with adjustable rate loans

Before I wrap up this discussion, let me mention one other thing. If you're working with a variable rate loan, you'll need to go to a bit more work. The reason, of course, is that every once in a while the bank will change the interest rate. As a result, your payment will change.

So, how do you deal with this real-life financial reality? Simple. Every time the interest rate changes, you need to update the loan payment amount, annual interest rate, total years remaining, and the date of the first payment after the interest rate change.

To do all this, follow these steps:

1. **Display the Edit Loan dialog box for the loan.**

   Display the Loans window by choosing the Loans command from the View menu. Then select the loan with the changing interest rate and click Edit. Quicken, ever the faithful servant, displays the Edit Loan dialog box, as shown in Figure 11-6.

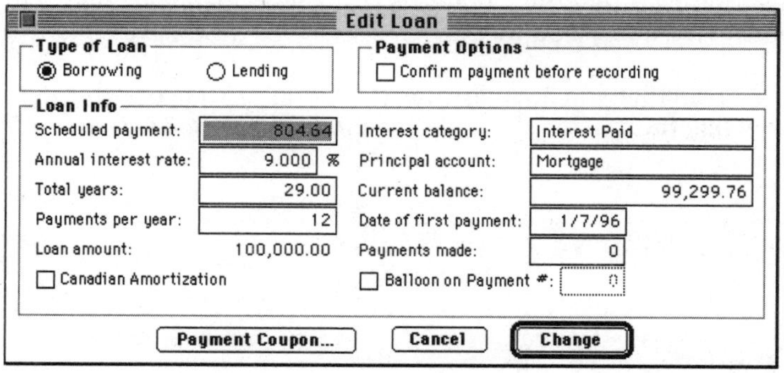

Figure 11-6:
The Edit
Loan dialog
box.

Edit Loan	
Type of Loan	**Payment Options**
● Borrowing ○ Lending	☐ Confirm payment before recording
Loan Info	
Scheduled payment: 804.64	Interest category: Interest Paid
Annual interest rate: 9.000 %	Principal account: Mortgage
Total years: 29.00	Current balance: 99,299.76
Payments per year: 12	Date of first payment: 1/7/96
Loan amount: 100,000.00	Payments made: 0
☐ Canadian Amortization	☐ Balloon on Payment #: 0
[Payment Coupon...]	[Cancel] [Change]

2. **Enter the new, adjusted payment amount.**

   Move the cursor to the Scheduled Payment text box and enter the new payment. You should be able to get this right off the friendly "your payment has changed" notice sent by the bank.

3. **Enter the new, adjusted interest rate.**

   Move the cursor to the Annual interest rate text box. Enter the new interest rate.

4. **Enter the total number of years of remaining payments.**

   Move the cursor to the Total Years text box and enter the number of years of payments that still remain. For example, if you've still got 29 and a half years left on a mortgage, enter **29.5**.

5. **Enter the loan balance at the time the interest rate adjustment occurred.**

   Move the cursor to the Current balance text box. Enter the current loan balance.

6. **Enter the date of the first payment after the interest rate change.**

   Move the cursor to the Date of First Payment text box. Then enter the date on which you'll make the first, adjusted payment.

7. **Click Change.**

   Quicken updates the loan information.

Does all this adjustment make sense? Here's another way to look at it. In effect, every time the loan interest rate changes, it's almost as if you set up a new loan equal to the loan balance at the time of the adjustment. And, this "new loan," of course, uses the new interest rate and payment amount.

Removing loans

You can delete loans by using the Loans window, too. (Remember that the Loans window is that thing that gets displayed when you choose the Loans command from the View menu.)

Delete a loan that you no longer need or shouldn't have added in the first place by selecting the loan on the Loans window. Then choose Delete.

Figure 11-7:
The Loans window. An old friend by now, no doubt.

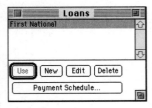

Delivering a Pound of Flesh (a.k.a. Making a Payment)

After you set up a liability account, you're ready to give the lender his pound of flesh — that is, make a payment. Before you say that this phrase is just some sort of populist bull-dweeble, I want to remind you that this metaphor comes from Shakespeare — Shylock uses it in *The Merchant of Venice*.

Recording the payment

After you set up the loan and the loan payment, you're ready to record the payment in (drum roll, please) . . . the register.

I'm trying to make the old Quicken register more exciting for you because you're probably becoming pretty darn familiar with it. And familiarity, as they say, breeds contempt.

Anyway, complete the following steps to record a payment:

1. **Display the register or Write Checks window.**

   If the bank account on which you write checks to make loan payments isn't selected, you must select it first. You can do so by clicking the Accounts icon on the iconbar.

2. **Enter the check date.**

3. **If you're using the register window, enter the check number. (If you're using the Write Checks window, of course, you don't enter the check number because Quicken will do this for you later.)**

4. **Start typing the lender's name in the Description or the Pay to the order of field text box.**

   As soon as Quicken figures out which loan you're talking about — and it shouldn't take too long — Quicken QuickFills the rest of the transaction with the loan information, as shown in Figure 11-8.

5. **Correct any bit of the transaction that is wrong.**

   Oh, I don't know. Let's say the county tax assessor just boosted your annual property taxes so the bank needs to collect more money. Yeah. That's a reasonable example. In that case, you would need to adjust both the payment amount and the split category fields that describe the property tax expense.

6. **Click Record.**

   Quicken enters the loan payment in the Bank Account register. You're done. Pretty easy, isn't it?

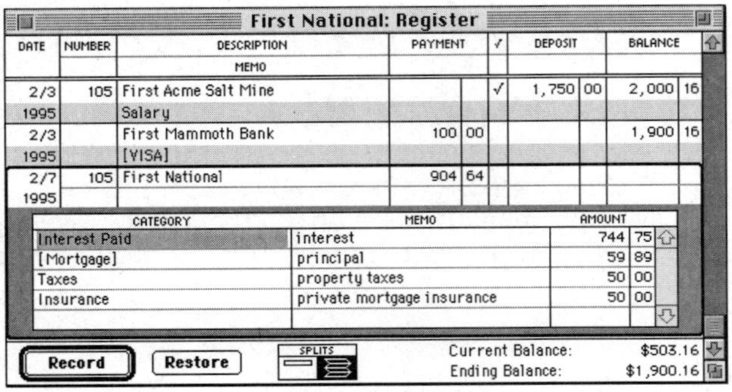

Figure 11-8:
The register window after Quicken has QuickFilled all the loan information.

Let me make one final observation. The reason that this transaction is tricky is because you're both assigning to an expense category and transferring to a liability account.

The interest expense thing probably makes sense to you. Paying interest you owe the bank is an expense — not altogether different from the amounts you pay the local supermarket for groceries.

The whole liability account transfer thing — well, that's a bit more involved. A bit more complicated. Really, what you're doing is moving money from your checking account (which decreases your checking account balance) to the lender (which decreases the amount you owe the lender).

Splitting loan payments is as close as you'll get to rocket science in your financial record-keeping.

Handling mortgage escrow accounts

We (you and I) should talk a bit more about one minor mortgage record-keeping annoyance — mortgage escrow accounts.

If you have a mortgage, you know the basic procedure. Although your mortgage payment may be $800 a month, your friendly mortgage company (while insisting that they trust you completely) makes you pay any extra $150 a month for property taxes and other such things. In other words, even though you're paying only $800 a month in principal and interest, your monthly payment to the mortgage company is, according to this example, $950 ($800 + $150).

The mortgage company, as you probably know, saves this money for you in an *escrow account* or a set of escrow accounts. A couple of times a year they pay your property taxes, and a time or two a year they pay your homeowner's insurance. If you have private mortgage insurance, they may pay this fee every month as well. And so it goes.

The question, then, is how to treat this stuff. As with most things, there's an easy way, which is rough, dirty, and unshaven, and there's a hard way, which is precise, sophisticated, and cumbersome.

You can choose whichever method you want. It's your life.

The rough, dirty, and unshaven method

Suppose that you do pay an extra $150 a month. You can treat this extra $150 as another expense category, such as Other Housing or Property Expenses. (I'm just making up these categories. If you can think of better ones, use your own.)

Nice. Easy. No fuss. These words and phrases pop into my head when I think about the rough, dirty, and unshaven method of mortgage escrow record-keeping. Figure 11-8 — which I showed a couple of pages ago — shows a sample Splits window filled out this way.

I use the rough, dirty, and unshaven method. Let me make a confession, though. This approach doesn't tell you how much moola you have stashed away in your escrow accounts. It also doesn't tell you how much you really spend in the way of homeowner's insurance, what you're entitled to claim as a property tax deduction, or how much they're bleeding you for private mortgage insurance.

To get these figures, you have to peruse the monthly and annual mortgage account statements — that is, if you get them. Or you have to call the mortgage lender and rattle a cage or two.

The precise, sophisticated, and cumbersome approach

You say you can't live with the uncertainty, the stress, the not knowing? There's another approach just for you.

You can set up an *asset account* for each of the escrow accounts for which the mortgage company collects money.

You set up asset accounts as you set up other liability accounts. Because I already explained this process, I'll just refresh your memory quickly. You need to set up an asset account with its starting balance equal to the current escrow account balance. To do so, display the My Accounts window and click the New button to indicate that you want to create a new account. Identify the account as an asset account and give it a name. Then, when Quicken displays the register for the account, tell Quicken how much money is in the account as of a specific date by adding an opening balance transaction.

If you've set up an account or two in your time, this process should take you about 40 seconds.

After you set up your asset account and record its current balance, you're ready to cruise. Record payments in the escrow as account transfers whenever you record the actual loan payment. Figure 11-9 shows an example of how the account register window looks when it shows splits information, assuming that there's only one escrow account.

First National: Register

DATE	NUMBER	DESCRIPTION	PAYMENT	✓	DEPOSIT	BALANCE
		MEMO				
2/3		First Mammoth Bank	100 00			1,900 16
1995		[VISA]				
2/7	105	First National	909 64			990 52
1995						

CATEGORY	MEMO	AMOUNT
Interest Paid	interest	744 75
[Mortgage]	principal	59 89
[Escrow]	property taxes & insurance	105 00

DATE	NUMBER	DESCRIPTION	PAYMENT	✓	DEPOSIT	BALANCE
2/7						
1995						

Record   Restore   SPLITS

Current Balance: $503.16
Ending Balance: $990.52

Figure 11-9: An account register showing transfers to an escrow account.

You need to do one other thing. When you set up an escrow account, you must record the payments that the bank makes from your escrow account to the county assessor (for property taxes) and to the insurance company (for things like homeowner's and private mortgage insurance). You don't know when these payments are really made, so watch your monthly mortgage account statements.

When the mortgage company disburses money from the escrow account to pay, for example, your first property tax assessment, you need to record a decrease equal to the payment for property taxes and then categorize the transaction as a property tax expense. This process isn't tricky in terms of mechanics, as shown in Figure 11-10, the escrow Account register. The account increases every loan payment (see the second transaction). The account decreases when there's a disbursement (see the third transaction).

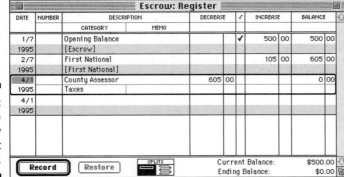

Escrow: Register

DATE	NUMBER	DESCRIPTION	DECREASE	✓	INCREASE	BALANCE
		CATEGORY MEMO				
1/7		Opening Balance		✓	500 00	500 00
1995		[Escrow]				
2/7		First National			105 00	605 00
1995		[First National]				
4/1		County Assessor	605 00			0 00
1995		Taxes				
4/1						
1995						

Record   Restore   SPLITS

Current Balance: $500.00
Ending Balance: $0.00

Figure 11-10: Here's the escrow account register.

Basically, the Escrow Account register mirrors the bank account register. The only difference is that the Payment and Deposit fields in the bank account register are labeled Decrease and Increase in the Escrow Account register.

This second approach doesn't seem like all that much work, does it? And if you use this approach, you can track escrow balances and escrow spending precisely. You can, for example, pull your property tax deduction right from Quicken. Jeepers, maybe I should try the sophisticated approach next year.

Your Principal-Interest Breakdown Won't Be Right

I don't want to bum you out, but your principal interest breakdown will often be wrong. You might calculate interest expense as $712.48, for example, when your bank calculates it as $712.47. A few pennies here, a few pennies there, and pretty soon your account balance and interest expense tallies are, well, a few pennies off.

So you can't change the world

You can try calling the bank, telling them what bozos they are, and then demanding that they correct your balance. If this approach works for you, let me know. You can write to me in care of the publisher. Or you can put your comment on the reader evaluation card that appears at the back of the book.

Or (and this method is really more practical) you can adjust your records to agree with the bank's. Here's how:

1. **Display the register for the liability.**

2. **Choose the Adjust Balance command from the Activities menu.**

   (Go ahead. Tap your keys very hard if you're angry that the bank won't adjust their records.) Quicken displays the Adjust Balance dialog box, as shown in Figure 11-11.

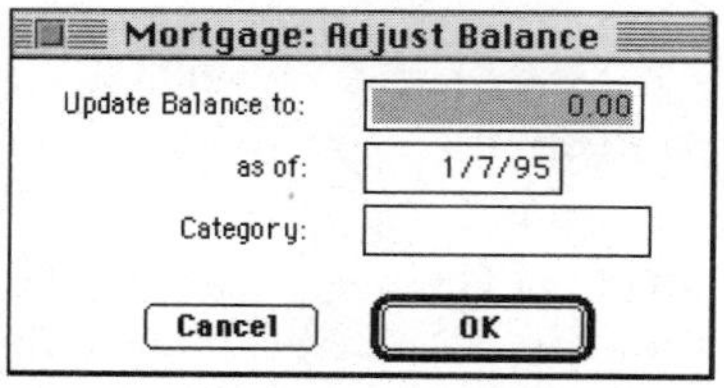

Figure 11-11:
The Adjust
Balance
dialog box.

Mortgage: Adjust Balance	
Update Balance to:	0.00
as of:	1/7/95
Category:	
Cancel	OK

3. **Enter the correct (that is, the one the bank says is correct) account balance.**

   Type the correct figure in the Update Balance To text box. (The amount probably comes from the year-end or month-end loan statement.)

4. **Enter the last day of the month or year for which you're making the adjustment.**

   Enter a transaction date in the As of text box. (The trick here is to use a transaction date that sticks the transaction that fixes the principal-interest split into the right month or year.)

5. **Enter your interest expense category.**

   Type the correct category name in the Category text box. Remember that all you need to do is type enough of the category name for Quicken to recognize. Once you do this, Quicken's QuickFill feature fills in the rest of the category information for you.

6. **Record the adjustment.**

   When the Adjust Balance dialog box correctly describes the needed adjustment, choose OK.

Do you think this adjustment business is kooky?

Does the whole adjustment transaction business make sense to you? At times it can seem kind of backwards, so let me throw out a quick observation.

Remember that as you record loan payments, you split the loan payment between the interest expense category and a principal account transfer that reduces the liability. Here's the tricky part: When the liability gets reduced either too much or not enough, you need to fix the both the liability balance *and* the principal-interest split.

Let me give you an example. Suppose that over the course of a year you record $.17 too little interest expense and therefore record $.17 too much principal reduction, despite your best efforts to be accurate. You need to increase the liability account balance by $.17 in this case, but you also need to increase the interest expense figure by $.17. By entering the interest expense category in the Category text box, Quicken does these adjustments for you. Pretty cool, huh?

Automatic Loan Payments

Quicken 5 adds a nifty new feature called the Financial Calendar. I wasn't exactly sure where or how you might want to use the Financial Calendar. After much wailing and gnashing of teeth, I figured that people would be most likely to use this feature for automatic loan payments.

The Financial Calendar feature may be useful in other instances as well. For example, a business might use the Financial Calendar to schedule and plan employee payroll checks, tax returns, and deposits.

Scheduling a loan payment with the Financial Calendar

If a loan payment occurs regularly, you can set it up as a future transaction. When you do so, Quicken automatically records the payment for you based on a schedule.

Consider this example: suppose that on the fifth day of every month your mortgage company taps your checking account for the full amount of your mortgage payment. (You, of course, have already authorized them to do so. They can't take your money willy-nilly.) In this case, you can tell Quicken to record the mortgage payment on the fifth of each month. Kind of handy, right?

Follow these steps to set up such a future transaction:

1. **Choose the Calendar command from the View menu or click the Calendar icon.**

    Quicken displays the Calendar, as shown in Figure 11-12. It shows a calendar for the current month and a list of transactions.

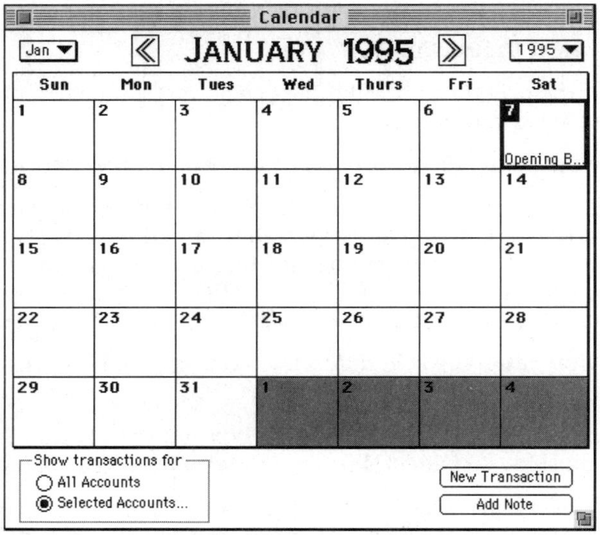

Figure 11-12:
The Calendar.

			Calendar			
Jan ▼	«	**JANUARY 1995**		»		1995 ▼
Sun	Mon	Tues	Wed	Thurs	Fri	Sat
1	2	3	4	5	6	**7** Opening B…
8	9	10	11	12	13	14
15	16	17	18	19	20	21
22	23	24	25	26	27	28
29	30	31	1	2	3	4

Show transactions for
○ All Accounts
◉ Selected Accounts…

[New Transaction]
[Add Note]

2. Display the first month for which you want to schedule the transaction.

Using the << and >> buttons, which appear to the left and right of the month name, select the starting month for the scheduled transaction. Or activate the month name drop-down list box, and select a month; then activate the year number drop-down list box and select a year.

3. Click the New Transaction command button.

When you do, Quicken displays the Schedule Future Transaction dialog box (see Figure 11-13).

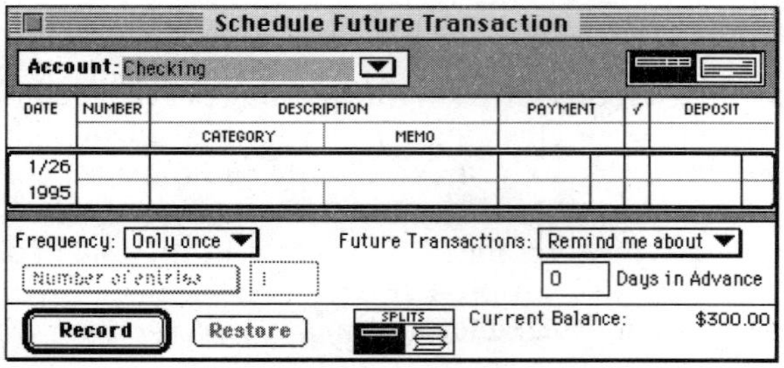

Figure 11-13:
The
Schedule
Future
Transaction
dialog box.

4. Verify the account.

Make sure that the Account drop-down list box at the top of the Schedule Future Transaction dialog box shows the right account. If you're going to record an automatic mortgage payment made from your First National checking account, the box should show "First National."

5. Enter the next transaction date.

You know the drill by now, right? Just click the Date field, and enter the date of the next transaction.

6. Enter the payee name and any other information needed.

Move the cursor to the Description field and begin typing the lender's name. As soon as Quicken knows which transaction you're talking about, it fills in the rest of the transaction fields for you. Change any of the information that needs to be changed. Also, note that if you hadn't ever recorded the transactions before, you would need to enter all the information.

7. Indicate how often the scheduled transaction should occur.

Activate the Frequency drop-down list box. Then select the frequency. (Initially, the Frequency drop-down list box shows Only Once.) For a monthly mortgage payment, for example, you would select Month.

Once you select a Frequency other than Only Once, Quicken enables another drop-down list box below the Frequency drop-down list. (Until this new drop-down list box is enabled, it's a little tough to see.) You can select this other Ongoing entry list box's setting to indicate, basically, that you want Quicken to just keep recording this transaction over and over again, until the cows come home. Or, you can select the Number of entries setting. In this case, Quicken opens up a previously hidden text box that lets you specify how many transactions it should record.

8. **(Optional) Tell Quicken you want it to remind you about this transaction whenever it should be entered or automatically enter the transaction for you.**

   Activate the FutureTransactions drop-down list box. Select the Remind Me About option. (This tells Quicken, "Hey, you! Yes, you! Remind me whenever this transaction should be entered.") Alternatively, you can select the Automatically Enter option. In this case, Quicken enters the transaction at the appointed time without telling you about the entry.

9. **Click Record.**

   Quicken adds the transaction to its future transactions list.

Quicken takes the Paul Masson approach to finance — it will enter no transaction before its time. So when the time is right — meaning next month on the fifth for this example — Quicken enters the transaction automatically.

More stuff about future transactions

You already know the most important thing about future transactions: how to set one up. Here are some other nuggets of knowledge that you might find useful.

Quicken identifies a calendar day for scheduled transactions by marking the day with the color green. You can see which transactions are scheduled for a day by clicking that day.

To change or delete a future transaction for a particular day, for example, select the day and then select the Edit Calendar Day command from the Edit menu. When Quicken displays the window listing transactions for that day, click the transaction (to select it) and then click either the Delete button (to remove the future transaction) or the Edit button (to change the future transaction). Figure 11-14 shows the Transactions dialog box.

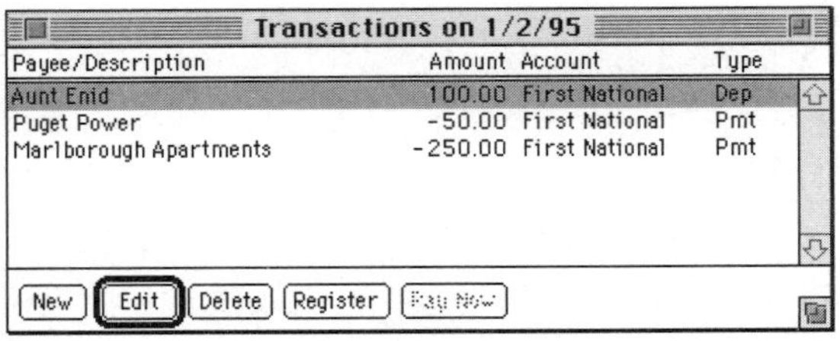

Figure 11-14:
The Transactions dialog box.

Payee/Description	Amount	Account	Type
Aunt Enid	100.00	First National	Dep
Puget Power	-50.00	First National	Pmt
Marlborough Apartments	-250.00	First National	Pmt

Transactions on 1/2/95

[New] [Edit] [Delete] [Register] [Pay Now]

More stuff about the Financial Calendar

The Financial Calendar provides some other buttons you may want to use. I'm not going to spend a lot of time on them; you'll have more fun trying them out yourself than you would reading about them. Nevertheless, let me give you a bird's-eye view:

- ✔ The Add Note button lets you post a note on a calendar day. You use this feature to create reminder notes. For example, you might want to post a note saying, "Remember Wedding Anniversary," on the big day. When you click this button, Quicken displays a dialog box in which you type the message and then click the close box. The program also marks the calendar day with a little square — a miniature Post-It Note. Click the square to read the message.

- ✔ The Show Transactions For buttons in the lower left corner of the dialog box let you choose which accounts' transactions appear on the register. Initially, the Financial Calendar includes all your accounts. (Quicken indicates this by marking the All Accounts option button.) If you want to pick and choose which accounts appear, mark the Selected Accounts option button. Quicken displays a window that lets you mark the accounts you want to see.

The 5th Wave   By Rich Tennant

"OH SURE, $1.8 MILLION DOLLARS SEEMS LIKE ALOT RIGHT NOW, BUT WHAT ABOUT RANDY? WHAT ABOUT HIS FUTURE? THINK WHAT A COMPUTER LIKE THIS WILL DO FOR HIS S.A.T. SCORE SOMEDAY."

Chapter 12
Mutual Funds

I don't mean to scare you, but I think investment record-keeping is Quicken's most complicated feature. So it's time to get down to business. Time to stop pussyfooting around. Time to earn my pay.

To Bother or Not to Bother?

Quicken's investment record-keeping feature lets you do three important things:

✔ Track your interest and dividend income

✔ Track real and potential capital gains and losses

✔ Measure an investment's performance by calculating an internal rate of return

If you're a serious investor, these things probably sound worthwhile. But before you invest any time learning how Quicken's investment record-keeping works, be sure that you need all this power.

Are your investments tax-deferred?

If your investments are tax-deferred (if you're using Individual Retirement Accounts (IRAs), 401Ks, or Keoghs, for example), you don't really need to track investment income and capital gains and losses. Tax-deferred investments have no effect on your personal income taxes. You get a tax deduction for the money you stick into IRAs, for example, and anything you take out is taxable.

With tax-deferred investments, you record all that you should need to know via your checking account. Checks earmarked for investment are categorized as "IRA Deductions," for example, while investment account withdrawals deposited into your checking account are categorized as "Income."

Are you a mutual fund fanatic?

If you're a fan of mutual funds, you won't need Quicken to measure the fund's annual returns. The fund manager provides these figures for you in quarterly and annual reports.

Some investors don't need Quicken

Let me give you an example of someone who doesn't need to use Quicken's investments feature — me. Once upon a time I bought and sold common stocks, fooled around with half a dozen mutual funds, and learned firsthand why junk bonds are called junk bonds. Over the last few years, though, I've simplified my financial affairs considerably.

I don't invest directly in stocks, bonds, or mutual funds these days; instead, I stick money in an IRA. My investments don't produce taxable dividends or interest income, nor taxable or tax-saving capital gains or losses. Money I put into the IRA is tax-deductible. And money I ultimately take out of the IRA will be taxable.

I'm also sticking with a handful of mutual funds, but I don't need to calculate the annual return — that's what mutual fund managers do. So I don't need to separately figure, for example, what my shares of Vanguard Index Trust delivered as an annual return when I include both the 3 percent dividend and the 10 percent price drop.

Because I don't need to track investment income, nor track capital gains and losses, nor calculate the progress of my investment portfolio, I don't need Quicken's investment record-keeping for my personal use.

Many investors do need Quicken

Of course, many people do benefit from Quicken's investment record-keeping. If you routinely buy stocks and bonds, you probably want to calculate your annual returns. What's more, if you try to monitor your capital gains and losses intelligently — and you should — you want to know which securities have gone up and which have gone done.

The size of your investment portfolio isn't an issue. For example, I have two daughters who are saving money for college. (Actually, in a cruel twist of fate, I am saving; they're simply accumulating.) Although Beth and Britt haven't saved much money, and although they use mutual funds to keep things simple, they do three things that cause nightmarishly complex record-keeping for their poor, overworked, and grossly underpaid accountant. (Can you say, "Daddy?") They reinvest their quarterly dividend income, pay annual maintenance fees, and coerce their parents into adding more money to their investment portfolios.

What's the big deal? All three things adjust the *basis* in the fund. And when Beth and Britt sell their mutual fund shares, their gain (or loss) will be determined by subtracting the basis from the sales proceeds.

The bottom line: Even though Beth and Britt don't have much money, I need to use Quicken to track their investments.

Tracking a Mutual Fund

If you still think that you need to track a mutual fund investment, you need to know how to set up a mutual fund account and then record your investment activities.

Even if you don't invest in mutual funds, you shouldn't skip this section.

Setting up a mutual fund investment account

Setting up an investment account works the same way as setting up any other account:

1. **Choose the Accounts icon from the iconbar.**

   Quicken, ever the faithful companion, displays the My Accounts window.

2. **Select the New button on the My Accounts window.**

   Quicken dutifully displays the Set Up Account window. If you've seen one Set Up Account window, you've seen them all — so I won't show them all as figures.

3. **Select the Mutual Fund option button.**

4. **Enter a name for the mutual fund.**

   Sure. You can do something totally outrageous. But I think it'll really be easiest if you just enter the name of the mutual fund. (Note, if you're like me and you use the same mutual fund for two different accounts—one for each of your two daughters, for example—you might instead enter the child's name.)

5. (Optional) Enter a description for the mutual fund.

Here again, you're pretty much on your own. I just leave this field blank. I figure I'll know what's what just by looking at the account name.

6. Choose Create.

Quicken displays the investment account register window. This account register looks a bit different than the one you're probably used to, however. Quicken adds some extra special fields for collecting the extra bits of information investment transactions involve: shares, share price, commissions, and so on (see Figure 12-1).

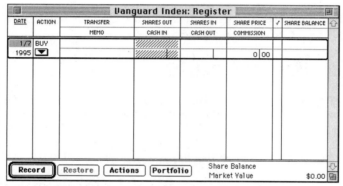

Figure 12-1:
The
investment
account
register
window.

Recording your initial investment

After you set up a mutual fund investment account, you can record an initial purchase of fund shares.

Of course, you need to know the original price of those first shares. So dig through that kitchen drawer where you stuff bank statements, financial records, and those kooky birthday cards from Aunt Enid.

When you find the proper paperwork that shows the number of shares you purchased and the price per share, here's what you do:

1. Select the investment account if it's not already shown in a register on your screen.

Display the My Accounts window; then highlight the investment account (with the arrow keys or by clicking the mouse). Select the Open button. Quicken displays the investment account register.

2. Enter the date you first purchased fund shares into the first row's Date field.

Move the cursor to the Date field and type the date using the MM/DD/YYYY format. Enter May 23, 1987, for example, as **5/23/1987**. You also may select the date from the pop-up calendar.

3. Indicate that you're recording the prior purchase of shares.

Activate the Action drop-down list box. From the drop-down list box, select Move Shares (MS) action. This tells Quicken, "Yeah, I've purchased some shares of this mutual fund, but I don't want you to adjust my checking account because I bought them a long, long time ago and I recorded the transaction then."

4. Enter the number of shares you purchased a long time ago in the Shares In field.

Move the cursor to the Shares In field. Type the number of shares you originally purchased.

5. Indicate what you paid per share.

Move the cursor on the Share Price field, and enter the share price. You can enter a fractional price — such as $10^1/_4$ — but your mutual fund shares probably cost something in dollars and cents — such as 10.25.

6. (Optional) Enter a memo description.

If you want to tie the purchase to a confirmation order number, for example, enter the data into the Memo field. I suppose you could use this field to record anything: Kilroy was here. Save the Whales. Don't tread on me.

7. Record the initial purchase of mutual fund shares.

Choose the Record button.

Quicken beeps in agony and then records the transaction into the register. Figure 12-2, for example, shows a register that records a $1,425.00 purchase of shares in the Vanguard Index mutual fund.

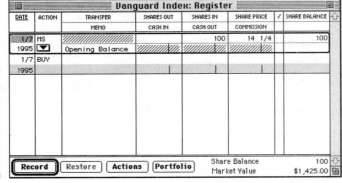

Figure 12-2:
The record
of an initial
purchase of
mutual fund
shares.

Buying near

As you purchase shares — by sending a check to the mutual fund management company or by reinvesting dividends and capital gain distributions — you should record these transactions in the Investment register.

By writing a check

If you buy shares by writing a check, there are two ways to enter a description of the shares you've purchased.

I think the easier way is to enter the transaction directly into the Investment register, much like you enter checks and deposits into a bank account register. To record the purchase this way:

1. **Enter the purchase date into the first empty row's Date field.**

2. **Indicate that you're purchasing new shares by check.**

   Activate the Action drop-down list box, and select the Buy action.

3. **Enter the bank account on which you'll write the check that pays for the shares.**

   Move the cursor to the Transfer field. Then type enough of the account name for Quicken to identify. Once you do, Quicken fills in the rest of the name for you. (Note that you can also display the My Accounts list window and double-click one of the accounts it lists.)

4. **Indicate what you paid per share.**

5. **Indicate the size of your purchase.**

   Tell Quicken the size of your investment. You need to enter two of the following three pieces of information: Shares In, Share Price, and Cash Out. Whatever piece of information you don't calculate, Quicken calculates for you. Pretty neat, right?

6. **(Optional) Enter a memo description.**

7. **Enter the commission or fee that you paid.**

   Move the cursor to the Commission field and enter the commission or fee you paid to purchase the shares. (This figure will be included in the amount shown in the Cash Out field.)

8. **Record the investment transaction and choose the Record button.**

   Figure 12-3 shows a new shares purchase transaction recorded in the Investment register.

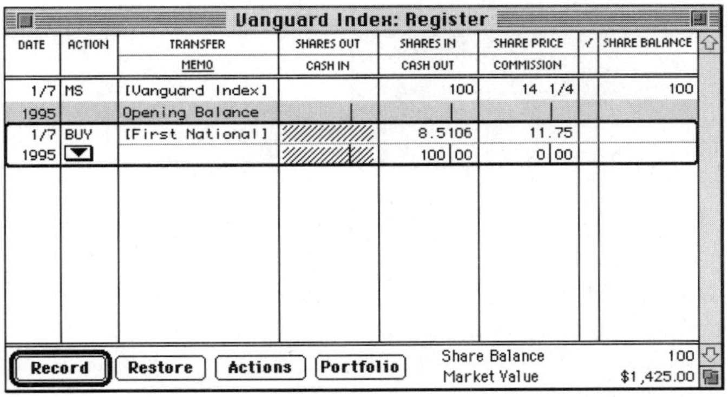

DATE	ACTION	TRANSFER	SHARES OUT	SHARES IN	SHARE PRICE	✓	SHARE BALANCE
		MEMO	CASH IN	CASH OUT	COMMISSION		
1/7	MS	[Vanguard Index]		100	14 1/4		100
1995		Opening Balance					
1/7	BUY	[First National]		8.5106	11.75		
1995	▼			100 00	0 00		

Record   Restore   Actions   Portfolio

Share Balance 100
Market Value $1,425.00

Figure 12-3:
Another
purchase of
new shares.

Quicken offers another way to record a shares purchase: the Buy dialog box. This dialog box prompts you to enter (in a dialog box) the same information that you record when entering a mutual shares purchase transaction directly into the Investment register. Quicken then records the transaction into the register.

To display the Buy dialog box, select the Actions button at the bottom of the investment account register. Quicken will display a window that lists all the possible actions (see Figure 12-4). Double-click the Buy action, and Quicken displays the Buy dialog box (see Figure 12-5).

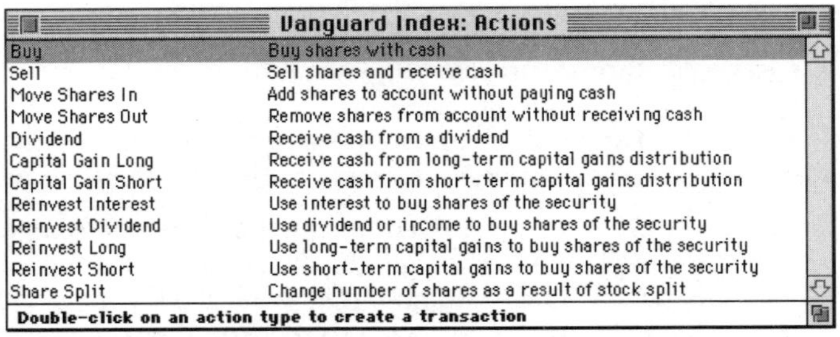

Vanguard Index: Actions

Buy	Buy shares with cash
Sell	Sell shares and receive cash
Move Shares In	Add shares to account without paying cash
Move Shares Out	Remove shares from account without receiving cash
Dividend	Receive cash from a dividend
Capital Gain Long	Receive cash from long-term capital gains distribution
Capital Gain Short	Receive cash from short-term capital gains distribution
Reinvest Interest	Use interest to buy shares of the security
Reinvest Dividend	Use dividend or income to buy shares of the security
Reinvest Long	Use long-term capital gains to buy shares of the security
Reinvest Short	Use short-term capital gains to buy shares of the security
Share Split	Change number of shares as a result of stock split

Double-click on an action type to create a transaction

Figure 12-4:
The Actions
window.

By reinvesting dividends, interest, or capital gains

When you reinvest your dividends, interest, or capital gains, you also have two methods available for recording the transaction: using the register or using the Reinvest dialog box you can get to using the Actions button. Here again, I like the register approach, so I'll describe it first.

```
┌─────────────────────────────────────┐
│ ▣▫  ▓▓▓▓ Vanguard Index: Buy ▓▓▓▓    │
├─────────────────────────────────────┤
│  Buy                    Date  1/7/95 │
│  _____ Shares Of   Vanguard Index  │
│              At  _____             │
│       Commission _____  0│00       │
│      Total Cost: _____  0│00       │
│   Source of Funds:[            ]     │
│ Memo: _____                │
│                                      │
│ ( Record )  [ Cancel ]               │
└─────────────────────────────────────┘
```

Figure 12-5:
The Buy
dialog box.

You can record your reinvestment transactions, which buy new shares, by first displaying the Investment register and then by following these steps:

1. **Enter the purchase date (in this case, the reinvestment date) into the next empty row's Date field.**

2. **Tell Quicken that you're purchasing new shares by reinvesting.**

   Activate the Action drop-down list box and select one of the following Reinvest actions:

   - Reinvest interest (RI)

   - Reinvest dividends (RD)

   - Reinvest long-term capital gains (RL)

   - Reinvest short-term capital gains (RS)

   Use the mouse to select the appropriate reinvestment action and press Enter. Quicken enters the reinvestment abbreviation in the Action field.

You don't need to determine whether the amounts you reinvest are dividends, interest, long-term capital gains, or short-term capital gains because the mutual fund statement tells you this. If you reinvest more than one type of gain, however, you need to record more than one transaction. For example, if the $50 you reinvest is part long-term capital gain and part dividend income, you need to record two transactions: one for the long-term capital gain reinvestment and one for the dividend income reinvestment.

3. **Indicate the number of shares you're purchasing by reinvesting profits.**

4. **Indicate the price per share that you paid.**

5. **Indicate the size of your purchase.**

   You either can give Quicken the number of shares you're purchasing or the total dollar amount of the transaction. If you haven't yet entered the number of shares, give the total dollar amount of your purchase.

6. (Optional) Type a brief explanation of the transaction into the Memo field.

7. Enter the commission or fee that you paid in the Commission field.

The commission fee is included in the figure shown in the Cash Out field.

8. Record the reinvestment transaction.

Select the Record button. Quicken records the reinvestment.

Figure 12-6 shows $61.25 of dividends being reinvested in the mutual fund by buying shares that cost $12.25 a piece. Other reinvestments work basically the same way — except you use a different reinvestment action.

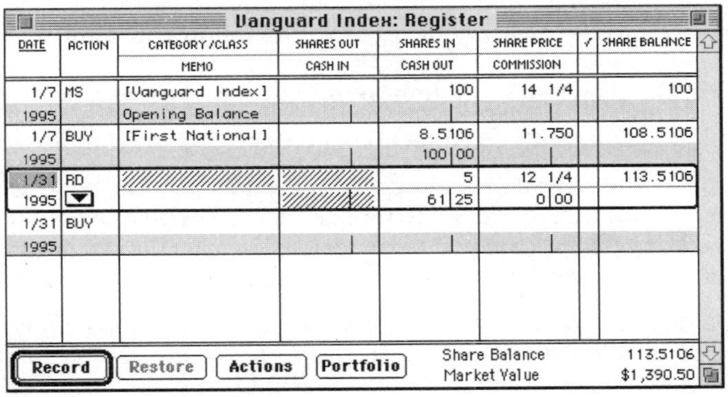

Figure 12-6:
How you record reinvestment of dividends.

DATE	ACTION	CATEGORY/CLASS	SHARES OUT	SHARES IN	SHARE PRICE	√	SHARE BALANCE
		MEMO	CASH IN	CASH OUT	COMMISSION		
1/7	MS	[Vanguard Index]		100	14 1/4		100
1995		Opening Balance					
1/7	BUY	[First National]		8.5106	11.750		108.5106
1995				100|00			
1/31	RD			5	12 1/4		113.5106
1995	▼			61|25	0|00		
1/31	BUY						
1995							

Share Balance 113.5106
Market Value $1,390.50

Record   Restore   Actions   Portfolio

As mentioned earlier, the second way to record amounts you reinvest is to use one of the Reinvest dialog boxes. To do this, select the Actions button (at the bottom of the investment account register) so that Quicken displays the Actions window. Then select the appropriate reinvestment action. (Which reinvestment action depends on what you're reinvesting: dividends, interest, long-term capital gains, or short-term capital gains.) After you make this selection, Quicken displays a Reinvest dialog box. Figure 12-7 shows the Reinvest Dividend dialog box.

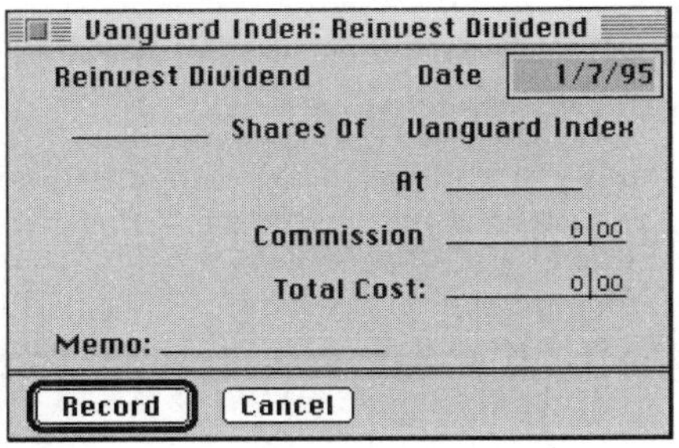

Figure 12-7:
The Reinvest Dividend dialog box.

Vanguard Index: Reinvest Dividend

Reinvest Dividend   Date   1/7/95

Shares Of   Vanguard Index

At   _____

Commission   _____ 0\|00

Total Cost: _____ 0\|00

Memo: _____

Record   Cancel

To describe an amount you're reinvesting, just fill in the text boxes, which are similar to the fields you fill in when you record the reinvestment directly into the register. When you select Record, Quicken takes the information you entered into the text boxes and records the reinvestment into the investment register.

Recording your profits

Every so often, you may receive distributions directly from the mutual fund company. Retirees, for example, often direct mutual fund managers to send dividend checks and capital gains directly to them rather than to have the amounts reinvested.

To record these kinds of distributions, you go through a process very similar to those described earlier. For example, if you want to record an income transaction directly into the Investment register, you follow these steps:

1. **Enter the distribution date into the next empty row's Date field.**

2. **Tell Quicken that you're receiving a distribution from the mutual fund.**

   Activate the Action drop-down list box and select the action to describe the distribution: Dividend, to indicate you're depositing dividends; Capital Gain Long, to indicate you're depositing long-term capital gains; or Capital Gain Short, to indicate you're depositing short-term capital gains.

   You don't need to determine for yourself whether a distribution is a dividend, a long-term capital gain, or a short-term capital gain because the mutual fund statement makes the distribution clear.

3. **Indicate into which bank account you deposited the distribution.**

   Move the cursor to the Transfer field. Then, type enough of the account name for Quicken to identify. Once you do, Quicken fills in the rest of the name for you. (Note that you can also display the My Accounts list window and double-click one of the accounts it lists.)

4. **Indicate the dividend or capital gains distribution amount.**

   Enter the amount in the Cash In text box.

5. **(Optional) Type a brief description of the distribution in the Memo field.**

   Be creative — type your wedding anniversary, the name of your dog, or even a piece of data related to the dividend or distribution.

6. **Record the dividend or distribution transaction.**

   You can record the dividend in a bunch of ways, but why not just click the Record button? Quicken records the reinvestment — *Bip, bap, boom* — it's just that quick.

Figure 12-8 shows $75 of dividends being deposited into a checking account named First National.

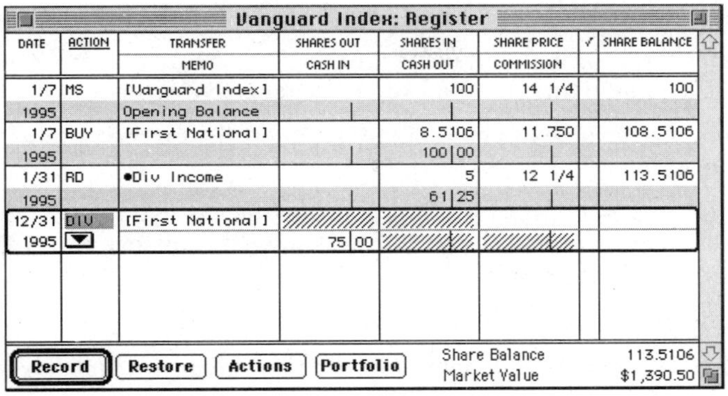

Figure 12-8:
How you
record a
dividend
distribution.

If you don't want to enter the transaction directly into the Investment register, you can also use the Income, Capital Gain Long, or Capital Gain Short dialog boxes. To do this, select the Actions button so Quicken displays the Actions window. Then, select the type of income you want to record: dividend, capital gain long, and capital gain short. Figure 12-9 shows the Dividend dialog box.

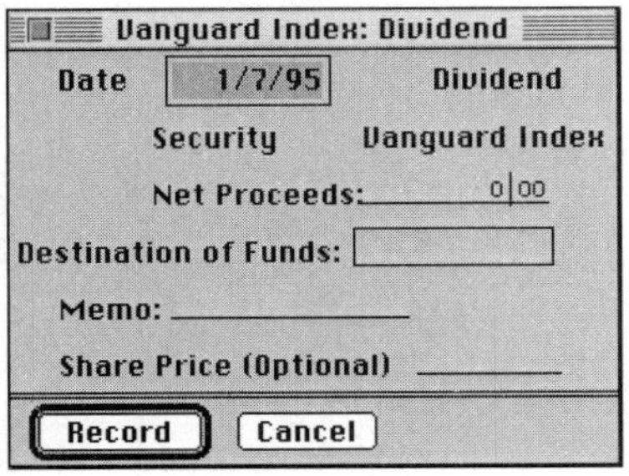

Figure 12-9:
The
Dividend
dialog box.

You record an income transaction in the Dividend dialog box in the same way that you record it directly in the register. You describe the income amount and the account into which the dividend or capital gains check is deposited.

Selling dear

Selling mutual fund shares works basically in the same way as buying them. You can record the sale of shares either directly into the register or by using a Sell dialog box.

If you want to record the sale of shares directly into the register, do the following:

1. **Enter the sale's date into the next empty row's Date field.**

2. **Tell Quicken that you're selling shares.**

    Activate the Action drop-down list box and select the Sell action.

3. Enter the bank account into which you'll deposit the sale's proceeds.

Enter the bank account name into the Transfer text box. Or type enough of the account name that Quicken will QuickFill the account name for you.

4. Indicate the size of your sale by giving Quicken the number of shares you sold.

You can also do this by telling Quicken the cash you received using the Cash In and Commission fields. I assume you can just give Quicken the number of shares sold, however. It's really the easiest way.

5. Indicate the price per share that you received.

With a little luck, your sale's price is more than you paid.

6. (Optional) Type a brief description of the sale in the Memo field.

7. Enter the commission or fee you paid to sell the shares in the Commission field.

No wonder Bernie, your broker, does so well, huh? He makes money whether you do or not.

8. Choose the Record button.

Figure 12-10 shows shares being sold to pay for Beth's first-quarter college tuition. Just a few pages ago, she was just a little girl. And now she's leaving home. She grew up fast.

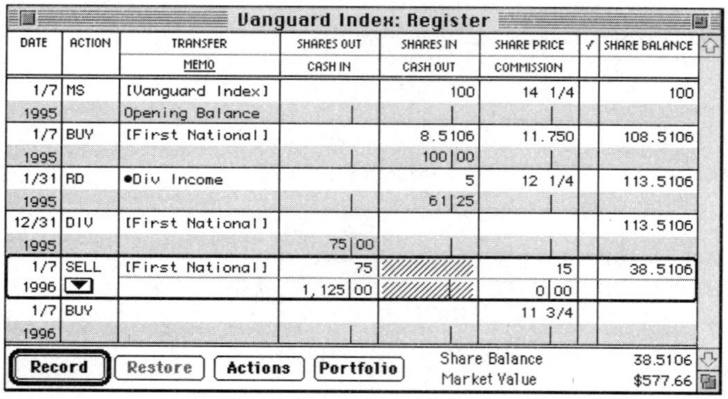

Figure 12-10:
How you record the sale of mutual fund shares.

DATE	ACTION	TRANSFER	SHARES OUT	SHARES IN	SHARE PRICE	√	SHARE BALANCE
		MEMO	CASH IN	CASH OUT	COMMISSION		
1/7	MS	[Vanguard Index]		100	14 1/4		100
1995		Opening Balance					
1/7	BUY	[First National]		8.5106	11.750		108.5106
1995				100 00			
1/31	RD	•Div Income		5	12 1/4		113.5106
1995				61 25			
12/31	DIV	[First National]					113.5106
1995			75 00				
1/7	SELL	[First National]	75	/////	15		38.5106
1996	▼		1,125 00	/////	0 00		
1/7	BUY				11 3/4		
1996							

Record	Restore	Actions	Portfolio	Share Balance	38.5106
				Market Value	$577.66

Vanguard Index: Register

If you don't want to record a sell transaction directly into the register, you can use a Sell dialog box. To do this, click the Actions button so Quicken displays the Actions window. Then double-click the Sell action. Quicken displays the Sell Shares dialog box, which collects the same information in its text boxes that you enter in the register's fields (see Figure 12-11).

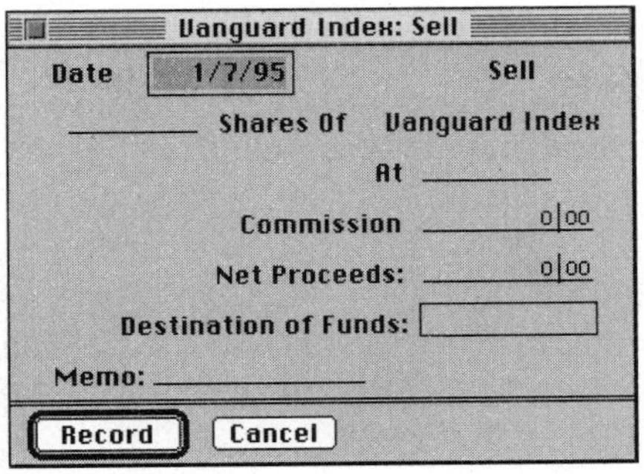

Figure 12-11:
The Sell
dialog box.

What if you make a mistake?

If you make a mistake, don't worry — it's not a problem. You can edit an investment transaction in the Investment register the same way you edit check and deposit transactions in a bank account register. For example, you can click the fields with the incorrect entries, fix them, and then record the new, corrected transaction.

Slightly tricky mutual fund transactions

I didn't describe every possible mutual fund transaction — although I have described every one I've encountered in the last 10 or 12 years. You should know, however, that Quicken does let you record two additional transactions: shares out and stock split transactions.

Removing shares from an account

You can tell Quicken to remove shares from an account without moving the money represented by the shares to some other account. Why would you want to remove a *move shares out* transaction? I can think of two situations: when you erroneously add shares to the account with the move shares action and now you need to remove them, or when you use an investment account to record old investment activity, such as activity from last year.

The first instance is self-explanatory because you are simply correcting an error that you made. In the second case, however, you don't want to transfer the proceeds of a mutual fund sale to a checking account because the money from the sale is already recorded as a deposit at some point in the past.

You can record a shares out transaction directly into the register by moving the cursor to the next empty row of the register and specifying the Action as move shares, or MS. Next, you fill in the rest of the fields in the investment register in the same way as you would for a regular ol' sell transaction—except enter the number of shares you're moving into the Shares Out field.

You also can record a shares out transaction with a Move Shares Out dialog box. Click the Actions button so Quicken displays the list of possible investment actions in the Actions window. Then, double-click the Move Shares Out action. When Quicken displays the Move Shares Out dialog box, fill in the Date text box and Shares Of field.

The stock split and then doubled

Stock splits don't occur very often with mutual funds; however, when they do occur, the mutual fund manager, in effect, gives you a certain number of new shares (such as two) for each old share you own.

To record a stock split, you use the Stock Split action. Then you indicate the ratio of new shares to old shares. For a two-for-one split, for example, you indicate that you get two new split shares for each old unsplit share. The whole process is really pretty easy.

You can record a stock split by moving the cursor to the next empty row of the register and using the Stock Split action. You also can click the Actions button, double click Share Split, and fill out the dialog box that asks about the split date, the new shares, the old shares, and optionally, the share price after the split.

Oops, my mutual fund shares are wrong

It's very possible that you may end up with share count errors in your mutual fund account. Sometimes the error occurs because calculations have been rounded differently in Quicken than by your mutual fund manager. If you sell shares for $13.65 and receive $838.89 for the transaction, for example, Quicken may calculate the number of shares sold in a different manner than your mutual fund manager.

To fix these sorts of errors, just make a *shares adjustment.* A shares adjustment just changes the number of shares Quicken shows for a mutual fund to whatever you set. To do this, choose the Adjust Balance command from the Activities menu. Quicken displays the Adjust Balance dialog box, shown in Figure 12-12.

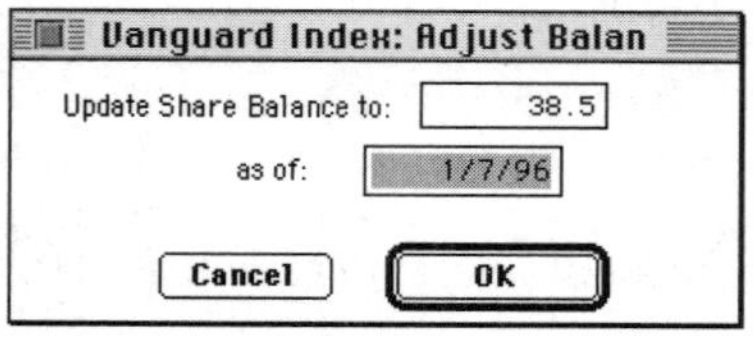

Figure 12-12:
The Adjust
Balance
dialog box.

To use this dialog box, just specify the correct number of shares, enter the date that reflects the corrected figure, and choose OK. Quicken adds a Move Shares transaction to the register to fix the shares balance for the mutual fund.

Reports

I just want to say one thing about Quicken reports as they relate to your investments: *remember the reports are there.* (For more information, see Chapter 6.)

Menu commands and other stuff

For the most part, the commands and menus available for an investment account are the same as those available for all the other accounts Quicken supplies. I've written about the commands that I think are most helpful to new users in the preceding chapters of this book. So if you have a question about how the Transaction command works, for example, refer to the Index, where you will be directed to a specific discussion of that command.

Updating Securities Prices

You can collect current market prices and store this information with your accounts. Just display the investment account that has the mutual fund shares. Then choose the Portfolio button or the Portfolio command from the View menu. Either way, Quicken displays the Portfolio window (see Figure 12-13).

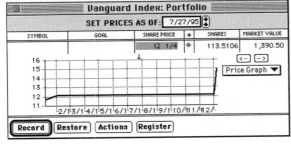

Figure 12-13: The Portfolio window.

To record the current market price for a security, or click the security. Then move the cursor to the Share Price field and enter the current price. You also can use the + and – keys to change the per share price incrementally by an eighth, or $.125.

Quicken updates the market value figure shown in the lower-right corner of the register window. After you update the market price, you can return to the register window by choosing the Register button.

The Portfolio window

You can do more with the Portfolio window than just update share prices. For example, if you take a close look at Figure 12-13, notice that there's an Actions button. If you click this, Quicken displays the same Actions window as when you click the Actions button on the investment account register window. You can use this window's list of actions to enter investment transactions directly from the Portfolio window.

The Set Prices As Of drop-down list box lets you specify the date on which you want to see and set market prices and values.

The drop-down list box that shows share price lets you change the portfolio information shown in the window. You can also choose to view market values in a graph and view price changes in a table. These other views, as they're called, don't make all that much sense for a mutual fund. They can, however, be very interesting when you start working with investment accounts that hold multiple securities. (I talk about this in the very next chapter.)

I'm not going to go into more detail here about what all these extra whistles and bells do. If you're a serious investor, however, take the time to explore these commands. You may gain some interesting insights into your investments.

This chapter described how you use the investments feature in Quicken for tracking your mutual funds. So if you invest exclusively in mutual funds, the information you've now picked up should be all you need.

If you also invest directly in such things as stocks and bonds, you may want to turn to the next chapter. It describes how you use a Quicken investment account to track a brokerage account.

Chapter 13
Stocks and Bonds

· ·

In This Chapter

▶ Setting up a portfolio account

▶ Describing the securities in a portfolio account

▶ Transferring cash to and from a portfolio account

▶ Buying stocks and bonds from a portfolio account

▶ Recording dividends, capital gains, and other investment income from securities held in a portfolio account

▶ Recording miscellaneous income and expenses, and return of capital

▶ Updating securities prices

▶ Adjusting your portfolio cash balance

▶ Adjusting your portfolio account shares

· ·

Tracking a Portfolio Account

When you understand how Quicken handles mutual fund investments, you'll find it a snap to work with what Quicken calls a portfolio account — an account for tracking stocks, bonds, all your other investments, and even the cash you hold in a brokerage account.

Because a portfolio account is really a supercharged version of Quicken's mutual fund account, I'm going to assume you've already read the previous chapter. I guess that means you need to read it if you haven't already. I'm sorry about this. I don't want to make you jump through unnecessary hoops. And I don't want you to waste time. But you really need to know what Chapter 12 talks about before you start fooling around with a portfolio account. Again, I'm sorry.

Setting up a portfolio account

Setting up a portfolio account is similar to setting up a regular mutual fund account except for a couple of minor but predictable differences. Because you're still fairly new to this process, I'll go through it step-by-step:

1. **Choose the Accounts icon from the iconbar.**

   Quicken, ever the faithful companion, displays the My Accounts window.

2. **Click the New button in the Account List window.**

   Quicken displays the familiar Set Up Account dialog box (see Figure 13-1).

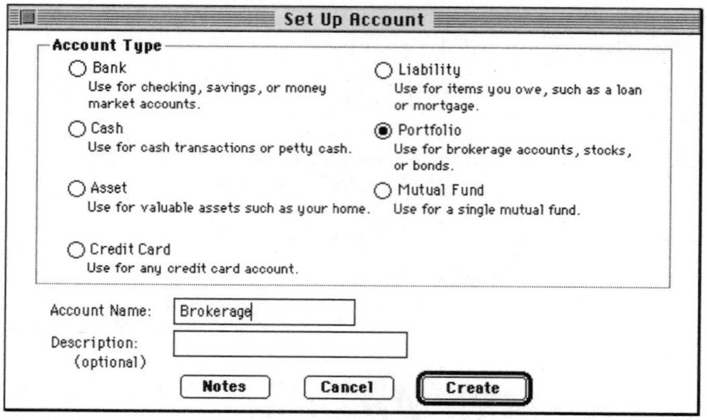

Figure 13-1:
The Set Up
Account
dialog box.

3. **Mark the Portfolio option button.**

   Doing so indicates that the account is an investment account that can hold a bunch of different stuff: stocks, bonds, mutual funds, and even cash.

4. **Name the investment.**

   Move the cursor to the Account Name field and type the name of the broker. Or, if you don't have trouble remembering your broker's name, you can identify this account as the one you use to track your brokerage account with a name like Brokerage. (I entered this name in Figure 13-1.)

5. **(Optional) Enter a description of the account.**

   You can use the Description text box to store extra information about the account.

6. **Click Create.**

   Quicken creates the new account and it displays an investment register window, as shown in Figure 13-2.

DATE	ACTION	SECURITY		SHARES OUT	SHARES IN	SHARE PRICE	√	CASH BALANCE
		TRANSFER	MEMO	CASH IN	CASH OUT	COMMISSION		
1/8 1995	BUY ▼			///////// /////////		0 00		

Cash Balance $0.00
Market Value $0.00

[Record] [Restore] [Actions] [Portfolio]

Figure 13-2:
The
investment
register
window.

Setting up security lists

Your account contains more than one type of *security*. You might have shares of
Boeing, General Motors, or Chase Manhattan. You name it, and someone owns it.

You need to create a list of the securities — stocks, bonds, and so on — that
your account holds.

To do so, complete the following steps after you set up the portfolio account:

1. **Choose the Securities command from the View menu.**

   Quicken displays the Securities window (see Figure 13-3). Note that any
   mutual funds you've already set up appear in the list as securities.

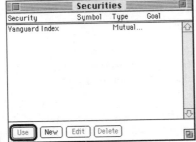

Security	Symbol	Type	Goal
Vanguard Index		Mutual...	

[Use] [New] [Edit] [Delete]

Figure 13-3:
The
Securities
window.

2. **Click the New button in the Securities window.**

   Quicken displays the Set Up Security dialog box, as shown in Figure 13-4.

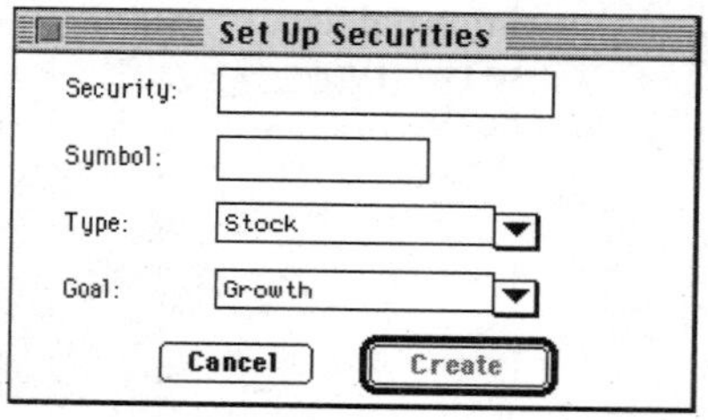

Figure 13-4:
The Set Up
Securities
dialog box.

```
┌──────────────────────────────────────┐
│ ▣      Set Up Securities             │
│  Security: ┌──────────────────────┐  │
│            └──────────────────────┘  │
│  Symbol:   ┌──────────────┐          │
│            └──────────────┘          │
│  Type:     │ Stock        │▼│        │
│  Goal:     │ Growth       │▼│        │
│            ┌────────┐ ┌──────────┐   │
│            │ Cancel │ │  Create  │   │
│            └────────┘ └──────────┘   │
└──────────────────────────────────────┘
```

3. Enter a name for the security by using the Security text box.

4. (Optional and probably crazy) Enter the stock symbol for the security in the Symbol text box.

This step allows you to download share price information from a modem.

5. Indicate which type of security you're setting up.

Activate the Type drop-down list box and then select one of the types listed: bond, CD, mutual fund, or stock.

6. Indicate the purpose for which you're investing.

Activate the Goal drop-down list box and then select one of the goals listed: college fund, growth, high risk, income, or low risk.

Both the Type and Goal drop-down list boxes include an Edit entry. If you select this entry, Quicken displays the Types or Goals window which lists the types or goals. You can add new types or goals — Sure-fire, Easy money, or Unconscionable profits, for example — to the list by clicking the New button and filling in the dialog box Quicken displays.

7. Choose Create.

Quicken redisplays the Security window. It now lists the new stock, bond, or any other item you added.

8. Practice, practice, practice.

As necessary, repeat steps 1 through 7 until you're sick to death of doing so or until you've described each of the securities in your portfolio account.

By the way, treat mutual fund shares that you hold in a portfolio account the same way that you treat other stocks and bonds that you hold in the account. If you're confused, think of it this way: while many mutual funds are sold by brokers to their clients, some mutual funds are sold by the mutual fund manager directly to the public.

I don't want to get into the subject of load mutual funds versus no-load mutual funds, but if you're interested in how these two types of funds work, flip open the *Wall Street Journal* and look for advertisements from no-load fund managers such as Vanguard, Scudder, and T. Rowe Price. Give one of them a call, and they'll tell you why they think you should bypass the middleman — your broker. Next, talk to a broker, who will tell you why you *shouldn't* bypass the middleman. Then you make the call.

What? You want *my* opinion? With much trepidation, I'll give it to you: I always use no-load mutual funds, so I'm a big fan of the do-it-yourself approach. However, I also think that a good broker — good being the key adjective — is well worth the commission fee if the broker helps you avoid expensive mistakes. I'm probably in enough hot water at this point from both sides, so I'll stop here.

Working with cash

There are really two differences between a mutual fund account and a portfolio account. One difference I've already alluded to: the fact that a portfolio account can hold a bunch of different securities instead of only one security.

But there's also another important difference. A portfolio account — such as the type you might have with a stock broker — often has a cash management, or *money market,* account is attached to the brokerage account.

When you initially set up a portfolio account, your money goes into this account. (The broker buys you a doughnut and coffee in this meeting so that you'll put lots and lots of money into your new account, remember?)

You purchase your first shares with the cash from this account. And when you sell shares, all cash proceeds go into this account.

Transferring cash to and from an account

Because you work with cash in a brokerage account, you need to know how to record the cash that flows in and out of the account.

To record the cash you transfer into a brokerage account, specify the action as Transfer Money, (identified with the secret code XFR.) To record the amount of a cash transfer, enter the dollar amount in the Cash In or Cash Out field. This is probably obvious to you, but money you stick into the account goes in the Cash In field and money you pull out of the account goes in the Cash Out field.

Figure 13-5 shows cash being transferred into a brokerage account. Notice that the lower right corner of the register window displays the cash balance.

DATE	ACTION	DESCRIPTION		SHARES OUT	SHARES IN	SHARE PRICE	✓	CASH BALANCE	
		TRANSFER	MEMO	CASH IN	CASH OUT	COMMISSION			
1/8	XFR	Initial Deposit		/////	/////	/////			
1995	▼	[First N		10,000 00		/////		10,000 00	
1/8	BUY								
1995									

Brokerage: Register

Record | Restore | Actions | Portfolio

Cash Balance $10,000.00
Market Value $10,000.00

Sure, it's not all that complicated. But you'll impress your friends.

Just for the benefit of those readers who have become accustomed to my step-by-step descriptions, here are the precise steps you need to follow to record the transaction shown in Figure 13-5.

1. **Indicate the action as Transfer Money.**

   Activate the Action drop-down list and choose the Transfer Money entry. Quicken inputs the secret code for a money transfer, XFR, into the Action field.

2. **(Optional) Enter a description for the transfer.**

   Move the cursor to the Description field, and then type something. In Figure 13-5, I just input "Initial Deposit." You can probably think of something better than that, though.

3. **Identify the account from which you transferred the money.**

   Move the cursor to the Transfer field and begin typing the account name. Remember that you only need to type enough of the name for Quicken to recognize. When Quicken recognizes what you're typing, it fills in the rest of the name for you.

4. **Tell Quicken how much you're transferring.**

   If you're moving money into the account, move the cursor to the Cash In field and enter an amount. If you're moving money out of an account, move the cursor to the Cash Out field and enter an amount.

5. Click Record.

Ever so gently, glide the mouse across the desktop. When the mouse pointer rests over the button labeled Record, click the mouse's left button decisively.

Adding shares to and Removing shares from a brokerage account

Add shares to your account when you need to store the shares in the account but don't want them to affect your brokerage account cash or other checking account. As with mutual fund Move Shares transactions, you would probably only add shares when you first set up a brokerage account.

You didn't read Chapter 12 carefully enough, by the way, if you're now saying to yourself, "Move Shares" transactions! What the heck are those? I don't remember this knucklehead talking about Move Shares transactions!"

I describe this process in detail in the preceding chapter, so I won't repeat that discussion here. But note that you can enter a Move Shares transaction either directly in the register or by using a dialog box that prompts you for needed bits of information. To access the Move Shares In or Move Shares Out dialog box, click the Actions button and then double-click either the Move Shares In or Move Shares Out transactions. When Quicken displays the dialog box, fill in its text boxes and click Record.

Figure 13-6 shows a Move Shares In transaction listing the amount and cost of shares previously purchased. I want to assure you that I'm not suffering delusions of grandeur. Nor have I won the lottery. These transactions are fake.

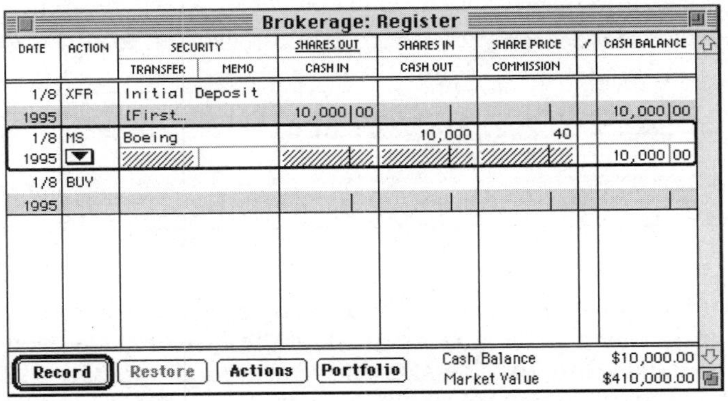

Figure 13-6:
A Move Shares In transaction.

Buying near and selling dear

Buying and selling securities in a brokerage account is very similar to buying and selling shares of a mutual fund. For example, you can enter buy and sell transactions in the register directly or click the Actions button and then double-click one of the Actions window's buy or sell entries. You fill out almost the exact same set of fields, but there are a couple of minor differences.

One difference is that because your account can have a whole bunch of different securities, you need to tell Quicken what you're buying or selling. To do this, enter the security name in the Security field. (If you haven't yet set up the security name, do this as described earlier in the chapter.)

The other difference between a portfolio account and a mutual fund account is that when you buy or sell a brokerage account share, Quicken wants to know where you got or stashed the cash.

If you just got the cash from the brokerage account (in the case of a purchase) or will leave the cash in the brokerage account (in the case of a sale), you leave the Transfer field blank. Quicken assumes, "Hey, if the boss didn't enter anything, it must just mean the money goes back in the pot." The first transaction shown in Figure 13-7 shows a purchase where the money comes from the portfolio account. The third transaction shown in Figure 13-7 shows a purchase where the money goes back into the portfolio account.

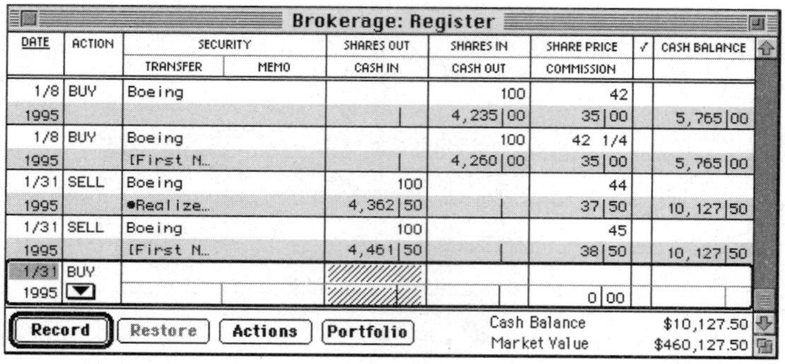

Figure 13-7: Sample buy and sell transactions.

If you got the money from another account (in the case of a purchase) or will move the money to another account (in the case of a sale), you enter the account name into the Transfer field. The second transaction shown in Figure 13-7 shows a purchase where the money comes from another bank account named First National. (You can only see the first part of the name. The rest of the name is cut off.) The fourth transaction shown in Figure 13-7 shows a purchase where the money goes into another bank account named First National.

One other thing. Notice that each of the transactions shown in Figure 13-7 names the security being purchased or sold. See that? Good.

You're now a churning hunk of burning funk. Your broker will love you.

Dividends, capital gains, and other goodies

You could probably guess as much, but the whole portfolio account cash business also comes into play with dividends and capital gains.

When an investment action involves cash, Quicken must know whether the cash goes into or out of the portfolio account or into or out of some other account (such as your checking account).

When you record dividends received on stock held in a brokerage account, you must specify where the dividend money goes — into the brokerage account or into some other account. To indicate that your dividend money goes into another account, you enter that account's name in the Transfer field. To indicate that your dividend money goes back into the portfolio account, just leave the Transfer field blank. Remember, too, to specify the security on which you received the dividend check.

Record capital gain distributions directly in the register in the same way that you record dividends directly in the register. Again, you must specify where the money ends up. To indicate that your capital gains distribution money goes back into the portfolio account as cash, leave the Transfer field blank. To indicate that your capital gains distribution goes into some other account, enter the account's name in the Transfer field.

When you describe a dividend, interest income amount, or capital gain using one of the dialog boxes you get to by clicking the Actions button, Quicken provides an optional Destination for Funds text box. If you fill in this text box, Quicken knows that you're moving the cash to another location. If you don't fill in this text box, Quicken knows that you're leaving the cash in your portfolio account.

I still don't get it — where's the cash?

I hope the logic of this "Where's the cash?" business makes sense. Again, the whole things boils down to one burning question: Where does the cash go or come from when you're talking about a portfolio account?

This advice is sort of funny, but let me suggest something. If this all seems terribly confusing, put this book down and think about this for a few minutes over the next day or so. I bet things will click for you, and suddenly the answer to the "Where's the cash?" question will become crystal clear.

Other not-so-tricky transactions

Quicken lets you record all sorts of transactions in a brokerage account. Not only can you do reminder and stock split actions (described for mutual fund accounts in Chapter 12), but you can also do a bunch of other things.

I'll briefly describe these other transactions and demonstrate them by using the register transactions shown in Figure 13-8.

Bonds, James Bonds

The first transaction shown in Figure 13-8 records the purchase of some bonds. Note that the bond price is given in dollars and cents.

Figure 13-8: Example transactions I'll use to explain some other record-keeping tricks.

DATE	ACTION	SECURITY		SHARES OUT	SHARES IN	SHARE PRICE	✓	CASH BALANCE	
		TRANSFER	MEMO	CASH IN	CASH OUT	COMMISSION			
1/1 1996	BUY ▼	WPPSS		/////	20 11,560 00	575 1/2 50 00		988,567 50	
1/1 1995	BUY	Krugerrands			1,000 400,250 00	400 250 00		588,317 50	
3/1 1996	II	WPPSS •Int Income		1,000 00				589,317 50	
4/15 1996	MISC	Krugerrands Investment ... storage			250 00			589,067 50	
4/15 1996	MISC	Cleat's REIT Rental Inco...		6,500 00				595,567 50	
6/30 1996	RC	Cleat's REIT	liquidation	2,200 00				597,767 50	

Record	Restore	Actions	Portfolio		Cash Balance	$597,767.50
					Market Value	$1,459,277.50

Why do I bring this up? If you invest in bonds, you know that a bond's price is actually quoted as a percentage of its face value. A bond that sells for $950 with a face value of $1,000, for example, is quoted as 95 because the $950 price is 95 percent of the $1,000 face value. Quicken, however, doesn't let you describe a bond's price as a percent. So you enter the bond price as its price in dollars and cents.

Going for the gold

The second transaction in Figure 13-8 shows the purchase of some Krugerrands (one-ounce gold coins minted by South Africa). For this transaction, the price is the price per Krugerrand, and the shares figure is actually the number of ounces (equal to the number of Krugerrands). Because Quicken doesn't supply price-per-ounce and number-of-ounces fields, you insert the information into the Share Price and Shares In fields. That makes sense, right?

Recording interest income

To record interest income directly in the register, use the Interest Income, or II, action (the third transaction shown in Figure 13-8). Note that you should identify the security paying the interest. (In the figure, the WPPSS bonds pay the interest.)

If you want to use the dialog box approach to record interest income, choose the Action button, double-click the Interest Income entry in the Actions window, and then complete the Interest Income dialog box.

By the way, you also use the Interest Income action for recording interest income of certificates of deposit and other debt securities you purchase.

Paying miscellaneous expense

Sometimes you need to pay an expense. I've never seen one occur for a stock or bond — but my investing has been pretty conventional. Expenses sometimes do arise with mutual fund shares (which can be stored in a brokerage account), real estate partnership interests (which can be treated like common stock shares), or precious metal investments (which can also be treated like common stock shares).

If you need to pay a fee for account handling or for storing those South African Krugerrands you've been hoarding, for example, you can record such an expense directly in the register by using the Miscellaneous Expense action. Categorize the expense by selecting an expense category from your regular category list. You can also click the Actions button, double-click the Miscellaneous Expense entry in the Actions window, and fill in the Miscellaneous Expense dialog box.

The fourth transaction listed in Figure 13-8 shows a miscellaneous expense associated with the Krugerrand investment. Note the category, Investment Exp.

Listing miscellaneous income

No big surprise here. Because you have a Miscellaneous Expense action, Quicken also provides a Miscellaneous Income action.

This investment transaction is very similar to the miscellaneous expense transaction. You use the miscellaneous income transaction to record investment income that can't be recorded by using one of the other investment income actions — dividends, interest income, or capital gains distributions.

I've seen this used mostly in relation to investments in things other than stocks and bonds. For example, in a real estate limited partnership the quarterly distributions that the general partner makes aren't interest or dividends; rather, they are rental income. In this case, you can use the Miscellaneous Income action. Quicken lets you specify an income category for the transaction, so that you can use the income category you set up to track rental income.

The fifth transaction in Figure 13-8 is a miscellaneous income transaction showing money you received for your share of a real estate investment trust's (Cleat's REIT) quarterly net rental income.

Recording a return of capital

One final thing: the old return of capital trick. Sometimes, the money you receive because you own a security isn't really income. Rather, it's a refund of part of the purchase price.

Consider this example. You buy a mortgage-backed security — such as a Ginnie Mae bond — for which the *mortgagee* (the person who borrowed the mortgage money) pays not only periodic interest but also a portion of the mortgage principal.

Obviously, you shouldn't record the principal portion of the payment you receive as income. You must record this payment as a mortgage principal reduction or — in the parlance of investment record-keeping — as a return of capital.

As another example, suppose you invest in a limited partnership or real estate investment trust that begins liquidating. Some of the money the investors receive in this case is really a return of their original investment, or a return of capital.

To record a return of capital action, specify the investment action as Return of Capital. The sixth transaction listed in Figure 13-8 shows a return of capital transaction associated with the Cleat's REIT security.

More Quick Stuff About Portfolio Accounts

Let me tell you a couple other quick things. You'll almost certainly find these tidbits helpful.

Monitoring and Updating Securities Values

Regardless of whether you're working with a mutual fund account or with securities in a portfolio account, you can collect current market prices and store them with Quicken's account information.

To do so, display the investment account with the mutual fund shares or the securities you want to update. Then choose the Portfolio command from the View menu or choose the Portfolio button at the bottom of the register window. Quicken displays the Portfolio window. (Check out Figure 13-9. I show this window in Chapter 12, but, heck, let's see it again.)

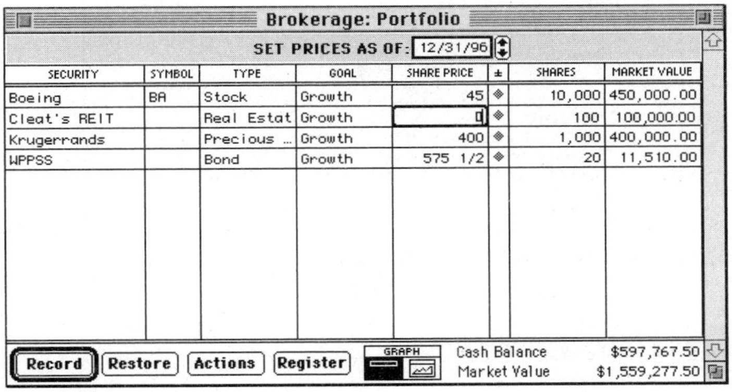

Figure 13-9: The Portfolio window.

SECURITY	SYMBOL	TYPE	GOAL	SHARE PRICE	±	SHARES	MARKET VALUE
Boeing	BA	Stock	Growth	45	◆	10,000	450,000.00
Cleat's REIT		Real Estat	Growth	0	◆	100	100,000.00
Krugerrands		Precious …	Growth	400	◆	1,000	400,000.00
WPPSS		Bond	Growth	575 1/2	◆	20	11,510.00

Brokerage: Portfolio
SET PRICES AS OF: 12/31/96

Record | Restore | Actions | Register | GRAPH | Cash Balance $597,767.50 | Market Value $1,559,277.50

Although I'm not a big fan of using the Portfolio window for looking at mutual funds, it makes a lot of sense for viewing a portfolio account. Why? Because it shows you the value of each of the securities in your portfolio. (You don't really need this information in a mutual fund account because you've got only one security. The account balance shows you the mutual fund investment's value.)

To record the current market price for a security, use the up- and down-arrow keys to highlight the security. Next, move the cursor to the Share Price field and enter the current price. You can also adjust a price by eighths by using the – and + keys. The – key subtracts an eighth, or $.125, from the price shown. The + key adds an eighth, or $.125, to the price shown.

After you update the market price for each security, choose Record. Quicken updates the market value figure shown in the lower right corner of the window.

If you want to enter transactions from the Portfolio window, click the Actions button to display the Actions window. I've shown this before, but Figure 13-10 shows it again. Then double-click the action you want to record. When Quicken displays a dialog box, you describe the transaction — it could be anything we've talked about in this or the preceding chapter — by filling in the dialog box

If you want to return to the register window, just click the Register button.

Brokerage: Actions	
Transfer Money	Move cash from one account to another
Buy	Buy shares with cash
Sell	Sell shares and receive cash
Misc. Income	Income from a miscellaneous source
Misc. Expense	Expense for various reasons
Move Shares In	Add shares to account without paying cash
Move Shares Out	Remove shares from account without receiving cash
Dividend	Receive cash from a dividend
Interest Income	Receive cash from interest income
Capital Gain Long	Receive cash from long-term capital gains distribution
Capital Gain Short	Receive cash from short-term capital gains distribution
Return of Capital	Receive cash from return of capital or principal
Reinvest Interest	Use interest to buy shares of the security
Reinvest Dividend	Use dividend or income to buy shares of the security
Reinvest Long	Use long-term capital gains to buy shares of the security
Reinvest Short	Use short-term capital gains to buy shares of the security
Stock Split	Change number of shares as a result of stock split
Double-click on an action type to create a transaction	

Figure 13-10:
The Portfolio
window.

Adjusting errors

You can adjust the cash balance in a portfolio account and the shares balance in portfolio accounts if for some reason the figures are incorrect.

Oops, my portfolio cash balance is wrong

To adjust the cash balance in a brokerage account, choose the Adjust Balance command from the Activities menu. Quicken next displays a dialog box that lets you specify the correct cash balance, the date as of which the figure you enter is correct, and the category which should be used to describe the adjustment. Fill in the text boxes and choose OK. Quicken adds an adjustment transaction to the register to fix the cash balance.

Oops, my portfolio account shares balance is wrong

To adjust the shares balance for a security in a brokerage account, you need to enter a Move Shares In or Move Shares Out transaction. I describe how you do this earlier this chapter and in the preceding chapter.

Chapter 14
Petty Cash and Mad Money

. . . .

In This Chapter

▶ Setting up a cash account

▶ Entering cash transactions

▶ Handling checks you cash

▶ Updating your petty cash or mad money balance

. . . .

*Y*ou can track petty cash in your business as well as the petty cash in your wallet (and we all have extra petty cash in our wallets, don't we?) by using a special Quicken cash account. To track the cash, you must set up a cash account and then enter the increases and decreases into the cash account's register. Sure — this isn't exactly rocket science — but shoot, I thought I'd just quickly go over this stuff to show you how easy it really is. OK?

Adding a Cash Account

To set up a cash account, you follow roughly the same steps as you do for a bank account. Because you've probably already set up a bank account, you can move quickly through the following steps for setting up a cash account:

1. **Choose the Accounts icon from the iconbar.**

    Quicken displays the My Accounts window. You remember this puppy, the one you've seen a thousand times already.

2. **Choose the New command button on the My Accounts window to set up a new account.**

    Quicken, of course, is no dummy; it displays the Set Up Account dialog box shown in Figure 14-1.

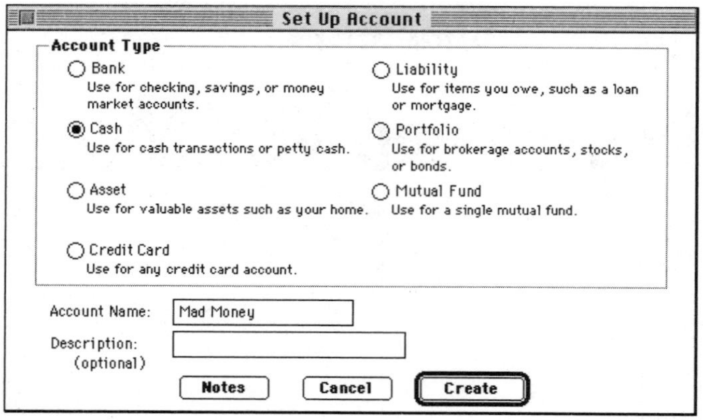

Figure 14-1:
The Set Up
Account
dialog box.

3. **Select the Cash option button.**

   You know how to do this, don't you? You click the button. Click.

4. **Name the account.**

   Move the cursor to the Account Name text box and type a name.

5. **(Optional) Provide a description for the money.**

6. **Click Create.**

   Quicken creates the account and opens an account register window for you (see Figure 14-2).

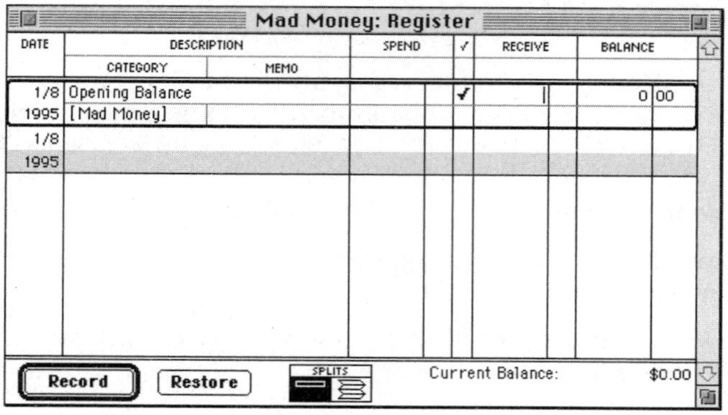

Figure 14-2:
The cash
account
version of
the register
window.

7. **Enter the starting cash balance you're holding.**

   With the cursor positioned in the Receive field, enter the cash balance you're currently holding by using the number keys.

8. **Enter the account balance date.**

   Move the cursor to the Date field and type the two-digit month number, the two-digit date number, and the two-digit year number (probably the current date.)

9. **Choose Record.**

   Quicken records the starting balance transaction.

Tracking Cash Inflows and Outflows

After you set up a cash account, you can use it to track the cash you receive and spend in the same way you track the deposits and checks for a bank account.

To record your cash inflows and outflows, use the Register window. To display the Register window for the cash account you just set up, for example, open the My Accounts window by choosing the Accounts icon from the iconbar and selecting the cash account from the Account list in the window. Figure 14-3 shows the cash account version of the register window with the starting balance transaction and a few others besides.

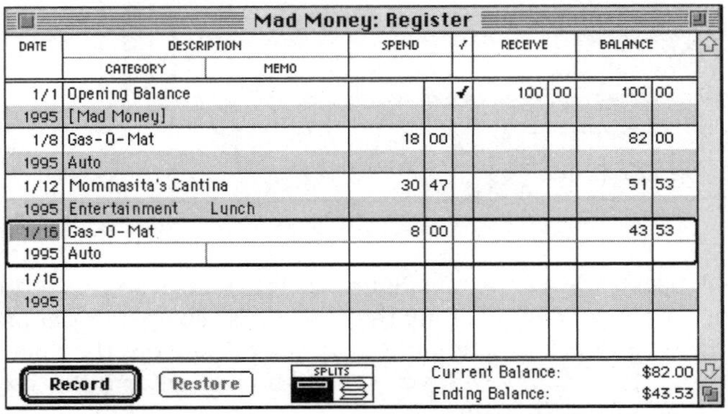

Figure 14-3: The cash account register after I've entered a handful of transactions.

To record the amount of money you spend, fill in the Date, Description, and Spend fields. To record the amount of money you receive, fill in the Date, Description, and Receive fields. To track the reasons you're receiving and spending the cash, use the Category and Memo fields.

About Checks You Cash Instead of Deposit

By the way, you don't necessarily need to set up a cash account if you like to spend cash (rather than, say, write checks or charge on a credit card). If you just cash a check and you do have a bank account set up, there's another way which may be simpler: just use the Splits window to show both the income category (Salary, for example, for an individual) and the way you're going to use the money.

For example, if you cash a $1,000 check and you plan to use the $1,000 for spending money, you may show a positive $1,000 in the Salary income category and a minus $1,000 in the Entertainment spending category. Figure 14-4 shows this trick.

Figure 14-4:
A zero-amount transaction is one handy trick.

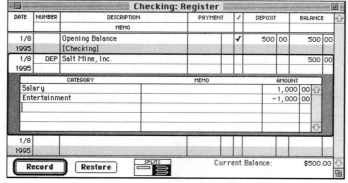

Note that the transaction shown in Figure 14-4 produces a transaction that equals zero. This is correct. Cashing the check that you never deposited doesn't affect your checking account balance. By filling out the Splits window as shown in Figure 14-4, however, you do end up recording both the $1,000 of income and the $1,000 of expense.

Don't worry. I won't ask why you're carrying around $1,000 in cash.

Updating Cash Balances

You can update a register's cash balance to reflect what you actually have in petty cash, your wallet, under the mattress, in the cookie jar, or wherever else you keep your cash by doing the following steps:

1. **Display the Cash register.**

2. **Choose the Adjust Balance command from the Activities menu.**

   Quicken displays the Adjust Account Balance dialog box, as shown in Figure 14-5.

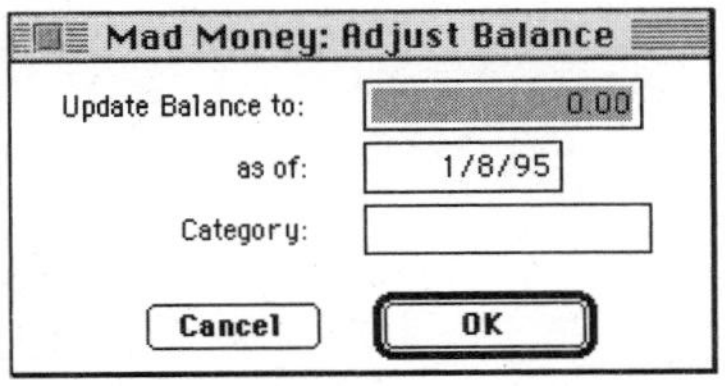

Figure 14-5:
The Adjust
Balance
dialog box.

Mad Money: Adjust Balance	
Update Balance to:	0.00
as of:	1/8/95
Category:	
Cancel	OK

3. **Enter the actual cash balance into the Update Balance To text box.**

4. **Enter the date of the adjustment in the As of text box.**

5. **Enter a category for the adjustment transaction into the Category text box.**

   One way to do this is to select a category from the list in the Categories window and then click the Use button.

6. **When you're finished, choose OK.**

   Quicken updates the cash account's balance.

Part IV
Serious Business

In this part...

*I*f you use Quicken in a business, you'll find it helpful to get some information about how to use it for payroll, customer receivables, and vendor payables. Sure, you could learn these things by sitting down with your certified public accountant, having a cup of coffee, and paying about $100 an hour.

Or you can read on, pretend that we're chitchatting over coffee, and save the $100.

Chapter 15
Payroll

• •

In This Chapter

▶ Creating categories and accounts you need to prepare payroll

▶ Getting an Employer ID Number

▶ Where to get Social Security, Medicare, and federal income taxes withholding information

▶ Calculating an employee's gross wages, payroll deductions, and net wages

▶ Recording a payroll check in Quicken

▶ Making federal tax deposits

▶ Filing quarterly and annual payroll tax returns

▶ Producing annual wage statements such as W-2s

▶ Handling state payroll taxes

• •

Many people use Quicken in a business. Many businesses have employees. Many employees want to be paid on a regular basis. Methinks, therefore, that many people will find help on preparing the payroll helpful.

Getting Ready for Payroll

To prepare payroll checks and summarize the payroll information that you need to prepare quarterly and annual returns, you need to set up some special accounts and categories. You also need to do some paperwork stuff. I'll describe how to do both things in this section.

Getting Quicken ready

To do payroll in Quicken, you'll need to set up several liability accounts, a payroll expense category, and several payroll expense subcategories. Fortunately, none of this is particularly difficult.

I'm going to describe how you do this for purposes of United States federal income and payroll taxes. If you employ people in one of the states that has a state income tax — California, say — you may also have state payroll taxes to deal with. But you can track and process these the same way you process the federal taxes.

I should say that the same thing is probable if you employ people outside the United States. But, hey, there are like a couple hundred countries in the world. So check with someone from the country of employment for specific advice.

Setting up liability accounts

You need to set up three liability accounts to deal with federal payroll and income taxes: one named Payroll-SS to track Social Security, one named Payroll-MCARE to track Medicare, and one named Payroll-FWH to track federal income taxes owed. (I should confess that these aren't my names. They're the sort of names Quicken expects you to use.)

To set up a liability account for any of these payroll tax liabilities, follow these steps:

1. **Choose the Accounts icon from the iconbar.**

   Quicken displays the My Accounts window. You've probably seen this dialog box about a hundred times before. If you want to see the dialog box right now, though, choose the Accounts icon and look at your screen.

2. **Choose the New command button in the My Accounts window.**

   Quicken displays the Set Up Account dialog box. If you've been reading this book cover-to-cover, you've seen this baby a bunch of times before. If you want or need to see it now, though, you can just follow along on-screen.

3. **Mark the Liability option button.**

   This tells Quicken you're going to set up an account.

4. **Enter the appropriate account name: Payroll-SS, Payroll-MCARE, or Payroll-FWH.**

   If your state has an income tax, you'll also want to set up a Payroll-SWH liability account. The only trick to naming other payroll tax liability accounts is that you need to start each liability account name with the word Payroll. No, this isn't some rule I made up arbitrarily. There really is a reason for this. The Quicken Payroll report prints information only on the accounts and categories that start with the word Payroll.

5. **(Optional) Enter a description.**

6. **Click Create.**

   Quicken displays an account register window for the new liability (see Figure 15-1).

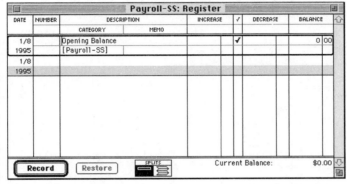

Figure 15-1:
The Quicken account register window showing a payroll tax liability.

7. **Enter the current amount you owe for the payroll tax liability.**

   Quicken positions the cursor at the Increase field so all you have to do is type the amount. Or if you're just starting and you owe nothing, enter **0**. (If you do owe something but you don't have a clue in the world as to how much, the easiest thing to do is to figure out what you owe now, before going any further. Sorry.)

8. **Enter the starting date.**

   Move the cursor to the Date text box. Enter the date on which you owe the balance you entered in step 7. This is probably the current date.

9. **Choose Record.**

   Quicken adds the new liability account.

10. **Repeat steps 2 through 9 for each of the other payroll tax liability accounts you want to add.**

   Remember that you need at least three payroll tax liability accounts — Payroll-SS, Payroll-MCARE, and Payroll-FWH — for the people you employ in the United States. And if you live in a state with income taxes, you either need to move or need to set up a fourth account: Payroll-SWH.

Setting up a payroll expense category

You'll also need to set up a payroll expense category, which isn't tough. Here's all you have do:

1. Choose the Cat icon from the ol' iconbar.

Quicken, with no hesitation, displays the Categories window. Figure 15-2 shows this happy puppy.

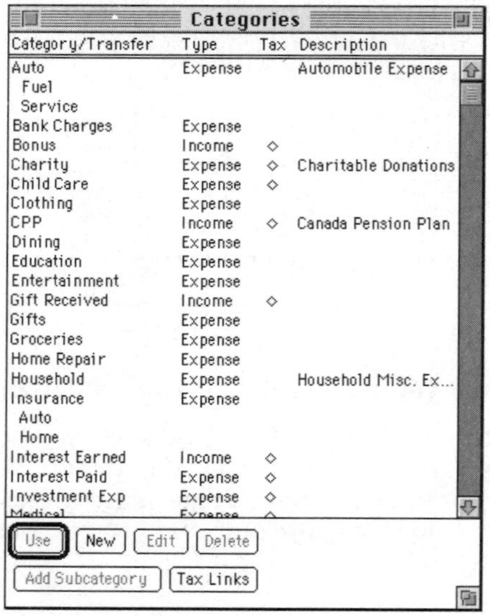

Figure 15-2: The Categories window.

2. Choose the New button.

Quicken displays the Set Up Categories dialog box (see Figure 15-3).

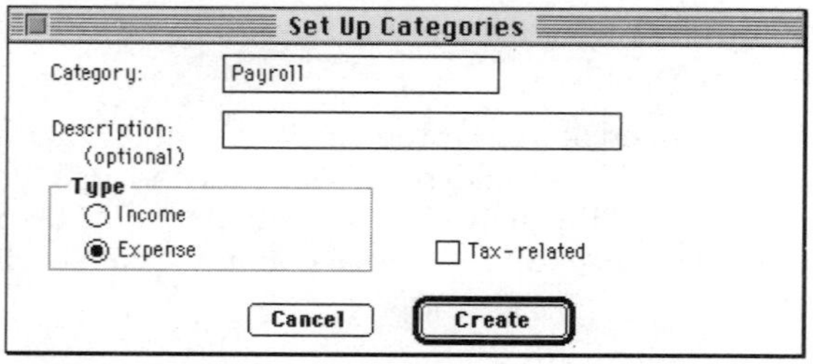

Figure 15-3: The Set Up Categories dialog box.

3. **Enter Payroll as the category name.**

   With the cursor positioned in the Name text box, type **Payroll**, as shown in Figure 15-3.

4. **Optionally, enter a description of the category.**

   If you want, you can type a description in the Description text box. Figure 15-3 doesn't show any description. But then I'm not particularly creative. You may be able to think of something.

5. **In the Type section, mark the Expense option button.**

   This tells Quicken you're setting up an expense category. But you probably know this, right?

6. **Indicate whether the payroll tax is tax deductible.**

   If you're going to be preparing payroll for a business, mark the Tax-related check box. If you're going to be preparing payroll for a household employee — like a nanny, say — don't mark the Tax-related check box. All this little check box really does is tell Quicken that this category should be included on the Tax Summary report. Household employee payroll expenses aren't tax deductible — as you probably know.

7. **Choose Create.**

   Quicken adds the category to the category list and redisplays the Categories window. You've almost completed this part of the mission, Commander Bond.

Setting up the payroll subcategories

There's one other thing you need to do to get Quicken ready for payroll. You need to set up subcategory expenses for employee gross wages, the company's share of the Social Security taxes, and the company's share of the Medicare taxes. Quicken expects you to use Gross, Comp FICA, and Comp MCARE as subcategory names. So that's what you'll do, okay?

1. **Open the Categories window if it isn't already displayed.**

   You can choose the Cat icon to display the window, as you probably know. If you can't remember what this dialog box looks like, refer to Figure 15-2.

2. **Select the Payroll category.**

   You can click the Payroll category or use the Up and Down arrow keys. You make the call.

3. **Choose the Add Subcategory button.**

   Quicken displays the Set Up Categories dialog box (refer to Figure 15-3).

4 **Enter the appropriate payroll expense subcategory name: Gross, Comp SS, or Comp MCARE.**

For example, move the cursor to the Name field and type **Gross** or **Comp SS** or **Comp MCARE**.

5. **Enter a description of the subcategory in the Description text box.**

Because the subcategory names are a little more cryptic, you may want to use the Description text box to document things such as the fact that Comp SS means employer Social Security.

6. **Mark or unmark the Tax-related check box as appropriate.**

If you marked the Tax-related check box for the payroll category, you should mark it for the subcategory, too.

7. **Choose Create.**

Quicken adds the subcategory to the category list and redisplays the Category & Transfer List window.

8. **Repeat steps 2 through 7 for each of the remaining payroll expense subcategories you need.**

Remember that for employees working in the United States, you need at least three subcategories: Gross (for tracking gross wages), Comp SS (for tracking employer Social Security taxes), and Comp MCARE for tracking employer Medicare taxes).

Congratulations, James! You saved the world again. You created the liability accounts and categories that you need to track the amounts you pay employees and the payroll taxes you withhold and owe.

Getting the taxes stuff right

There are also a couple of other things you need if you want to do payroll the right way.

Requesting (or demanding) an Employer ID Number

First, you need to file an SS-4, or Request for Employer Identification Number form, with the Internal Revenue Service (IRS) so you can get an employer identification number. You can get this form by calling the IRS and asking for one. Or if you have a friend who's an accountant, he or she may have one of these forms. (See, there is a reason to invite people like me to your dinner parties.)

In one of its cooler moves, the IRS changed its ways and now lets you apply for and receive an employer identification number over the telephone. You still need to fill out the SS-4 form, however, so you can answer questions the IRS asks during the short telephone-application process. (You also need to mail or fax the form to the Service after you have your little telephone conversation.)

So what about Social Security, Medicare, and withholding taxes?

You need to do two things before you can know how to handle all those taxes. First, you need your employees to fill out a W-4 form to let you know what filing status they will use and how many personal exemptions they will claim. Guess where you get blank W-4 forms? That's right . . . from your friendly IRS agent.

The second thing you need to do is get a Circular E Employer's Tax Guide publication. The Circular E publication is the pamphlet that tells you how much you should withhold in federal income taxes, Social Security, and Medicare from a person's salary. You can get this form and the additional Federal and State forms that you must fill out to satisfy the government requirements for hiring employees, too, just by calling those friendly people at the Internal Revenue Service.

Paying someone for a job well done

After you tell Quicken to get ready to do payroll and you collect the needed tax information, you're ready to pay someone.

Figuring out the gross wages figure

This should be pretty easy. Does Raoul make $14-an-hour? Did he work 40 hours? Then you owe him $560 because $14 times 40 equals $560. Is Betty's salary $400-a-week? Then you owe her $400 for the week.

All that deductions stuff

Your next step — after you know how much you're supposed to pay Raoul or Betty — is to figure out what big brother says you must withhold.

To figure this out, you need both Raoul's and Betty's W-4s to find out their filing status and personal exemptions. Then just flip to the page in the Circular E that describes withholding for a person claiming the filing status and paid by the week.

If Raoul is single and claims just one personal exemption, for example, you would flip to the page like the one shown in Figure 15-4. Remember that Raoul is paid weekly. I circled the number in the table in Figure 15-4 that shows what Raoul is supposed to pay in federal income taxes, Social Security, and Medicare.

And about Betty? Remember that Betty's pay is $400-a-week. If Betty's filing status is married filing joint and with three personal exemptions, you would flip to the page that resembles Figure 15-4. Again, I circled the number in the table in Figure 15-4 that shows what Betty is supposed to pay.

Always use up-to-date information. The numbers you use for federal income tax withholding change annually. Therefore, don't use the table shown in Figure 15-4. It will be out-of-date by the time you read this.

Social Security and Medicare amounts are figured by multiplying the gross wage figure by a set percentage. Social Security is 6.2 percent of the gross wages up to a specified limit — $60,600 in 1994 and probably roughly $62,000 in 1995. The Medicare tax is 1.45 percent of the gross wages. (Be sure to check your faithful Circular E if you think limits come into play for a particular employee. Note, too, that as I'm writing this, Congress is fiddle-faddling with the tax laws again.)

Figuring out someones net wages

Table 15-1 summarizes the payroll calculations shown in Figure 15-4.

Does Table 15-1 make sense? If it doesn't, take another look at the marked information in Figure 15-4 and read my earlier discussion of how to figure out deductions stuff. All I've really done in the table is reorganize some information, calculate the Social Security and Medicare taxes, and show how Raoul's and Betty's gross pay gets nickeled and dimed by the various taxes they owe.

Table 15-1	Payroll for Raoul and Betty		
Item	*Raoul*	*Betty*	*Explanation*
Gross wages	$560.00	$400.00	Hey, it's their pay
Withholding	$075.00	$032.00	From Circular E
Social Security wages	$034.72	$024.80	6.2 percent of gross
Medicare wages	$008.12	$005.80	1.45 percent of gross
Net Wages	$442.16	$337.40	What's left over

SINGLE Persons—WEEKLY Payroll Period
(For Wages Paid After December 1990)

And the wages are—		And the number of withholding allowances claimed is—										
At least	But less than	0	1	2	3	4	5	6	7	8	9	10
		The amount of income tax to be withheld shall be—										
$540	$550	$95	$83	$72	$60	$53	$47	$41	$35	$29	$22	$16
550	560	98	86	75	63	55	49	42	36	30	24	18
560	570	101	89	77	66	56	50	44	38	32	25	19
570	580	103	92	80	69	58	52	45	39	33	27	21
580	590	106	95	83	71	60	53	47	41	35	28	22
590	600	109	97	86	74	63	55	48	42	36	30	24
600	610	112	100	89	77	65	56	50	44	38	31	25
610	620	115	103	91	80	68	58	51	45	39	33	27
620	630	117	106	94	83	71	60	53	47	41	34	28
630	640	120	109	97	85	74	62	54	48	42	36	30
640	650	123	111	100	88	77	65	56	50	44	37	31
650	660	126	114	103	91	79	68	57	51	45	39	33
660	670	129	117	105	94	82	71	59	53	47	40	34
670	680	131	120	108	97	85	74	62	54	48	42	36
680	690	134	123	111	99	88	76	65	56	50	43	37
690	700	137	125	114	102	91	79	68	57	51	45	39
700	710	140	128	117	105	93	82	70	59	53	46	40
710	720	143	131	119	108	96	85	73	62	54	48	42
720	730	145	134	122	111	99	88	76	64	56	49	43
730	740	148	137	125	113	102	90	79	67	57	51	45
740	750	151	139	128	116	105	93	82	70	59	52	46
750	760	154	142	131	119	107	96	84	73	61	54	48
760	770	157	145	133	122	110	99	87	76	64	55	49
770	780	159	148	136	125	113	102	90	78	67	57	51
780	790	162	151	139	127	116	104	93	81	70	58	52
790	800	165	153	142	130	119	107	96	84	72	61	54
800	810	168	156	145	133	121	110	98	87	75	64	55
810	820	171	159	147	136	124	113	101	90	78	66	57
820	830	173	162	150	139	127	116	104	92	81	69	58
830	840	176	165	153	141	130	118	107	95	84	72	60
840	850	179	167	156	144	133	121	110	98	86	75	63
850	860	182	170	159	147	135	124	112	101	89	78	66
860	870	185	173	161	150	138	127	115	104	92	80	69
870	880	187	176	164	153	141	130	118	106	95	83	72
880	890	190	179	167	155	144	132	121	109	98	86	74
890	900	193	181	170	158	147	135	124	112	100	89	77
900	910	196	184	173	161	149	138	126	115	103	92	80
910	920	199	187	175	164	152	141	129	118	106	94	83
920	930	201	190	178	167	155	144	132	120	109	97	86
930	940	204	193	181	169	158	146	135	123	112	100	88
940	950	207	195	184	172	161	149	138	126	114	103	91
950	960	210	198	187	175	163	152	140	129	117	106	94
960	970	213	201	189	178	166	155	143	132	120	108	97
970	980	215	204	192	181	169	158	146	134	123	111	100
980	990	219	207	195	183	172	160	149	137	126	114	102
990	1,000	222	209	198	186	175	163	152	140	128	117	105
1,000	1,010	225	212	201	189	177	166	154	143	131	120	108
1,010	1,020	228	215	203	192	180	169	157	146	134	122	111
1,020	1,030	231	218	206	195	183	172	160	148	137	125	114
1,030	1,040	234	221	209	197	186	174	163	151	140	128	116
1,040	1,050	237	224	212	200	189	177	166	154	142	131	119
1,050	1,060	240	227	215	203	191	180	168	157	145	134	122
1,060	1,070	243	231	218	206	194	183	171	160	148	136	125
1,070	1,080	246	234	221	209	197	186	174	162	151	139	128
1,080	1,090	250	237	224	211	200	188	177	165	154	142	130
1,090	1,100	253	240	227	214	203	191	180	168	156	145	133
1,100	1,110	256	243	230	217	205	194	182	171	159	148	136
1,110	1,120	259	246	233	220	208	197	185	174	162	150	139
1,120	1,130	262	249	236	224	211	200	188	176	165	153	142
1,130	1,140	265	252	239	227	214	202	191	179	168	156	144
1,140	1,150	268	255	243	230	217	205	194	182	170	159	147
1,150	1,160	271	258	246	233	220	208	196	185	173	162	150
1,160	1,170	274	262	249	236	223	211	199	188	176	164	153
1,170	1,180	277	265	252	239	226	214	202	190	179	167	156
1,180	1,190	281	268	255	242	229	216	205	193	182	170	158

$1,190 and over — Use Table 1(a) for a **SINGLE person** on page 22. Also see the instructions on page 20.

Page 25

Figure 15-4:
A payroll report.

What about other taxes and deductions?

If you have other taxes and deductions and you understand how the federal income taxes, Social Security taxes, and Medicare taxes work, you won't have any problem working with the other taxes — no matter what they are.

State income tax withholding, for example, works like the federal income tax withholding. (Of course, you need to get the state's equivalent to the Circular E guide.)

In general, other taxes and amounts paid by the employee get treated similarly.

WARNING!

In fact, the only thing that you need to be careful about is what affects employees' gross pay for income taxes but not their Social Security taxes — things like 401K deductions and certain fringe benefits. If you have these kinds of things to deal with and you need help, just ask your accountant. (It's just too difficult — and actually kind of dangerous, too — for me to provide general answers that will work for everyone who reads this paragraph. Sorry.)

Recording a payroll check

After you make the tax deduction and net wages calculation, you're ready to record the check. This is a little bit complicated, but stick with me, partner. We'll get through it in no time.

If Raoul and Betty are milling around your computer, whining and saying things like, "Gee, Boss, how much longer? I want to get to the bank before it closes," tell them to cool their heels for about three minutes.

Suppose that you're going to record the check using the register window for the bank account (see Figure 15-5). As you know, recording the check into the Write Checks window works the same basic way. The difference is that by using the Write Checks window for the bank account, you can print the payroll check.

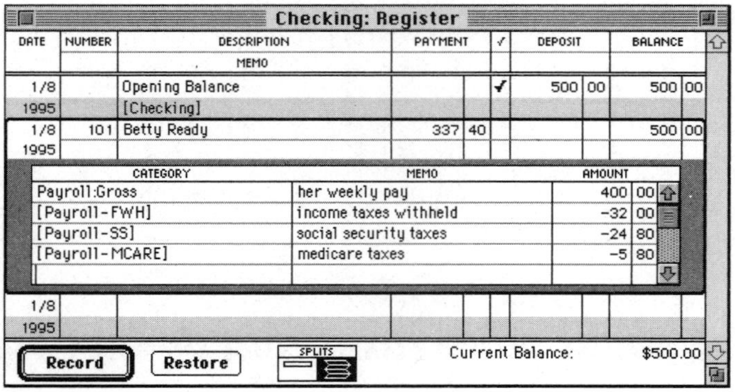

Figure 15-5:
The register window for your checking account.

After you display the register window and highlight the first empty row of the register, follow these steps.

1. **Enter the date of the payroll check in the Date field.**

2. **Enter the payroll check number in the Number field.**

3. **Enter the employee name in the Description field.**

4. **Enter the net wages amount in the Payment field.**

5. **If needed, click the Splits button so you can see the Split field information.**

6. **In the first row of the Splits window, enter the category and gross wages amount in the correct fields.**

   Enter the category Payroll:Gross. The amount, of course, should be the gross wages figure (400.00 in the example).

7. **Enter the employee's federal income taxes in the second row of the Splits window.**

   Enter the liability account Payroll-FWH. The amount should be –32.00.

8. **Enter the employee's Social Security tax withheld and account in the second row of the Splits window.**

   Instead of a category in the Category section, enter the liability account Payroll-SS. The amount of the Social Security tax withheld should be 6.2 percent of the employee's gross wages (32.00 in this example). Enter this in the Amount section.

9. **Enter the employee's Medicare tax withheld and account in the third row of the Splits window.**

   In the Category section, enter the liability account Payroll-MCARE. The amount of the Medicare tax withheld should be 1.45 percent of the employee's gross wages (–5.80 in this example).

   Figure 15-5 shows the checking account register window and the Splits window filled out to record Betty's $400 of wages, the taxes poor Betty has to pay on these earnings, and the net wages figure of $337.40. If you have questions about any of these figures, take a peek again at Table 15-1, shown earlier.

10. **On the next two empty lines of the Splits window, enter the employer's matching share of the Social Security taxes you have to pay.**

    If the employee pays $24.80 of Social Security, for example, use the first empty line to enter $24.80 of expense categorized to the Payroll:Comp SS expense category. Enter 24.80 in the Amount section and Payroll:Comp SS in the Category section.

    Then use the second empty line to record $24.80 of payroll FICA tax liability using the [Payroll-FICA] account. Enter **–24.80** in the Amount section and Payroll-SS in the Category section.

11. **On the next two empty lines of the Splits window, enter the employer's matching share of the Medicare you have to pay.**

    If the employer pays $5.80 of Medicare, for example, use the first empty line to enter $5.80 of expense categorized to the Payroll:Comp MCARE expense category. Enter **–5.80** in the Amount section and Payroll:Comp MCARE in the Category section.

    Then use the second empty line to record $5.80 of payroll FICA tax liability using the Payroll-MCARE account. Enter **–5.80** in the Amount section and Payroll-MCARE in the Category section.

    Figure 15-6 shows the Social Security and Medicare payroll tax information.

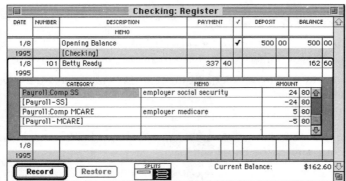

Figure 15-6:
The
employer's
matching
share of
Social
Security and
Medicare
taxes.

The accounts you use to show the payroll taxes withheld and owed are liability accounts. By looking at the account balances of these accounts, you can easily see how much you owe the government.

12. **If you have other employer-paid payroll taxes, record these following the employer's matching share of Social Security and Medicare.**

    You can use this same basic approach to record federal and state unemployment taxes.

13. **To record the payroll check and related employer-paid payroll tax information, choose Record.**

You did it! You recorded a payroll check and the related payroll taxes. Maybe it wasn't all that much fun. But at least it wasn't very difficult.

Making Tax Deposits

Make no mistake. Big Brother wants the money you withhold from an employee's payroll check for federal income taxes, and Social Security and Medicare. Big brother also wants the payroll taxes you owe — the matching Social Security and Medicare taxes, federal unemployment taxes, and so on.

Then every so often, you need to pay Big Brother the amounts you owe.

Making this payment is actually simple. Just write a check for the account balances shown in the payroll tax liability accounts. If you have only written the one check to Betty (as shown in Figures 15-5 and 15-6), for example, your payroll liability accounts would show balances as follows:

Liability Account	Amount
Payroll-FICA	$49.60
Payroll-MCARE	$11.60
Payroll-FWH	$32.00
	———
Total	$93.20

Notice that the Payroll-SS account balance and the Payroll-MCARE account balance include both the employee's Social Security and Medicare taxes and the employer's Social Security and Medicare taxes.

Then you write a check for the $93.20 you owe (see Figure 15-7). The only tricky thing about this transaction is that you're transferring the check amount to the

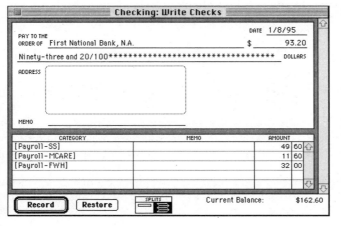

Figure 15-7:
The check and split transaction information when you pay the IRS.

payroll liability accounts rather than assigning the check amount to a payroll tax category. In effect, you're transferring money from your checking account to the government to pay off the payroll taxes you owe.

The first time you see this sort of transfer, it can be a little confusing. So take a minute to think about this. If you write the check to the government, your checking account doesn't have the money in it any more, and you don't owe them the money any more. Therefore, the checking account balance and the liability account balance both need to be decreased. In Quicken, the way you do this is with an account transfer.

When do you make payroll tax deposits? The general rule about United States federal tax deposits is this: If your accumulated payroll taxes are less than $500 for the quarter, you can just pay the taxes the following month with your quarterly return. (This is called the De Minimis rule. I guess the rule was named after a Congresswoman named Dee Minimis or something.) If you owe $500 or more, other special rules come into play that determine how quickly you need to pay deposits.

By the way, you'll always be OK if the last payroll check you write (every time you process payroll) is for the payroll taxes you've withheld or owe. Just make sure you run the check down to the bank the same day.

To make a payroll tax deposit, just deposit your check with a federal tax deposit coupon to a financial institution qualified as a depository for federal taxes or to the Federal Reserve bank serving your geographical area. The IRS should have already sent you a book of coupons as a result of your asking for an Employer ID Number. And one other thing: Make your check payable to the depository or to the Federal Reserve.

Filing Quarterly Payroll Tax Returns

At the end of every quarter, you need to file a quarterly payroll tax return. (By quarters here, I'm referring to calendar quarters. You don't do this four times on a Sunday afternoon as you or your couch-potato spouse watch football.)

If you're a business, for example, you must file a Form 941 — which is just a form you fill out to say how much you paid in gross wages, how much you withheld in federal taxes, and how much you owe for employer payroll taxes.

If you're not a business but you have got household employees — such as a nanny — you must file a Form 942. Again, this is just a form you fill out to say how much you paid in gross wages, withheld in federal taxes, and owe in payroll taxes.

Now, all these numbered forms may make you feel like you're watching a rerun of "Adam 12" ("One Adam 12 . . . One Adam 12 . . . We've got a 941 in progress . . . Backup units on the way . . . Officer requests assistance . . ."). But you'll find that filling out these forms is darn simple. All you really need to know is what the gross wages totals are.

To get the gross wages totals and the balances in each of the payroll tax liability accounts, print the Business Payroll report. To do this, activate the Report

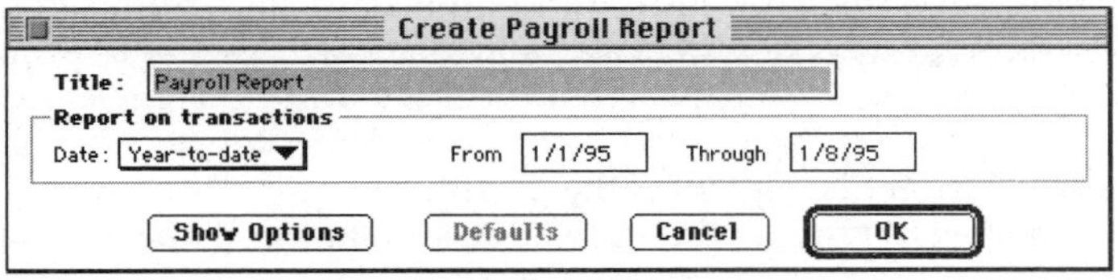

Figure 15-8: The Create Payroll Report dialog box.

menu, choose the Business command to display the Business Reports menu. Then double-click the Payroll report command. Quicken displays the Create Payroll Report dialog box, as shown in Figure 15-8.

Specify the range of dates as the start and end of the quarter for which you're preparing a quarterly report. Then choose OK. Quicken produces a payroll report, which you can easily use to fill out the quarterly payroll tax return. Figure 15-9 shows the Payroll report. (As I mentioned earlier, what this report really does is summarize all the transactions that were categorized as falling into the Payroll expense category or transferred to an account named Payroll (something).)

The Overall Total shown for the Payroll:Gross category — $400 in the example — is the gross wages upon which your employer payroll taxes are calculated.

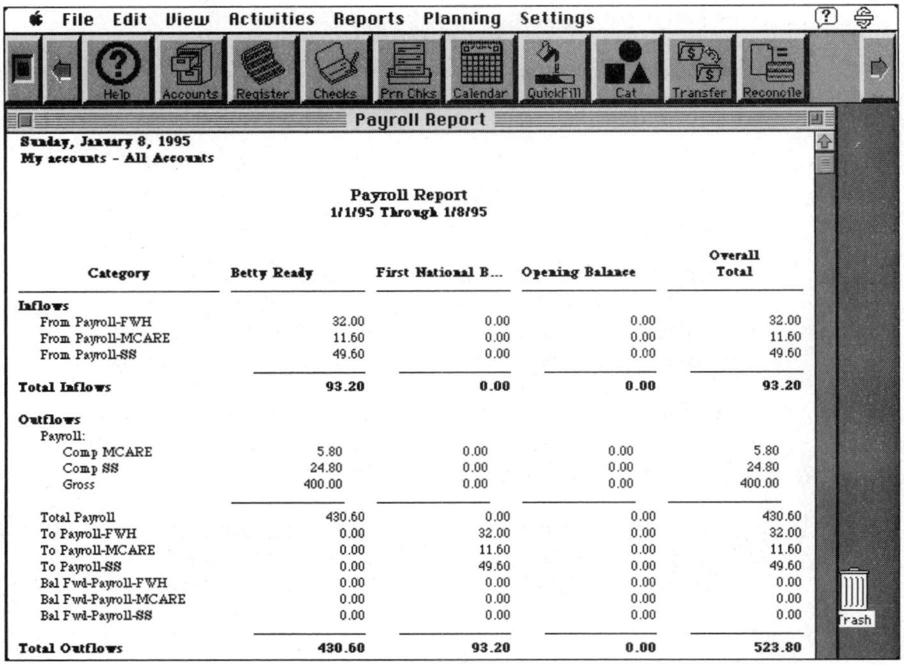

Sunday, January 8, 1995
My accounts - All Accounts

Payroll Report
1/1/95 Through 1/8/95

Category	Betty Ready	First National B...	Opening Balance	Overall Total
Inflows				
From Payroll-FWH	32.00	0.00	0.00	32.00
From Payroll-MCARE	11.60	0.00	0.00	11.60
From Payroll-SS	49.60	0.00	0.00	49.60
Total Inflows	**93.20**	**0.00**	**0.00**	**93.20**
Outflows				
Payroll:				
Comp MCARE	5.80	0.00	0.00	5.80
Comp SS	24.80	0.00	0.00	24.80
Gross	400.00	0.00	0.00	400.00
Total Payroll	430.60	0.00	0.00	430.60
To Payroll-FWH	0.00	32.00	0.00	32.00
To Payroll-MCARE	0.00	11.60	0.00	11.60
To Payroll-SS	0.00	49.60	0.00	49.60
Bal Fwd-Payroll-FWH	0.00	0.00	0.00	0.00
Bal Fwd-Payroll-MCARE	0.00	0.00	0.00	0.00
Bal Fwd-Payroll-SS	0.00	0.00	0.00	0.00
Total Outflows	**430.60**	**93.20**	**0.00**	**523.80**

Figure 15-9: The Payroll Report window.

The Comp SS and Comp MCARE contributions are the amounts you recorded to date for the employer Social Security and Medicare taxes — so you need to double these figures to get the actual Social Security and Medicare taxes owed.

By the way, if your accountant is the person who will fill out the 941 or 942, you don't even need to read this stuff. Your accountant won't have any problem completing the quarterly payroll tax return using the Quicken Payroll report and in fact — I kid you not — will probably even enjoy it.

Those Pesky Annual Returns and Wage Statements

At the end of the year, there are some annual returns — like the 940 federal unemployment tax return — and the W-2 and W-3 wages statements you'll need to file.

As a practical matter, the only thing that's different about filling out these reports is that you need to use a payroll report that covers the entire year — not just a single quarter. So you need to enter the range of dates in the Payroll Report dialog box as January 1 and December 31.

The 940 annual return is darn easy if you've been wrestling with the 941 or 942 quarterly returns. The 940 annual return works the same basic way as those more difficult quarterly tax returns. You print the old payroll report, enter a few numbers, and then write a check for the amount you owe.

Note that you need to prepare any state unemployment annual summary first before preparing the 940 because the 940 requires information from the state returns.

For the W-2 statements and the summary W-3 (which summarizes your W-2s), you just print the old payroll report and then, carefully following directions, enter the gross wages, the Social Security and Medicare taxes withheld, and the federal income taxes withheld into the appropriate blanks.

If you have a little trouble, call the IRS. If you have a lot of trouble, splurge and have someone else do it for you. It doesn't take a rocket scientist to fill out these forms, by the way. Any experienced bookkeeper can do it for you.

Please don't construe my "rocket scientist" comment as personal criticism if this payroll taxes business seems terribly complicated. My experience is that some people — and you may very well be one of them — just don't have an interest for things like payroll accounting. If, on the other hand, you're a "numbers-are-my-friend" kind of person, you'll have no trouble at all once you learn the ropes.

Doing the State Payroll Taxes Thing

Yeah. I haven't talked about state payroll taxes — at least not in any great detail. I wish I could provide this sort of detailed, state-specific help to you. Unfortunately, doing so would make this chapter about 150 pages long. It would also cause me to go stark, raving mad.

My sanity and laziness aside, however, you still need to deal with the state payroll taxes. Let me say, however, that you apply to state payroll taxes the same basic mechanics you apply to the federal payroll taxes. For example, a state income tax works the same way as the federal income tax, employer-paid state unemployment taxes work like the employer-paid federal taxes, and employee-paid state taxes work like the employee-paid Social Security and Medicare taxes.

If you've tuned in to how federal payroll taxes work in Quicken, you really shouldn't have a problem with the state payroll taxes — at least, not in terms of mechanics.

The 5th Wave   By Rich Tennant

"WE OFFER A CREATIVE MIS ENVIRONMENT WORKING WITH STATE-OF-THE-ART PROCESSING AND COMMUNICATIONS EQUIPMENT; A COMPREHENSIVE BENEFITS PACKAGE, GENEROUS PROFIT SHARING, STOCK OPTIONS, AND, IF YOU'RE FEELING FUNKY AND NEED TO CHILL OUT AND RAP, WE CAN DO THAT TOO."

Chapter 16
Receivables and Payables

· ·

In This Chapter

▶ Setting up an account to track customer receivables

▶ Recording customer invoices

▶ Recording customer payments

▶ Tracking amounts your customers owe

▶ Handling customer receivables: a problem

▶ Describing vendor payables

▶ Handling vendor payables

▶ Tracking vendor payables

▶ Using the Billminder™ utility

· ·

*Q*uicken, as a checkbook program, isn't really built for tracking the amounts that clients and customers owe you or that you owe your vendors, but you can do both if you don't have a long list of receivables or payables. This short chapter describes how you can handle both situations.

Preparing to Track Customer Receivables

To track customer receivables, you must set up an asset account just for tracking customer receivables. If you know how to set up an asset account, just do it. If you don't, follow the steps outlined below:

1. **Display the My Accounts window.**

   Choose the Accounts icon from the iconbar to display the window.

2. **Choose the New button on the My Accounts window.**

   Quicken displays the Set Up Account dialog box (see Figure 16-1).

3. **Mark the Asset option button.**

   This button tells Quicken that you're setting up a catch-all asset account to track something besides a bank account, cash, or your investments.

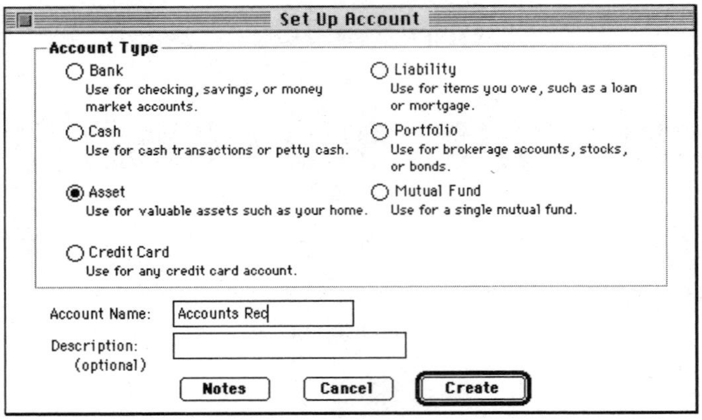

Figure 16-1:
The Set Up
Account
dialog box
filled out to
set up an
accounts
receivable
account.

4. Name the account.

Move the cursor to the Account Name text box and type a name, such as
Accounts Rec, to identify the account as the one that holds your accounts
receivable. But one of the fun things about being in your own business is
that *you* get to make the decisions about what you name your accounts —
so go for it, dude, and be creative.

5. Click Create.

Quicken creates the account and displays an account register for it (see
Figure 16-2).

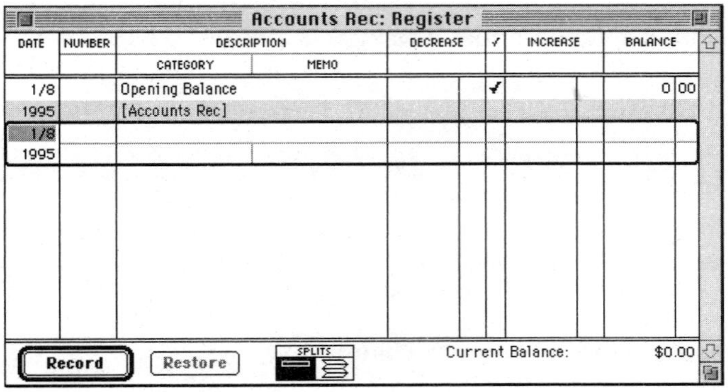

Figure 16-2:
The
accounts
receivable
register.

6. Enter the starting balance as 0.00.

With the cursor positioned on the Increase field, enter the starting balance
as zero.

7. Choose Record.

Recording Customer Invoices and Payments

Because Quicken isn't designed to keep track of lots of receivables and doesn't generate its own invoices (see Chapter 2 for a refresher on what Quicken does and doesn't do), I think that the easiest approach to setting up an account is just to use Quicken to keep a list of your unpaid customer invoices. You could use a Quicken asset account to bill customers and track their invoices, but this approach requires Rube Goldberg*esque* complexity. What's more, if you do want to do all this complex stuff, you're really better off with a real small-business accounting system.

Now, back to the chase. . . .

Recording customer invoices

After you bill a customer, you just enter a transaction for the invoice amount in your Accounts Receivable account register. You can follow these steps for recording a customer invoice in the next empty slot in the Accounts Receivable register:

1. **Display the Register window for the Accounts Receivable account.**

   To display the Register window, choose the Accounts icon from the iconbar and double-click the Accounts Receivable account.

2. **Enter the invoice date — the date you bill your customer or client — in the Date field.**

3. **Enter the invoice number in the Number field.**

   The invoice number you enter is the number of the invoice you create yourself.

4. **Enter the customer or client name in the Description field.**

   Remember that after the first time you enter the customer or client name the first time, subsequent times you enter the customer or client name you only need to enter enough of it for Quicken to recognize. Ah, yes. Your old friend QuickFill comes to the rescue again.

Make sure that you use the same spelling of the customer's name every time you enter it because Quicken summarizes accounts receivable information by payee name; Quicken interprets *John Doe* and *Jonh Doe* as two different customers. In addition, you must take care with names because Quicken's QuickFill works quickly in assuming that you mean a particular account name. If you first enter a customer name as *Mowgli's Lawn Mower Repair,* for example, and then later you type **Mowg** as an account name, Quicken assumes that you're entering another transaction for *Mowgli's Lawn Mower Repair* and fills the Description field with the complete name.

5. **Enter the invoice amount in the Increase field.**

6. **Choose Record to record the transaction.**

   If Quicken reminds you to enter a category, save the transaction with the category. You don't want to use a category in this step because you later categorize the invoice by using an income category when you record the customer deposit.

Figure 16-3 shows a register entry for a $750 invoice to Mowgli's Lawn Mower Repair. The ending balance, shown in the lower-right corner, is actually the sum of all the transactions shown in the register.

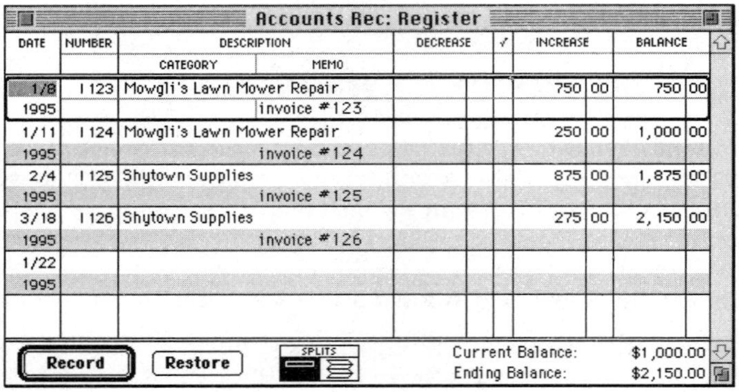

Figure 16-3:
An invoice entry in the accounts receivable register.

DATE	NUMBER	DESCRIPTION		DECREASE	√	INCREASE	BALANCE
		CATEGORY	MEMO				
1/8 1995	1 123	Mowgli's Lawn Mower Repair	invoice #123			750 00	750 00
1/11 1995	1 124	Mowgli's Lawn Mower Repair	invoice #124			250 00	1,000 00
2/4 1995	1 125	Shytown Supplies	invoice #125			875 00	1,875 00
3/18 1995	1 126	Shytown Supplies	invoice #126			275 00	2,150 00
1/22 1995							

Accounts Rec: Register

[Record] [Restore] SPLITS

Current Balance: $1,000.00
Ending Balance: $2,150.00

Recording customer payments

When you work with customer payments in Quicken, you actually need to do two things. First, you record the customer check as a deposit in your bank account and categorize it as falling into one of the your income categories. Because you probably can record this information with your eyes closed and one hand tied behind your back, I won't describe the process again here.

Second, you must update your accounts receivable list for the customer's payment. To update the list, display the Accounts Receivable account in the Register window and mark the existing invoice the customer has paid by putting a check mark in the cleared field. Figure 16-4 shows that the first $750 invoice to Mowgli's Lawn Mower Repair has been paid.

Note that I've gotten pretty crazy and entered some other invoices, too. (Hey, it's my job.)

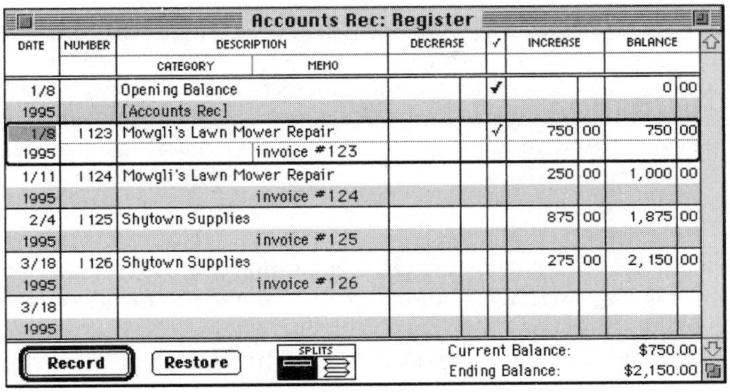

Figure 16-4:
The
accounts
receivable
register
with invoice
#123 marked
as paid.

Tracking Your Receivables

When you look at the Accounts Receivable register at this point, you can't tell the total of what your customers owe you. In Figure 16-4, for example, even though I've marked invoice #123 as paid, the account balance still shows $2,150 (the balance of all four invoices shown).

Discovering a dirty little secret about Quicken's A/R reporting

You have just discovered an unfortunate quirk in the way Quicken handles accounts receivable: the account balance for an asset account includes all the transactions entered in the register — even those you mark as being cleared. This quirk causes some problems. For example, you can't print an accurate balance sheet report because Quicken uses the account balance from an asset account on the balance sheet report, and this balance is not accurate. If you again use the example data from Figure 16-4, a balance sheet would show your accounts receivable as $2,150, even though your customers really owe you only $1,400. Yikes!

Oh m' gosh — does this mean you can't track receivables this way? — naw. It does mean, however, that you can't use the accounts receivable account balance for anything because the balance is really a meaningless number. What's more, the accounts receivable, total assets, and net worth figures on the balance sheet reports are also meaningless numbers because the report uses the goofy accounts receivable account balances, too.

Producing an accurate balance sheet

Suppose that you do want to produce an accurate balance sheet. What do you do? You simply strip out the cleared transactions in a receivables register by deleting them one by one. Before you begin your deletions, however, print a copy of the Customer Receivables register. You may want to have a record someplace of the customer invoices that you billed.

What's that? You don't like the idea of stripping out the transactions? OK. If you're willing to go to slightly more work, you can fix the accounts receivable balance in another way. Using the Splits button (see Chapter 14), go through and add split transaction detail that shows a reduction in the invoice total that results when the customer makes a payment.

For a $400 invoice on which the customer pays the $400, for example, the Splits window includes one line that records a positive number for the initial $400 invoice and another line that records a negative number for the $400 customer payment. So what you're left with is a transaction that equals zero because the split transaction amounts add up to zero.

You can overcome the problem of producing an accurate balance sheet with Quicken by simply printing an A/R by Customer business report to summarize who owes you and how much they owe.

The A/R by Customer report summarizes all uncleared transactions. To Quicken, however, the first transaction in this register, Opening Balance, looks like a customer — even though it is not a real account. So that this phantom customer doesn't appear on your report, either delete it or mark it as cleared.

To print the A/R by Customer business report, follow these simple steps:

1. **Display the Reports menu.**

2. **Choose the Business command to display the Business Reports window.**

3. **In the Business Reports list, double-click A/R by Customer.**

   Quicken displays the Create A/R by Customer Report dialog box.

4. **Choose Show Options if you've already created other asset accounts.**

   Quicken displays the expanded Create A/R by Customer Report dialog box.

5. **Select which accounts with uncleared transactions you want on the accounts receivable report.**

   Use the Restrict by options so that the report includes only your accounts receivable account, as shown in Figure 16-5.

6. **Choose OK.**

Quicken produces a report that summarizes the uncleared transactions by payee names. Figure 16-6 shows the A/R by Customer report based on the three uncleared invoices shown in Figure 16-3.

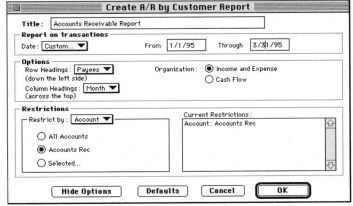

Figure 16-5: The expanded Create A/R by Customer Report dialog box.

Accounts Receivable Report

Sunday, January 8, 1995
My accounts - Accounts Rec

Accounts Receivable Report
1/1/95 Through 3/31/95

Payee	1/95	2/95	3/95	Overall Total
Mowgli's Lawn Mower Repair	1,000.00	0.00	0.00	1,000.00
Shytown Supplies	0.00	875.00	275.00	1,150.00
Overall Total	**1,000.00**	**875.00**	**275.00**	**2,150.00**

Show Page Breaks | Full Columns

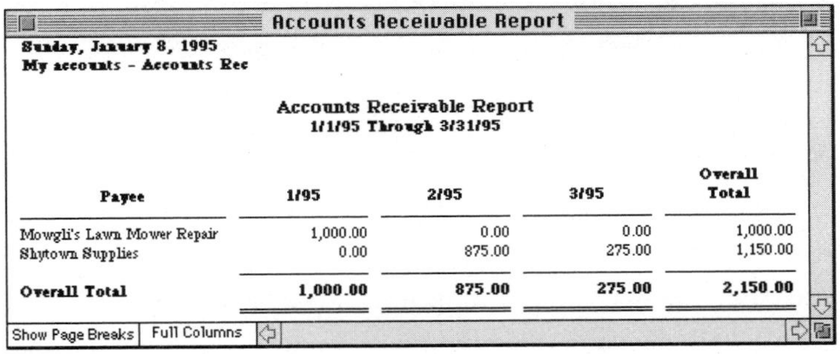

Figure 16-6: The A/R by Customer report.

Preparing to Track Vendor Payables

You really don't have to do anything special to begin tracking the amounts you know that you'll pay; however, you do need to have a bank account already set up. (I'm assuming you already have a bank account set up. If you don't — and it's almost impossible to believe that you don't — refer to Chapters 1 and 2.)

Describing your vendor payables

You describe your vendor payables by filling in the checks you use to pay a vendor's bills in the Write Checks window. Don't print the checks, though. Quicken tracks these unprinted checks because they represent your unpaid vendor invoices. That's it.

I'm super tempted to describe how you fill out the blanks of the Write Checks window — the result of the first tenet in the boring old computer writer's code of honor, "When in doubt, describe in detail." But really — and you probably know this — filling out the Write Checks window is darn easy.

If you're not sure about how to fill out the Write Checks window, don't feel that you're stupid or that the process requires an advanced degree. After all, you're still getting your feet wet. So if you feel like you may fall in this category, peruse Chapter 5 and then go ahead and wail away at your keyboard.

Tracking your vendor payables

Whenever you want to know how much money you owe someone, just print a report that summarizes the unprinted checks by payee name. Pretty easy, huh? All you have to do is print the A/P by Vendor business report. If you know how to print the report, go ahead. If you need a little help, here's a blow-by-blow account of the steps you need to follow:

1. **Display the Reports menu.**

2. **Choose the Business command to display the Business Reports menu.**

3. **Choose the A/P by Vendor entry in the list.**

   Quicken displays the Create A/P by Vendor Report dialog box, already filled out so that Quicken can print an A/P by Vendor report. Because I have explained this dialog box in Chapter 6, I didn't include it as a figure in this chapter.

4. **Choose OK.**

   Quicken summarizes the unprinted checks in your bank, cash, and credit card accounts in a cute little report.

How Quicken identifies an unprinted check

Here's a little tidbit of information you may (or may not) find useful. When you describe a check you want to print by using the Write Checks window, Quicken records the check in the register but uses the word *Print* in place of the check number.

The word *Print* identifies the check as the one that you want to print and signals Quicken to look at the check and say to itself, "Aha! — an unprinted check!" *Print* is, to say the least, an important word.

Explaining how Quicken handles payables

Before I conclude this wonderfully interesting, terribly exciting discussion about how you track unpaid bills in Quicken, let me make one final, quick point: an unprinted check gets counted as an expense only after you print it. Does this sound like much ado about nothing? It probably is.

But let's take a minute to explain the accounting system that Quicken uses. For example, if you record a $1,000 check to your landlord on December 31 but you don't print the check until January, Quicken doesn't count the $1,000 as an expense in December. It instead counts the $1,000 as an expense in January of the next year.

By the way, the Quicken register will show two balances: the current balance, which shows, well, the current balance—the balance that's in your account even as you read this sentence; and the ending balance, which shows the unprinted checks.

If you know a little about cash-basis accounting versus accrual-basis accounting, you've probably already said to yourself, "Hey, man, Quicken uses cash-basis accounting." And you're right, of course.

This little subtlety between the two accounting systems can cause confusion, especially if you've already been working with a regular, full-featured accounting system that uses an accounts payable module with accrual-basis accounting. In one of these systems, the $1,000 check to your landlord probably gets counted as an expense as soon as you enter it in the system.

Meeting a New Friend Named Billminder

Bill, my affectionate nickname for Billminder, is a separate program in Quicken that will soon become a good friend of yours, too. You can tell Quicken to fix your computer so that the Billminder program runs every time you turn on your computer — a nice feature.

What Bill does is simple: it looks through your unprinted checks for any checks with dates falling on or before the current date. If Bill finds a check with such a date, it displays a message that says, "Hey, dude, you have checks that you need to print." Or, in the case where you have overdue checks, Bill displays a message that says, "Dude, the situation is getting gnarly — you've got some seriously overdue checks." (The messages don't use these exact words, by the way.)

To tell Bill you want him reminding you of the checks you need to print, follow these steps:

1. Choose the Billminder command from the Settings menu.

In a surprising move, Quicken displays the Billminder Settings dialog box (see Figure 16-7).

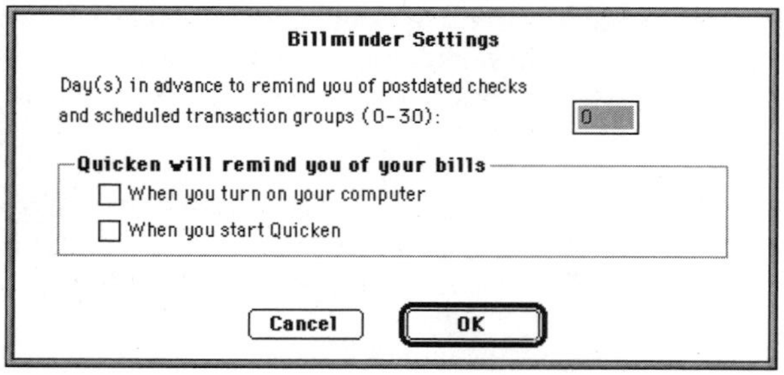

Figure 16-7:
The
Billminder
Settings
dialog box.

Billminder Settings

Day(s) in advance to remind you of postdated checks
and scheduled transaction groups (0-30):   [0]

┌─ **Quicken will remind you of your bills** ─────────┐
│ ☐ When you turn on your computer   │
│ ☐ When you start Quicken   │
└──┘

[Cancel]   [**OK**]

2. Enter a value in the only text box on the dialog box.

This value tells Bill how many days in advance you want to be reminded of unprinted checks. The value tells Quicken how many days in advance you want to be queried about scheduled transactions and Investment reminder messages.

3. Turn on the Billminder reminder feature.

To turn on Bill, just mark one of the check boxes on the Billminder Settings dialog box: When you turn on your computer or When you start Quicken.

4. Choose OK.

Well, that about wraps up the main part of tonight's show. If you're thinking that it's still a little too early to go to bed, flip through the following chapters. They provide 10-item lists of a bunch of eclectic topics: 10 things to do when you visit Acapulco, 10 things you should never do during a commercial airline flight, and so on. Time flies when you're having fun, doesn't it?

Part V
The Part of Tens

In this part...

As a writing tool, laundry lists aren't something that high school English teachers encourage. But you know what? The old laundry list format is pretty handy for certain sorts of information.

With this idea in mind (and, of course, deepest apologies to my high school English teacher, Mrs. O'Rourke), the next and final part simply provides you with lists of information about Quicken: answers to ten commonly asked questions about Quicken, ten things every business owner using Quicken should know, ten things you should (or should not) do if you are audited, and so on.

Chapter 17

Ten Questions I'm Frequently Asked about Quicken

*W*hen people find out that I've written a book about Quicken, they always ask a question or two. In this chapter, I list the most common questions and their answers.

Does Quicken Work for a Corporation?

Sure. But let's talk for a minute about what's unique — at least from an accountant's perspective — about a corporation.

In addition to recording assets (like bank accounts and receivables) and liabilities (like mortgages and trade payables), a corporation needs to *track,* or keep records for, the stockholders' equity.

Stockholders' equity includes the amount people originally paid for their stock, any earnings the corporation has retained, cumulative income for the current year, and sometimes other stuff, too.

"Ugh," you're probably saying to yourself. "Ugh" is right. Accounting for stockholders' equity of a corporation is mighty complicated at times. So complicated, in fact, that Quicken can't track a corporation's stockholders' equity.

I'm not saying that you can't use Quicken if you're a corporation, and I'm not saying that you shouldn't. (I do business as a corporation and I use Quicken.) Just remember that someone — probably your poor accountant — periodically needs to calculate your stockholders' equity.

Fortunately, the financial information you collect with Quicken provides, in rough form, much of the information that your poor accountant needs to do things manually.

What Happens to Stockholders' Equity in Quicken?

Quicken doesn't exactly ignore a corporation's stockholders' equity. In an Account Balances report, the difference between the total assets and the total liabilities actually represents the total stockholders' equity. (Quicken labels this total Net Worth.) So, to the extent that your total assets and total liabilities figures are correct, you know your total stockholders' equity.

Does Quicken Work for a Partnership?

Yep, it does. But a partnership that uses Quicken faces the same basic problem as a corporation that uses Quicken. In a partnership, the partners want to track their partnership capital accounts (or at least they should). A partnership capital account simply shows what a partner has put into and taken out of a business.

As noted in the preceding section, Quicken calculates a net worth figure for you by subtracting total liabilities from total assets. So, to the extent that your total assets and total liabilities are accurately accounted for in Quicken, you know roughly the total partnership capital.

To solve this problem, you — or someone else — need to track what each partner puts into the business, earns as a partner in the business, and then takes out of the business.

Can I Use Quicken for More than One Business?

Yeah, but be very careful. *Very* careful. You must be especially diligent in keeping the two businesses' financial records separate.

Quicken provides a handy tool for keeping them straight: you can work with more than one file. Each file, in effect, is like a separate set of financial records. You can't record automatic transfers between accounts in different files; instead, you must record each side of the transaction separately. You can, however, keep truly separate business records.

To create a separate file, use the New File command on the File menu.

If you've been using Quicken for a while, you can probably figure out for yourself how the File New File command works. If you need help, refer to my discussion of this command in Chapter 1.

Separate bank accounts are usually a must. If you keep separate records for two distinct businesses in Quicken, you need to set up separate bank accounts for them. In fact, my attorney tells me that in the case of a corporation, you must set up a separate corporate bank account for the corporation to truly be considered an independent legal entity. Talk to your attorney if you have questions; attorneys can tell you the specifics that apply to a particular state and situation.

What Kind of Business Shouldn't Use Quicken?

You're probably saying to yourself, "Quicken works for corporations (sort of), and it works for partnerships (sort of). Does that mean that it works for just about any kind of business?"

The answer is no. Quicken is a darn good product. In fact, for many small businesses, it's a great product. But it doesn't work in every situation.

Here's a three-part test you can use to determine whether your business should use Quicken. If you answer yes to two or three of the questions, you should seriously consider moving up to a full-featured small-business accounting system.

1. Do you regularly need to produce business forms other than checks?

If you answer no to this question, you're in good shape with Quicken, which produces checks easily. And if all you need is an occasional invoice, you can create them easily enough on your computer. I, for example, produce a handful of invoices a month. I do them on my word processor and never have any problems.

If you do produce a lot of forms besides checks, you should probably consider moving up to a small-business accounting system that produces the forms you want. If you've been using Quicken, for example, take a look at M.Y.O.B. for the Macintosh. (If it isn't out yet, it should be soon.) Another more powerful but wonderfully designed product you might try is Peachtree Accounting.

2. Do you need to track assets other than cash or investments?

For example, do you have a long list of customer receivables that you need to monitor? Or do you buy and resell inventory? In these situations, an accounting system is usually helpful in tracking these items. Quicken doesn't do a very good job of tracking these other assets, so you may want to look at one of the other small-business accounting products.

3. Are you having problems measuring your profits with cash-basis accounting?

I'm not going to get into a big, tangled discussion of cash-basis versus accrual-basis accounting. It wouldn't be any fun for you. It wouldn't be any fun for me, either. Nevertheless, you should know that if you can't accurately measure your business profits by using cash-basis accounting (which is what Quicken uses) you may be able to more accurately measure your business profits by using accrual-basis accounting. To do so, use an accounting system that supports accrual-basis accounting. I should be totally honest with you and tell you that to measure your profits the right way, you (or your accountant) need to use — horror of horrors — double-entry bookkeeping.

One final comment. If you are a Quicken user but realize that you're outgrowing the checkbook-on-a-computer scene, verify there isn't a version of QuickBooks for the Macintosh. (No, I don't get a kickback from Intuit.) Here's the deal: QuickBooks looks and feels a lot like Quicken. Plus, it uses the data you've already collected with Quicken. So you'll find that moving from Quicken to QuickBooks is only slightly more complicated than rolling off a log. The only problem is that there isn't, at least as I'm writing this, a version of QuickBooks for the Macintosh. There are only versions for Windows and DOS personal computers. My guess, though, is that there will be a version for the Mac, too — and probably someday soon.

Can I Use Quicken Retroactively?

Yeah. And the idea is better than it might seem at first.

It doesn't take long to enter a year's worth of transactions in Quicken (as long as you have decent records to work with). If you're, like, a millionaire, it might take you a couple days. (Of course, in this case you can probably hire someone to do it for you.) If you're a regular, ordinary person, I bet you can get it done on a rainy Saturday afternoon.

After you enter all the information into a Quicken register, you can easily monitor your spending in various categories, track your income and outgo, and reconcile your bank accounts. I know one professional who uses Quicken records to do these things every year. Hey, it's not the most efficient way to do things. And it's not a very good way to manage business or personal financial affairs. But it works. Sort of. (Sorry, Jimbo.)

Can I Do Payroll with Quicken?

Yes. See Chapter 15 for more details.

It may also be that by the time you read this, there will be a version of QuickPay for the Macintosh. (Currently, there are only versions for Windows and DOS personal computers.) I mention this because you can also use the QuickPay to do payroll in Quicken. If you've only got one or two salaried employees who always earn the same amount — a nanny, for example — then you don't need QuickPay. (Even if it's available.) But if you have a bunch of employees or even a single hourly employee, QuickPay saves you a great deal of time.

Can I Prepare Invoices?

No. This is a good example of when you should consider moving up to a full-featured small-business accounting system.

Can I Import Data from an Old Accounting System?

Someone had to ask this question, I guess. (Imagine me taking a deep breath here.) Yes, you can import data from your old accounting system. To do so, export the old system's data into a file that matches the Quicken Interchange Format, or QIF, specification. Then import this file into an empty Quicken file.

- ✔ This process isn't for the timid or faint of heart.
- ✔ I would also claim that it isn't for people who have better things to do with their time.
- ✔ My advice to you? Go to a movie. Mow your lawn. Read a trashy novel. Forget all about this importing business.

Wait until the new year to switch programs

If you're moving to Quicken, your transaction volumes probably aren't so incredibly mammoth that you have gazillions of transactions to enter anyway. Given this, it probably makes sense to convert, or switch, programs at the beginning of your fiscal, or accounting, year—usually January 1. By waiting until the next fiscal year, the only data you absolutely have to load into Quicken are the asset and liability account balances. And you can do so easily enough when you set up the accounts.

What Do You Think about Quicken?

I think it's great. But I bet your question isn't really whether Quicken is good or not. Heck, the package sells something like two million copies a year. So we both know that the package is pretty good, right? My guess is that what you really want is my opinion about using Quicken in particular business or personal situations.

It's tough to answer this question in a one-way conversation. Even so, let me give you some of the best reasons for using Quicken:

- You always know your bank account balances, so you won't ever have to wonder whether you have enough money to pay a bill or charge a purchase.
- Reconciling your account takes about two minutes. (I'm not joking. It really does take a couple minutes.)
- You get a firm handle on what you're really making and spending.
- You can budget your spending and then track your spending against your budget.
- If you're a business, you can measure your profits as often as you want by using cash-basis accounting.
- If you're an investor, you can monitor your investments and measure their actual returns.

I hope these answers help. My guess is that if you think a program like Quicken will help you better manage your financial affairs, it probably will.

Chapter 18

Ten Tips for Bookkeepers Who Use Quicken

An amazing number of people use Quicken for small-business accounting: dentists, contractors, lawyers, and so on. And, not surprisingly, a great number of bookkeepers use Quicken.

If you're jumping up and down, waving your hands, saying, "I do, I do, I do," this chapter is for you. I tell you here what you need to know to make your use of Quicken smooth and sure.

Tricks for Learning Quicken if You're New on the Job

First of all, let me congratulate you on your new job. Let me also remind you how thankful you should be that you'll be using Quicken and not one of the super-powerful-but-frightening, complex accounting packages.

If you're new to computers, you need to know a thing or two about them. Don't worry. This isn't as difficult as you may think. (Remember that a bunch of anxious folks have gone before you.)

Turning on the computer

Before you use the computer, you need to:

1. **Press the Mac's On switch. (It's either a switch on the back of the Mac or a key in the upper right corner of the keyboard.)**

2. **Push a switch to turn on your monitor (the television-like screen).**

3. **Flip a switch to turn on the printer.**

Even if you're a little timid, go ahead and ask your boss how to turn on the computer and its peripherals. This won't be considered a stupid question. Different computers get turned on in different ways. For example, the computer and its peripherals may already be on and plugged into a fancy-schmancy extension cord called a *power strip* — but this power strip thing is turned off.

By the way, the word *peripherals* refers to things that work with the computer, such as the printer.

Starting Quicken

After you turn on the computer, you should see something on the screen that looks like what I've shown in Figure 18-1.

This "something" is called the Quicken 5 folder window, but you don't have to remember this bit of trivia. To start Quicken, double-click the icon labeled "My accounts." Quicken starts, and it opens the Quicken data files.

If you don't see the Quicken 5 folder window or some other window that has the Quicken icon in it, you'll need to look for the folder that has the Quicken program and data files in it. This isn't difficult, but you'll probably need some help. Don't feel ashamed or embarrassed about this. People organize their hard disks and folders in all sorts of different ways — some of them pretty ugly. So it's OK to ask questions.

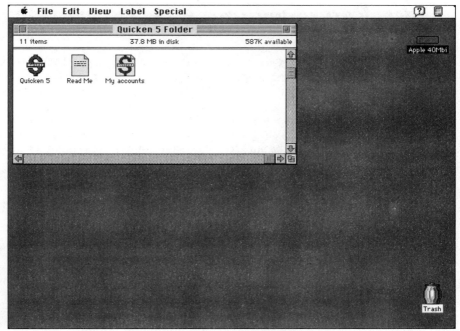

Figure 18-1:
The Quicken
5 Folder
window.

If you can't find a file named "My accounts" which is the default suggestion Quicken supplies, go ahead and ask for help, too. You can't know with absolute certainty what name people have used for the Quicken files.

Learning Quicken

When you know how to turn on the computer and how to start Quicken, you're ready to rock. Give Part II of this book a quick read. Then carefully read those chapters in Part IV that apply to your daily work.

One last thing: This is a lot easier than you think. Remember when you learned how to drive a car? Sure it was confusing at first: all those gauges and meters . . . the tremendous power at your fingertips . . . traffic. After you gained some experience, though, you loosened your death grip on the wheel. Heck, you even started driving in the left lane.

Give yourself a little time. Before long you'll be zipping around Quicken, changing lanes three at a time.

Cross-Reference and File Source Documents

Be sure to cross-reference and file (neatly!) the source documents (checks, deposit slips, and so on) you use to enter transactions. I won't tell you how to set up a document filing system. There's a pretty good chance you can do this better than I — in fact, I usually use a crude, alphabetical scheme.)

Check forms (the check source documents) are numbered, so you can cross-reference checks simply by entering check numbers when recording a check transaction. But be sure to do the same for deposits and other withdrawals, too.

Cross-referencing enables you to answer any questions about a transaction that appears in a register. All you have to do is find the source document you used to enter the transaction.

Always Categorize

Always categorize a transaction. In an account transfer, specify the account to which an amount has been transferred.

A favorite but sloppy accounting trick is to assign funny transactions to a *suspense account.* Suspense accounts, however, often become financial landfills where you (and anyone else using Quicken) dump transactions you don't know what do to with.

Quickly, the suspense grows and grows. And pretty soon, it's a huge mess and no one has the energy to clean it up.

By the way, you can tell Quicken to remind you to enter a category every time you enter a transaction. Here's how to get this reminder:

1. **Choose the General command from the Settings menu.**

   Quicken, in a surprise move, displays the General Settings dialog box (see Figure 18-2).

2. **Specify that Quicken warn you if a transaction has no category.**

   Click the Require category on transactions check box with the mouse.

3. **Choose OK.**

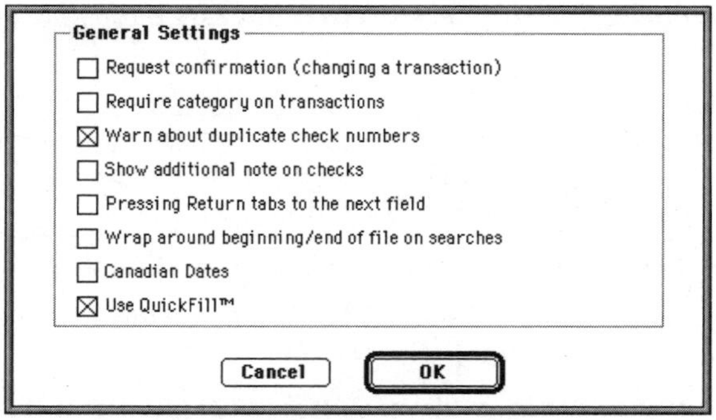

General Settings
- ☐ Request confirmation (changing a transaction)
- ☐ Require category on transactions
- ☒ Warn about duplicate check numbers
- ☐ Show additional note on checks
- ☐ Pressing Return tabs to the next field
- ☐ Wrap around beginning/end of file on searches
- ☐ Canadian Dates
- ☒ Use QuickFill™

[Cancel] (**OK**)

Figure 18-2:
The General
Settings
stuff. You
get the
general
idea.

Reconcile Promptly

This is a pet peeve, so bear with me if I get a little huffy.

I think you should always reconcile, or balance, a business's bank accounts within a day or two after you get the bank statement. You'll catch any errors you or the bank has made.

You also minimize the chance that you'll suffer financial losses from check forgery. Here's why: if a business or individual promptly alerts a bank about a check forgery, the bank rather than the business suffers the loss in most cases.

Reconciling in Quicken is fast and easy, so there's no good excuse not to reconcile promptly. Chapter 7 describes how to reconcile accounts in Quicken.

Things You Should Do Every Month

In a business, everyone has some routine tasks: Go through the In basket. Return phone messages. Clean the coffee machine.

Here are six bookkeeping chores you should probably do at the end of every month:

1. **If the business uses a petty cash system, replenish the petty cash fund. Make sure that you have receipts for all withdrawals.**

2. **Reconcile the bank and credit card accounts.**

3. **If you're preparing payroll, be sure to remit any payroll tax deposit money owed.**

   For businesses in the United States, you can get information about how this works from the Internal Revenue Service. Note that you may need to remit payroll tax deposit money more quickly than this. (If you want to be really save, remit the money every payday.)

4. **Print a copy of each of the account registers for the month.**

   Set these copies aside as permanent financial records. Chapter 5 describes how to print reports, including the account registers.

5. **Print two copies of the monthly cash flow statement and the P&L statement.**

   Give one copy to the business's owner or manager. Put the other copy with the permanent financial records.

6. **If you haven't done so already during the month, back up the file containing the Quicken accounts to a floppy disk.**

   You can reuse the floppy disk every other month. Chapter 8 describes how to back up files.

Don't view the preceding list as all-inclusive. There may be other things you need to do. I'd hate for people to say, "Well, it doesn't appear on Nelson's list, so I don't have to do it." Yikes!

Things You Should Do Every Year

Here are the things I think you should do at the end of every year:

1. **Do all the usual month-end chores for the last month in the year.**

   See the list in the preceding section.

2. **Prepare and file any state and federal end-of-year payroll tax returns.**

   Businesses in the United States, for example, need to prepare the annual federal unemployment tax return (Form 940).

3. **Print two copies of the annual cash flow statement and the annual P&L statement.**

   Give one copy to the business's owner or manager. Put the other copy with the permanent financial records.

4. **If the business is a corporation, print a copy of the Business Balance Sheet report.**

   This report will help whoever prepares the corporate tax return.

5. **Back up the file containing the Quicken accounts to a floppy disk.**

   Store the floppy disk as a permanent archive copy.

6. **If the business's accounts are full — you notice that Quicken runs slower — use Quicken's Year End command to shrink the file.**

   Quicken creates a new version of the file, keeping only the current year's transactions. See Chapter 8.

Again, don't view the preceding list as all-inclusive. If you think of other things to do, do them.

About Debits and Credits (if You're Used to These)

If you've worked with a regular small-business accounting system, you may have missed your old friends, debit and credit. (Is it just me, or do *debit* and *credit* sound like the neighbor kid's pet frogs to you, too?)

Quicken is a single-entry accounting system and, as a result, doesn't really have debits and credits. Double-entry systems have debits and credits. (As you may know, the two entries in a double-entry system are your old friends: debit and credit. For every debit, you have equal credit.)

Quicken does supply a sort of chart of accounts, which you can use to describe accounting transactions. The Categories window, which you can usually display by clicking the Cat icon, actually parallels a regular accounting system's chart of accounts. Figure 18-3 shows the Categories window.

Accordingly, when you record a transaction that increases or decreases one account, you record the offsetting debit or credit when you categorize or transfer the account.

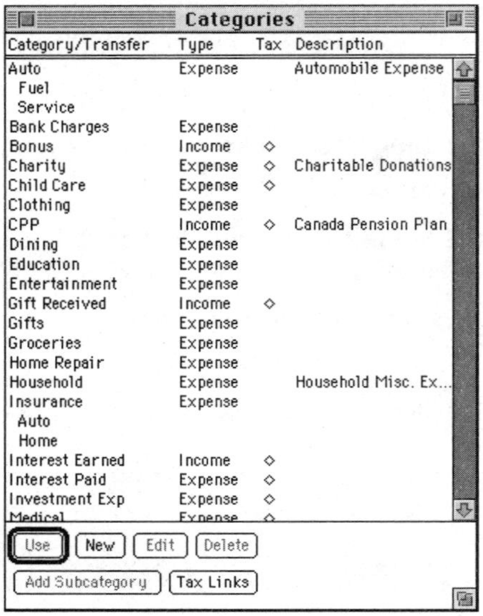

Figure 18-3: Quicken's Categories list is pretty much the same thing as a chart of accounts — if you're used to these.

Converting to Quicken

If you're converting to Quicken from a manual system or from another more complicated small-business accounting system, here are two important tips:

1. **Start using Quicken at the beginning of a year.**

   The year's financial records are then in one place — the Quicken registers.

2. **If it's not the beginning of the year, go back and enter the year's transactions.**

   Again, the year's financial records are then in one place — the Quicken registers. (This will take time if you have a bunch of transactions to enter. In fact, you may want to postpone your conversion to Quicken.)

Income Tax Evasion

A nice fellow wandered into my office the other day and told me that he had inadvertently gotten entangled in his employer's income tax evasion. He didn't know what to do.

He had unwittingly helped his employer file fraudulent income tax returns. Then, already sucked into the tar pit, he had lied to the IRS during an audit.

I didn't have anything good to tell him.

And I never did get the fellow's name, so I'll just call him *Chump*.

But I want to share this fellow's story with you. It really didn't make any financial sense for Chump to help his employer steal. Chump didn't get a share of the loot; he just helped his employer commit a felony. For free. (What a guy!)

Although Chump didn't receive any of the booty, he probably still is in serious trouble with the IRS. The criminal penalties can be enormous; prison, I understand, is not fun.

I'm not going to spend any more time talking about this. But I do have a piece of advice for you. Don't be a Chump.

Segregating Payroll Tax Money

While I'm on the subject of terrible things the IRS can do to you, let me touch on the problem of payroll tax deposits — the money you withhold from employee checks for federal income taxes, Social Security, and Medicare.

If you have the authority to spend the money you withhold, don't — even if the company will go out of business. If you can't repay the payroll tax money, the IRS will go after the business owners and also after *you*.

It doesn't matter that you're just the bookkeeper; it doesn't matter whether you regularly attend church. The IRS doesn't take kindly to those who take what belongs to the IRS.

By the way, I should mention that the IRS is more lenient in cases where you don't have any authority to dip into the payroll tax money and the business owner or your boss does this. If this is happening to you, however, be darn careful not to get involved. And start looking for a new job.

Chapter 19

Ten Tips for Business Owners

*I*f you run a business and you use Quicken, you need to know some stuff. You can learn these things by sitting down with your certified public accountant over a cup of coffee at $100 an hour. Or you can read this chapter.

Sign All Your Own Checks

I have nothing against your bookkeeper. In a small business, however, it's just too darn easy for people — especially full-charge bookkeepers — to bamboozle you. By signing all the checks yourself, you keep your fingers on the pulse of your cash outflow.

Yeah, I know this can be a hassle. I know this means you can't easily spend three months in Hawaii. I know this means you have to wade through paperwork every time you sign a stack of checks.

By the way, if you're in a partnership, I think you should have at least a couple of the partners co-sign checks.

Don't Sign a Check the Wrong Way

If you sign many checks, you may be tempted to use a John Hancock-like signature. Although this makes great sense if you're autographing baseballs, don't do it when you're signing checks. A wavy line with a cross and a couple of dots is really easy to forge.

Which leads me to my next tip. . .

Review Canceled Checks Before Your Bookkeeper Does

Be sure you review your canceled checks — before anybody else sees the monthly bank statement.

This chapter isn't about browbeating bookkeepers. But a business owner will discover whether someone is forging signatures on checks only by being the first to open the bank statement and reviewing each of the canceled check signatures.

If you don't do this, unscrupulous employees — especially bookkeepers who can update the bank account records — can forge your signature with impunity. And they won't get caught if they never overdraw the account.

Another thing: if you don't follow these procedures, *you* will probably eat the losses, not the bank.

How to Choose a Bookkeeper if You Use Quicken

Don't worry. You don't need to request an FBI background check.

In fact, if you use Quicken, you don't need to hire people who are familiar with small-business accounting systems. Just find people who know how to keep a checkbook and work with a computer; you shouldn't have a problem getting them to understand Quicken.

Of course, you don't want someone who just fell off the turnip truck. But even if you do hire someone who rode into town this way, you're not going to have much trouble getting him up to speed with Quicken.

But when you hire someone, find someone who knows how to do payroll — not just the federal payroll tax stuff (see Chapter 15) — but also the state payroll tax monkey business.

Get Smart about Passwords

In Chapter 8, I got all hot and bothered about passwords. Let me add here that I suggest you use a password to keep your financial records confidential if you use Quicken in a business and it's you who does the Quicken *thang.* (Especially if you have employees who know how to operate a PC and have access to the PC you use for Quicken.)

Leave Your Password Record at Home

To assign a file password, see Chapter 8. But be sure that you don't lose your financial records by forgetting your password. (I think it's a good idea to keep *at home* a record of the password you use for the computer at work.)

Cash-Basis Accounting Doesn't Work for All Businesses

When you use Quicken, you employ an accounting convention called *cash-basis accounting* to measure your profits. When money comes in, you count it as revenue. When money goes out, you count it as expense.

Cash-basis accounting is fine when a business's cash inflow mirrors its sales and its cash outflow mirrors its expenses. This isn't the case, however, in many businesses. A single-family home contractor, for example, may have cash coming in (by borrowing from banks) but may not make any money. A pawn-shop owner who loans money at 22 percent may make scads of money even if cash pours out of the business daily. As a rule of thumb, when you're buying and selling inventory, accrual-basis accounting works better than cash-basis accounting.

So this isn't earthshaking. It's still something you should think about.

When to Switch to Accrual-Basis Accounting

If tracking cash flows doesn't indicate whether your business is making a profit or a loss, then you probably need to switch to accrual-basis accounting. Almost certainly you need to switch accounting systems.

What to Do if Quicken Doesn't Work for Your Business

Quicken is a great checkbook program. In fact, my friends at some of the other financial software companies won't like me saying this, but Quicken is probably the best checkbook program.

However, if Quicken doesn't seem to fit your needs — for example, you need accrual-basis accounting (see preceding section) — you may want one of the more complicated but also more powerful small-business accounting packages.

If you like using Quicken, look at QuickBooks for Windows. (Although QuickBooks for Windows wasn't available when I wrote this, I hear it will be ready soon.)

You also should look at other more powerful programs, such as the full-featured Peachtree Accounting products. (There are several. Just read one of those annual reviews of accounting software that appear every year in magazines like MacWorld or MacUser.)

I am amazed that PC accounting software remains so affordable. You can buy a great accounting package — one you can use to manage a $5 million or a $25 million business — for a few hundred bucks. This is truly one of the great bargains.

Keep Things Simple

Let me share one last comment about managing small-business financial affairs. *Keep things as simple as possible.* In fact, keep your business affairs simple enough that it's easy to tell if you're making money and if the business is healthy.

This may sound like strange advice, but as a CPA I've worked for some very bright people who built monstrously complex financial structures for their businesses, including complicated leasing arrangements, labyrinth-like partnership and corporate structures, and sophisticated profit-sharing and cost-sharing arrangements with other businesses.

I can only offer anecdotal evidence, of course, but I strongly believe that these super-sophisticated financial arrangements don't produce a profit when you consider all the costs. What's more, these super-sophisticated arrangements almost always turn into management and record-keeping headaches.

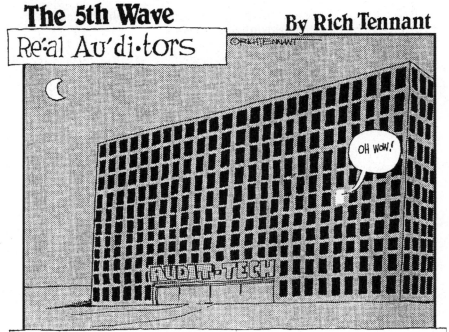

Real Auditors always do their best work between 1 and 5 a.m.

Chapter 20

Ten Things You Should Do If You're Audited

*B*ecause you may use Quicken to track things like your income tax deductions, I want to mention some of the things you should do if you get audited.

Leave Quicken at Home

Don't bring Quicken with you to an IRS audit. Even if you're really proud of that new laptop.

Here's the problem: Quicken's reporting capabilities are incredibly powerful. If you've been using Quicken diligently, you own a rich database describing almost all your financial affairs. When you bring Quicken (and your Quicken file) to the IRS, you're spilling your financial guts.

Now I'm not one who recommends sneaking stuff by the IRS. But it is dumb to give an IRS agent the opportunity to go on a fishing expedition. Remember, the agent isn't going to be looking for additional deductions.

I know of a young, inexperienced CPA who took Quicken to an audit. After the IRS agent would ask a question, the CPA would proudly tap a few keys on the laptop, smile broadly, and then show the agent on-screen, for example, all the individual entertainment expenses claimed by the taxpayer in question.

Funny thing, though, the IRS agent also saw some other things. Such as money that should have been claimed as income. Reporting requirements the taxpayer failed to meet. Obvious out-of-line deductions.

Print Summary Reports for Tax Deductions

Ol' Quicken can be your friend, though, if you're audited.

Before you go to the audit, find out what the IRS is questioning. Print a summary report of every questioned deduction: charitable giving, medical expenses, travel and entertainment, and so on. You'll have an easy-to-understand report explaining how you came up with every number the IRS wants to examine.

By the way, I know a very clever tax attorney who used Quicken in this manner. The audit lasted half an hour.

Collect All Source Documents

After you print a summary report of every questioned deduction, collect all the source documents — usually canceled checks — that prove or indicate a transaction in question.

For example, if you claim $600 in charitable giving, the report summarizing this deduction may show 12 $50 checks written to your church or the local United Way agency. To verify this report, find the 12 canceled checks.

Call a Tax Attorney if the Agent Is Special

An IRS *special agent* isn't an agent endorsed by Mr. Rogers. Internal Revenue Service special agents investigate criminal tax code violations. If a special agent is auditing your return, you're in a heap of trouble. So get a tax attorney.

In my mind, being audited by a special agent is like being arrested for murder. Call me a scaredy-cat, but I'd want legal representation even if I were innocent.

Don't Volunteer Information

Loose lips sink ships. Don't volunteer any information — even if it seems innocuous. Just answer the questions you're asked.

Again, I'm not suggesting that you lie. The agent, however, is looking for income you forgot or deductions you overstated. The more information you provide, the more likely you'll reveal something damaging.

For example, if you offhandedly tell the agent about your other business — where you knit socks for golf clubs — you may wind up debating whether that cute little business is really a business (and not a hobby) and whether knitting golf socks entitles you to deduct those country club dues and green fees.

Consider Using a Pinch Hitter

I don't think an audit should terrify you. And I'm someone who's scared of everything: dinner parties where I don't know anyone, stormy nights when the neighborhood seems particularly deserted, driving on bald tires. You get the idea. Nonetheless, if you used a paid-preparer, think about sending that person in your place.

You'll pay for this service, of course. But it may help if the person who prepared your return does the talking.

Understand Everything on Your Return

Be sure you understand everything on your return. You won't help yourself if you tell an agent that you don't have a clue about some number on your return.

Be Friendly

Be nice to the IRS. Remember, the agents actually work for you. In fact, the more taxes that the agents collect from people who owe the federal government, the less the rest of us have to pay. (An article in *Money* magazine a few years ago suggested that we end up paying several hundred dollars more a year in income taxes because so many people cheat.)

Don't Worry

If you've been honest and careful, you've got nothing to worry about. Sure, maybe you made a mistake. Maybe the agent will find the mistake. And maybe you'll have to pay some additional taxes.

If you haven't been honest and careful, I offer my condolences. Sorry.

Don't Lie

Don't lie; it may be perjury. You could go to jail and share a cell with someone named Skull-crusher. Develop a close, personal relationship.

You get the picture. And it's not pretty.

So don't lie.

Chapter 21

Ten Things I Didn't Talk About (Or so)

*T*he *...For Dummies* series books aren't supposed to be monster books. In fact, I hear that authors that turn in 600-page manuscripts are severely punished. (No one will say exactly what the punishment is. One rumor suggests they make you watch endless reruns of "The A Team.") For this reason, there's some stuff I left out of the preceding chapters.

Yet, a big part of understanding is knowing what you don't know. So, I wanted to end this book with short descriptions of the Quicken features I didn't talk about.

If you read something here that piques your interest and you understand most of the stuff I've already talked about, you should probably be able to figure out how to use any of these features on your own. (I say this assuming you've read much of this book and spent some time getting your feet wet.)

Let me make one final point, too. If you see something in this chapter that you're really frustrated doesn't appear in the book, let me know. The registration card which appears as the last page of this book includes space for you to comment on the book. There's a special space for "What I would change, add, delete, etc." If you fill out that card and send it in, the publisher will send me a photocopy of the card. No, I'm not looking for abuse. But I do want to do right by you. So, I'll carefully consider your suggestions. And if you make a compelling argument that some feature should have been described, I'll add it to the next edition of the book

Memorized Transactions

Memorized Transactions are copies of existing transactions you've added to a list. (The list goes by two names: the memorized transactions list and the QuickFill transactions list.) Any time you want to re-record one of these transactions, you can do so simply by using the same transaction description. When Quicken realizes the description matches one of the memorized transactions list, it'll fill in the rest of the transaction using the memorized transaction.

"Steve-buddy," you're saying to yourself, "This sounds pretty cool, so what gives? Where's the coverage?"

OK, I didn't really talk about memorized transactions. But here's why. Quicken automatically adds transactions to the memorized, or QuickFill, transactions list. So, you really never need to use the Edit menu's Memorize command which is the way you—Joe or Jane User—add transactions to the list.

Plus, Quicken automatically does the QuickFill thing for you.

By the way, if you want to see the memorized, or QuickFill, transactions list, click the QuickFill button on the iconbar. (The window that Quicken displays will let you add, edit, and remove memorized transactions from the list.)

Transaction Groups

Ah, yes. Transaction Groups. OK, here's the scope. Transaction groups are sets of memorized transactions that you can enter as a group. If you were running a business and had, like, 37 payroll transactions to record each week and these checks were all pretty much the same, you could create a transaction group. Then, once you had done this, you could just tell Quicken "Hey, Quicken, enter all the transactions in the group." This would, for the obvious reason, be quicker than individually entering 37 transactions.

Why didn't I cover transaction groups? Good question. I guess I figured that most people aren't going to have big sets of identical transactions they're going to be regularly entering.

If you think transaction groups sound interesting and you've been working with Quicken for, say, a few months, you can probably figure them out yourself. To create a transaction group, you use the View menu's Transaction Groups command.

Publishing

Your Macintosh's operating system supports easy sharing of documents and chunks of documents between programs—Quicken and Excel, for example—using its Publish/Subscribe capability.

If you've worked with publications and subscriptions in other programs, you'll have no problem doing it in Quicken.

Quicken Quotes

With the newest version of Quicken, you can retrieve relatively recent securities prices using an on-line service called Quicken Quotes.

I don't doubt that some users will want to do this. It all sounds pretty neat, right? Here's my scrooge-like perspective, however: First, you're not really getting up-to-the-minute information. There's at least a 20-minute delay. So, you can't use the information for trading. (You need real-time quotes and the ability to immediately execute transactions to actually trade.)

Second, if you're not trading, I think there are probably better things to do with your time. Every bit of research I've seen supports the view that successful investing requires long-term planning horizons and patience. So, I'm not sure you should be checking the value of your securities on a daily basis, which you can do with the newspaper. And I'm very confident that it's not a good use of your time to check (delayed!) security prices several times each day.

I'm also not sure the delayed security prices are worth the $1/minute connect time charges.

If you're now mad at me for being so bold—after all, who am I to say how you should spend your time or money—let me give you the birds-eye view. You can describe how you want to connect to the Quicken Quotes service by using the Settings menu's Quicken Quotes command. Once you've done this, you make your on-line connection to the Quicken Quotes service using the Activities menu's Retrieve Quotes command.

Forecasting

The newest version of Quicken also includes a forecasting tool. If you choose the Forecast command on the Planning menu, Quicken forecasts account balances using future transactions you've created using the Financial Calendar and, optionally, forecasted income and expense events you manually add to the forecast.

The Forecasting tool is pretty neat. And it's kind of fun. But, it's not something you need to worry about or work with until you're darn familiar with most of Quicken's other capabilities.

Electronic Payments with CheckFree

CheckFree enables you to pay your bills electronically.

First, you enter the bills you want to pay like you enter a check in the Write Checks screen. If you need to write a $52 check to the electric company, for example, you fill out the Write Checks screen with this information.

Then you connect to the CheckFree service — through a modem — and send the payment information, including the date the bill should be paid. The CheckFree people look through their records and find everyone who's supposed to pay the same electric company on the same day. They then send the electric company one big check and a list of the people whose payments are included in the big check. A day or two later, the CheckFree people deduct what you owed from your checking account.

"Hmmm," you're thinking, "this CheckFree thing sounds pretty cool. Why don't you cover it someplace?"

Well, while some people love CheckFree, I think it's a little complicated for a new Quicken user to handle right off the bat. And it costs several dollars a month. And you need a modem. And you need to give Quicken a bunch of rather technical information so it can use your modem to successfully connect to the CheckFree computer. What's more, some businesses may not accept the one big check approach.

Exporting Tax Information

You can export tax deduction information to Intuit's MacInTax program and other, tax preparation programs like TaxCut. But, frankly, I don't think this process is worth your time.

For one thing, you don't pull that many numbers from the Quicken registers anyway. When you complete a business tax return, for example, you only pull two or three dozen category totals. (You import the category totals into a tax preparation program—nothing else.) And a personal return probably needs only half a dozen category totals, maybe fewer. I think it's easier to just pull these totals from a Quicken report.

Let me also point out another problem with the whole exporting thing. Just because your Quicken register's show a category total doesn't mean you can use it. And I'm not even talking about input errors or miscategorizations. No, I'm talking about the problem where your Quicken registers say one thing and an informational return (like the 1099 the bank sends you) or year-end statement (like the mortgage company's or county assessor's) says something else. You'll need to report as income and claim as deductions what any informational returns or year-end statements show. So you're going to need to compare Quicken's numbers to any year-end statements or returns you get anyway. My feeling is why go to the work? Why not just use the numbers on the year-end statements and returns?

The Settings General Command

The Settings menu's General command displays a dialog box that lets you change the way Quicken works. You customize Quicken by marking and unmarking self-explanatory check boxes.

If you're in the mood, go for it.

The Reports and Report Fonts Commands

These Settings menu commands let you change the way Quicken's reports work by clicking buttons. I could have written some truly boring chapter which you could have slogged your way, through. But, it'll really be much easier for you and much more fun if you just experiment.

The Graphs and Graph Fonts Commands

My excuse here—I mean, rationale—is the same one as given in the preceding confession.

The Check Printing Command

This Settings menu command lets you change the check style and font for printed checks. You can also specify whether categories should print on the check and which check date to use.

If you want to make these sorts of changes, just choose the command and experiment.

Appendix A

How to Install Quicken in Nine Easy Steps

*1*f you haven't already installed Quicken, let's get it over with right now:

1. Turn on your Mac.

How you do this will depend on your Mac. On mine, there's this button in the upper, right corner of the keyboard. I push, and, *viola!* My Mac comes to life.

2. Get the Quicken floppy disks.

Rip open the Quicken package and get out the floppy disks (those plastic or 3 ¹/₂-inch squares).

3. Insert the first floppy disk.

Stick the floppy disk that's labeled "Install Disk 1" into your floppy drive slot. Your Mac, sensing you're about to start something big, opens the Quicken 5 folder (See Figure A-1).

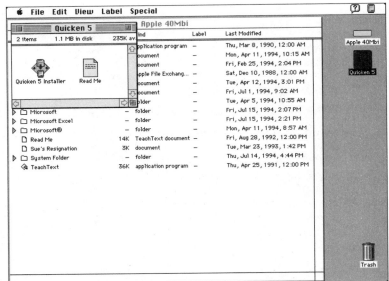

Figure A-1:
The Quicken
5 folder.

4. Double-click the Quicken 5 Installed icon.

You know how to do this, right? You click the mouse twice in row. Quickly. Suddenly, with little or no warning, you see the Quicken copyright screen, as shown in Figure A-2.

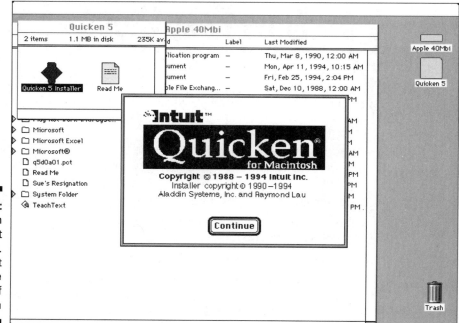

Figure A-2:
The Quicken copyright screen. You're about to enter the world of Quicken

5. Click the Continue button.

It's the one labeled Continue, as you probably guessed. Quicken asks, politely, where you want to stick it. (Quicken, I mean.) To be helpful, it even makes a suggestion: A new folder named the "Quicken 5 Folder" (See Figure A-3).

6. Tell the Quicken Installer where you want Quicken.

I don't have any earth-shaking advice for you here, but I think it's probably OK advice to just go with the Quicken Installer's suggestion. So, I'd just click Install. If you're someone who likes having it your way, however, you can use the pop-up menu shown at the top of the dialog box to pick the disk and folder for the new folder. (You can also pick an existing folder. You might do this if you already use Quicken and want to have the new Quicken go into the old Quicken folder. Does that make sense? I think so.)

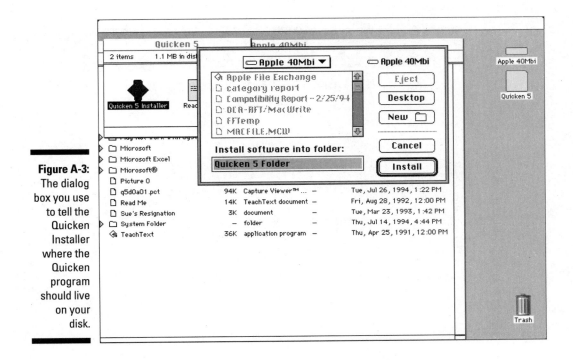

Figure A-3:
The dialog box you use to tell the Quicken Installer where the Quicken program should live on your disk.

7. Click Install.

You'll see a little message box on the screen that tells you the Quicken installer is busily working, fast as its little feet will run. When the installation process is over, done, complete, the Quicken installer displays another message box, as shown in Figure A-4.

8. Click OK.

You'll now see the new Quicken folder with a couple of items: The Quicken 5 icon, cleverly labeled "Quicken 5," and a Readme file (See Figure A-5).

9. (Optional) Celebrate.

Stand up at your desk, click your heels together three times, and repeat the phrase, "There's no place like home, Toto; there's no place like home."

Oh. One other thing. If you're ready to start using Quicken and you're not tired of reading, you should now flip to Chapter 1. It'll tell you how to start Quicken and start using Quicken. (OK. You may already know that you start Quicken by double-clicking its icon, but there are a few things I want to tell you about how to use Quicken.

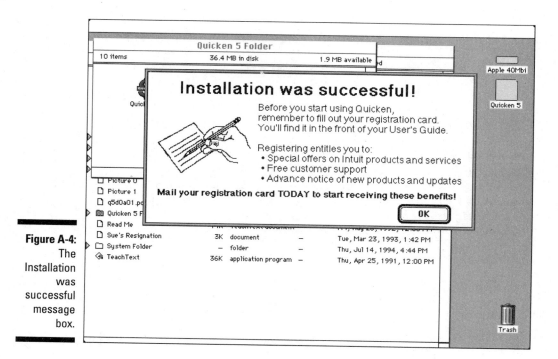

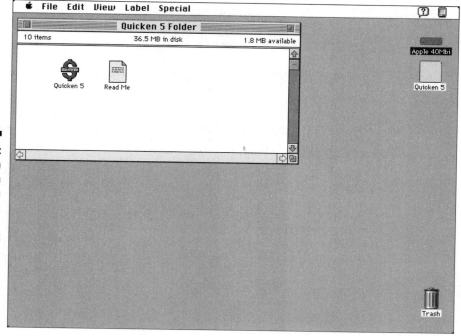

Glossary of Business and Financial Terms

940 Payroll Tax Form

The annual federal unemployment tax return. There's also a 940EZ version that is supposed to be EZier to fill out.

941 Payroll Tax Form

The quarterly federal payroll tax form that tells the IRS what federal employee payroll taxes (Social Security and Medicare) you've collected and remitted.

942 Payroll Tax Form

The quarterly payroll tax form that tells the IRS what domestic employee payroll taxes you've collected and remitted. (Use the 942, for example, if you employ a nanny and you want to be the U.S. Attorney General someday.)

Account

In Quicken, a list of the increases and decreases in an asset's value or in a liability's balance.

Account Balance

The value of asset or the outstanding principal owed for a liability. For example, the value of a checking account is the cash value of the account. The balance of a mortgage liability is the principal you still owe.

Account Transfer

An amount you move from one account (such as a checking account) to another (such as a savings account).

Account Type

Quicken provides several versions, or types, of accounts: four for keeping records of the things you own and two for keeping records of the amounts you owe.

- Bank accounts — for tracking checking and savings accounts
- Cash accounts — for tracking the cash in your pocket or wallet
- Mutual fund accounts — for tracking an individual mutual fund
- Portfolio accounts — for tracking all your investments: stocks, bonds, Krugerrands, and even mutual funds
- Asset accounts — for tracking anything else you own
- Credit card accounts — for tracking your plastic
- Liability accounts — for tracking everything else you owe: mortgages, car loans, and so forth

Accounts Payable

In a business, the amounts you owe your trade creditors — your landlord, the office supplies store, the distributor from whom you purchase your inventory, and so on. People who prefer monosyllabic speech often refer to accounts payable as A/P.

Accounts Receivable

In a business, the amounts your customers or clients owe you. People who prefer monosyllabic speech often refer to accounts receivable as A/R.

Amortization

The itsy-bitsy principal payments you make over the course of repaying a loan. Eventually, these principal reductions pay off the loan.

Backing Up

Making a copy. If something terrible happens — fire, hard disk failure, thermonuclear exchange — you still have a copy on floppy disk.

Balancing an Account

The steps you take to explain the difference between what your records show as a balance and what the bank's records (statement) show. Also referred to as "reconciling an account."

Billminder

A program that comes with Quicken. When asked by you, Billminder looks through your postdated checks whenever you start your computer. If there's a check that needs to be paid, Billminder tells you.

Bookkeeper

Someone who keeps the "books," or financial records.

Budget

A plan that says how you plan to make and spend money.

Capital Accounts

The money a sole proprietor leaves in or contributes to the sole proprietorship. Also, the money a partner leaves in or contributes to a partnership.

Capital Gain

What you earn by selling an investment for more than you paid for it.

Capital Loss

What you lose by selling an investment for less than you paid.

Category

In Quicken, how you summarize income and outgo. For example, you might use a category such as "Wages" to summarize your payroll check deposits. And you might use categories such as "Housing," "Food," and "Fun" to summarize your checks.

Category List

The list of categories you can use. While setting up the first account in a file, Quicken suggests category lists for home users and for business users.

Certified Public Accountant

Someone who's taken a bunch of undergraduate or graduate accounting courses, passed a rather challenging two-and-a-half day test, and worked for at least a year or two under a CPA doing things like auditing, tax planning and preparation, or consulting.

Chart

A picture that shows numbers. In Quicken, you can produce pie charts, bar charts, line charts, and so on.

Check Date

The date you write your payment instructions, or check. Technically, the check date is the date on which your payment instructions to the bank become valid.

Check Form

The preprinted form you use to provide payment instructions to your bank: "OK, Mammoth National, pay Joe Shmoe $32 from my account, 00704-844." Theoretically, you could use just about anything as a check form — a scrap of paper, a block of wood, and so on. In fact, rumor has it that someone once used a cowhide. It's easier for your poor bank, though, if you use check forms that follow the usual style and provide OCR characters along the form's bottom edge.

Circular E

Instructions from the Internal Revenue Service to employers. This publication tells how much federal income tax to withhold and other stuff like that. Call the IRS and request a copy if you need one.

Cleared

When a check or deposit has been received by the bank. An *uncleared* transaction hasn't been received by the bank.

Click

The process of pointing to something on a screen with a mouse and then pressing the mouse's left button. Occasional secondary usage (spelled "clique") refers to a snobbish group of adolescents.

Commands

What you use to tell Quicken what it should do. For example, "Quicken, I command thee to print a report."

Controller

A business's chief accountant — and usually the brunt of most accountant jokes. Also known as a *comptroller*.

Corporation

A legal business entity created by state law, owned by shareholders, and managed by directors and officers. As a business entity, a corporation has unique advantages and some disadvantages. Ask your attorney for more information.

Credit Card Accounts

An account specifically set up to track credit card charges, payments, and balances.

Cursor

Someone who uses vulgar language habitually. Also, the little blinking line or square (mouse pointer) that shows where what you type will go.

Deleted Transaction

A transaction that Quicken has removed from the register. *See also* **Voided Transaction.**

Disk

The thing-a-ma-jig in your computer on which your Mac stores your programs (like Quicken) and your data files (like the Quicken file for your financial records). A hard disk (inside your computer) can store a great deal of information; floppy disks, which can be removed, store less data than a hard disk.

Double-Click

Two clicks of the mouse in quick succession.

Exit

To quit, shut down, terminate, or stop a program.

Field

Where bunnies hop around. Also, input blanks on a screen.

File

Where data is stored. Your Quicken financial records, for example, are stored in a file.

Filename

The name of the file, or document, in which Quicken stores data.

Financial Wizards

People who believe that they know so much about the world of finance that it is actually their God-given duty to share their expertise with you.

Find

A tremendous bargain, as in "At $22,000, the five-bedroom house was a real find." In Quicken, also an Edit menu command that you can use to locate transactions. *See also* **Search Criteria**.

Folder

Basically, a drawer (like a filing cabinet drawer) that your Mac uses to organize your hard disk.

Help

A program's on-line documentation — which can almost always be accessed by choosing one of the Balloon Help menu commands. Also a verbalized cry for assistance.

Intelli Charge

A credit card especially for Quicken users that lets you receive your monthly statement on disk or via a modem. As a result, you need not enter your monthly credit card charges.

Internal Rate of Return

An investment's profit expressed as a percentage of the investment. If you go down to the bank and buy a certificate of deposit earning 7 percent interest, for example, 7 percent is the CD's internal rate of return. I don't want to give you the heebie-jeebies, but internal rates of return can get really complicated really fast.

Liability Accounts

An account specifically set up for tracking loans, payments, the principal and interest portions of these payments, and the outstanding balance.

Memo

A brief description of a transaction. Because you also give the payee and category for a transaction, it usually makes sense to use the Memo field to record some other bit of information about a check or deposit.

Menu

In Quicken, a list of commands. In a restaurant, a list of things you can order from the kitchen.

Menu Bar

Although it sounds like a place where menus go after work for a drink, a menu bar is a horizontally arranged row, or bar, of menus.

Missing Check

A gap in the check numbers. For example, if your register shows a check 101 and a check 103, check 102 is a missing check. The term also refers to missing persons of Czechoslovakian ancestry. (In this case, however, the usual spelling is "missing Czech.")

Mouse

A furry little rodent. Also, a pointing device you can use to select menu commands and fields.

Mutual Fund Account

An account specifically set up to track a mutual fund investment.

Partnership

A business entity that combines two or more former friends. In general, each partner is liable for the entire debts of the partnership.

Password

A word you have to give Quicken before Quicken will give you access to a file. The original password, "Open sesame," was used by Ali Baba.

Payee

The person to whom a check is made payable. (If you write a check to me, Steve Nelson, for example, I'm the payee.) In Quicken, you give the payee name by filling in the description field.

Portfolio Account

An account specifically set up to track all your investments. Unlike a mutual fund account, a portfolio account includes a cash element. Since we're talking about this, let me mention a couple other things to you, too. (1) Quicken used to call portfolio accounts, "brokerage accounts." (2) Typically, you will want to set up one portfolio account for each brokerage account statement you receive.

Power User

Someone who's spent far more time than is healthy fooling around with a computer. Power users are good people to have as friends, though, because they can often solve your worst technical nightmares. However, note that most people who describe themselves as power users aren't.

Register

The list of increases and decreases in an account balance. Quicken displays a register in a window that looks remarkably similar to a crummy old paper register — your checkbook. To print a copy of the register you see on your screen, choose the File menu's Print Register command; then press Return.

Report

An on-screen or printed summary of financial information from one or more registers.

Restore

Replace the current version of a file with the backup version. You may want to do this after a fire, hard disk failure, or thermonuclear exchange. *See also* **Backing Up**.

QIF

An acronym standing for Quicken Interchange Format. Basically, QIF is a set of rules that prescribes how a file must look if you want Quicken to read it. If you're a clever sort, you can import category lists and even transactions from files that follow the QIF rules.

Quicken

The name of the checkbook-on-a-computer program that this book is about. You didn't really need to look this up, did you?

QuickFill

A clever little feature. If Quicken can guess what you're going to type next in a field, it'll type, or QuickFill, the field for you. QuickFill types in transactions, payee names, category names, security names, and just about anything else it can guess.

QuickZoom

A clever big feature. If you have a question about a figure on an on-screen report, click the figure. Quicken then lists all the individual transactions that go together to make the figure.

Scroll Bars

The vertical bars along the window's right edge and the horizontal bars along the window's bottom edge. Use them to scroll, or page, through your view of something that's too big to fit on one page.

Search Criteria

A description of the transaction you want to locate. *See also **Find**.*

Sole Proprietor

A business that's owned by just one person and that doesn't have a separate legal identity. In general, businesses are sole proprietorships, partnerships, or corporations.

Spacebar

An intergalactic cocktail lounge. Also, the big long key on your keyboard that produces a blank space.

Split Transactions

A transaction assigned to more than one category or transferred to more than one account. A split check transaction, for example, might show a $50 check to the grocery store paying for both groceries and automobile expenses.

Stockholders Equity

The money that shareholders have contributed to a corporation or allowed to be retained in the corporation. You can't track stockholders equity with Quicken.

Subcategory

A category within a category. For example, the suggested Quicken home categories list breaks down utilities spending into a Gas and Electric subcategory and a Water subcategory.

Tax Deduction

For an individual, an amount that can be deducted from total income (such as alimony or Individual Retirement Account contributions) or used as an itemized deduction and deducted from adjusted gross income (such as home mortgage interest or charitable contributions). For a business, any amount that represents an ordinary and necessary business expense.

Transposition

Flip-flopped numbers — for example, 23.45 entered as **24.35** (the 3 and 4 are flip-flopped as a 4 and 3). These common little mistakes have caused many bookkeepers and accountants to go insane.

Techno-Geek

Someone who believes that fooling around with a computer is more fun than anything else in the world.

Voided Transaction

A transaction that Quicken has marked as void (using the Payee field), marked as cleared, and set to zero. Void transactions appear in a register, but because they are set to zero, they don't affect the account balance. *See also **Deleted Transaction***.

W-2 and W-3

A W-2 is the annual wages statement you use to tell employees what they made and to tell the IRS what your employees made. When you send in a stack of W-2s to the IRS, you also fill out a W-3 form that summarizes all your individual W-2s. W-2s and W-3s aren't much fun, but they're not hard to fill out.

Zen Buddhism

A Chinese and Japanese religion that says enlightenment comes from things like meditation, self-contemplation, and intuition — not from faith, devotion, or material things. I don't really know very much about Zen Buddhism. I did need a Z entry for the glossary, though.

Appendix C
Secret Business Formulas

· ·

I have some good news and some bad news for you. The good news is that there are some powerful formulas you can use to better your chances of business success and increase your profits. I'm not joking. There really are formulas like this. You can and should use them. And in the pages that follow, I'm going to explain how you do all this.

Now for the bad news. To use these formulas, you'll need to feel comfortable with a bit of arithmetic. You don't need to be a serious mathematician or anything. But you do need to feel comfortable with percentages and calculators.

Even so, I want to encourage you to skim through this chapter. Even if you're not particularly fond of or all that good at arithmetic, you'll pick up some weird insights into the world of finance.

You can use the Macintosh Calculator accessory to calculate any of the secret formulas. To access the Calculator, choose the Calculator command from the Apple menu.

1. The First "Most Expensive Money You Can Borrow" Formula

Here's something you may not know. The most expensive money you borrow is from vendors offering early payment discounts you don't take. Let me explain why this is. Say your friendly office supplies store offers you a 2% discount if you pay at the time of purchase rather than in the usual 30 days. In this case, you're paying 2% more by paying 30 days later. In effect, you're paying a 2% monthly interest charge. A 2% monthly interest charge works out to a 24% annual interest charge. That's a lot of money.

Here's another example which is only slightly more complicated. Many, many vendors offer a 2% discount if you pay within the first 10 days an invoice is due rather than 30 days later. (These payment terms are often described and printed at the bottom of the invoice as "2/10, Net 30.")

In these cases, you're paying 2% more by paying 20 days later. (The 20 days later business is the difference between 10 days and 30 days.) 2% for 20 days is roughly equivalent to 3% for 30 days, or a month. So, a 2% 20-day interest charge works out to a 36% annual interest charge. Now we're talking serious money.

The following table shows how some common early payment discounts translate into annual interest rates. By the way, I've been a bit more precise in my calculations for this table, so these numbers vary slightly (and are larger) than those I've given in the preceding paragraph.

Early payment discount	For paying 20 days early	For paying 30 days early
1%	0.1843	0.1229
2%	0.3724	0.2483
3%	0.5644	0.3763
4%	0.7604	0.5069
5%	0.9605	0.6404

Is it just me, or do those numbers blow you away, too? The 2% for 20 days early payment discount you always see works out to over 37% annual interest (if you do the math really precisely). Man, that hurts. And if you don't take a 5% for 20 days early payment discount when it's offered, you're effectively borrowing money at an annual rate of 96%. You didn't read that last number wrong. Yes, a 5% for 20 days early payment discount works out to an annual interest rate of almost 100%.

I should make a couple more observations, too. A 1% discount for paying 30 days early isn't such a bad deal in many cases. Look at the table. It shows the 1% discount for paying 30 days early as 12.29 percent. Sure. That's pretty high. But that interest rate is less than many credit cards. And that interest rate is less than many small business credit lines.

The bottom line on all this is that early payment discounts, if not taken, represent one of the most expensive ways to borrow money. I'm not saying there won't be times when you need to do this. I can guess that your cash flow gets pretty tight sometimes. (This is true is most businesses, as you probably know.) I am saying that you should never skip taking an early payment discount unless it makes sense to borrow money at outrageous interest rates.

Oh, yes. The secret formula. To figure out the effective annual interest rate you're paying by not taking an early payment discount, you use this formula:

$$\text{Discount percent} / (1 - \text{Discount percent}) * (365 / \text{Days of early payment})$$

So to calculate the effective annual interest rate you're paying by not taking a 2% discount for paying 20 days early, you calculate this formula:

$$.02 / (1 - .02) * (365/20)$$

Work out the mathematics, and you'll get .3724 which is the same thing as 37.24% interest rate. (Note that the discount percents are entered as their equivalent decimal values.)

Unfortunately, the Mac's Calculator doesn't include parentheses keys. So if you're using it, you'll need to calculate the stuff inside the parentheses first. Then, you'll need to use these results to calculate the entire formula. You may have another calculator installed on your Mac that has parentheses keys, however.

2. The Second "Most Expensive Money You Can Borrow" Formula

You know that "most expensive money you can borrow" stuff I talked about in the preceding paragraphs? There's a very tragic flip side to the story if you're offering your customers early payment discounts and they're taking them. In effect, if you offer people early payment discounts and they take them, you're borrowing money from your customers. And at the same outrageous interest rates. If customer Joe Schmoe gets a 2% early payment discount for paying 20 days early, for example, you've in effect paid ol' Joe a roughly 2% interest charge for a 20-day loan. Using the same formula I gave for the first "most expensive money you can borrow" formula, that works out to 37.24%.

I should say that in some industries, customers expect early payment discounts. You may have to offer them. But you should never do this willingly. You should never do this for fun. It's just too expensive a way to borrow money. 37.24%. Yikes.

Let me also offer a rather dour observation. In my experience, any time someone is offering big early payment discounts — I've seem them as big as 5% — they're either stupid or desperate and probably both.

What about Cash Payment Discounts?

Good question. These are actually different. My doctor, for example, offers me a 2% discount if I pay him in cash at the end of my visit rather than 30 days later. Is my doctor stupid or desperate? No. Here's the reason. First, if I pay him on the spot, he doesn't have to bill me or the insurance company and that saves his bookkeeper time. If it takes the $12/hour bookkeeper a quarter hour to prepare the invoice, send it out to both me and the insurance company, and then record and deposit the payment, he has to pay $3 real money to invoice me. So, he'll save that if he gets the cash up front.

There's also a more subtle thing—something the good doctor is too polite to bring up. If my doctor collects his cash from patients up front, he'll probably have fewer uncollectible accounts receivable later on. This is a tricky equation. There's no formula I can give you. But the logic is that he'll collect at least some of the cash — 98% of the cash, to be precise — from deadbeats from whom otherwise he would collect nothing. And the deadbeats who will pay 98% up front rather than stiffing him more than make up for the 2% discount that the non-dead-beats enjoy.

3. The "How Do I Break Even" Formula

I know you're not interested in just "breaking even." I know you want to make money in your business. But, that said, it's often super-helpful to know how much stuff you need to sell just to cover your expenses. If you're a one-person accounting firm (or some other service business), for example, how many hours do you need to work to pay your expenses and perhaps a small salary. Or, if you're a retailer of, say, toys, how many toys do you need to sell to pay your overhead, the rent, and sales clerks.

You see my point, right? Knowing how much revenue you need to generate just to stay in the game is really useful information. Knowing your break-even point, as it's known, lets you benchmark your performance. (Any time you're not breaking even, you know you have a serious problem which will need to be resolved quickly to stay in business.) And considering break-even points is invaluable when you think about new businesses or new ventures. (As you ponder any new opportunity and its potential income and expenses, you will want to know how much income needs to be generated just to pay those expenses.)

To calculate a break-even point, you need to know just three pieces of information. You need to know your *fixed costs* — the expenses you must pay regardless of the business's revenue, or income. You need to know the *revenue* you generate for each sale. And you need to know the *variable costs* you incur in each sale. (These variable costs, also called direct expenses in case you care, aren't the same thing as the fixed costs.)

Let's take the book-writing business as an example. Suppose that as you've been reading this book, you keep thinking, "Man, that guy is having too much fun...Writing about accounting programs...working day-in and day-out with buggy beta software....Yeah, that would be the life."

Let's further suppose that for every book you write you think you can make $5,000 but that you'll probably end up paying around $1,000 a book for things like long distance telephone charges, overnight courier charges, and extra hardware and software. And let's suppose that you need to pay yourself a salary of $20,000 a year. (We'll say this is your only fixed cost since you'll be writing at home at a small desk in your bedroom.)

OK, here's how the situation breaks down.

Variable	Amount	Explanation
Revenue	$5,000	It's what you can squeeze out of the publisher
Variable Costs	$1,000	All the little things add up
Fixed Costs	$20,000	You need someplace to live and food to eat

With these three bits of data, you can easily calculate how many books you need to break-even. Here's the formula:

Fixed Costs/(Revenue – Variable Costs)

If you plug in the writing business example data, things look like this:

$20,000/($5,000 – $1,000)

Work through the math and you get 5. That means you need to write (and get paid for) 5 books a year to pay both the $1,000 per book variable costs and your $20,000 salary. Just to prove that I didn't make up this formula and that it really works, here's how things look if you do write 5 books.

Description	Amount	Explanation
Revenue	$25,000	5 books at $5,000 each
Variable Costs	(5,000)	5 books at $1,000 each
Fixed Costs	(20,000)	A little food money, a little rent money, a little beer money
Profits	$0	Subtract the costs from the revenue, and there's nothing left

So to break even in a book writing business like the one described here, you need to be able to sell and write 5 books a year. If you didn't think you could sell 5 books or didn't think you could write 5 books, it would make no sense for you to get into the book writing business.

Your business is probably more complicated than book writing, but the same formula and logic applies. You need just three pieces of information: the revenue you receive from the sale of a single item, the variable costs of selling (and possibly making) the item, and the fixed costs you pay just to be in business.

Quicken doesn't collect or present its information in a way that lets you easily pull the revenue per item and variable costs per item off some report. Nor does it provide a fixed costs total on some report. But if you understand the logic of the preceding discussion, you can easily massage the Quicken data to get the information you need. Whatever you sell — be it hours of consulting services, thingamajigs, or corporate jets — has a price. So, that's your revenue per item input.

Most of the time, what you sell has a cost, too. If you buy and resell thingamajigs, those thingamajigs cost you some amount of money. If manufacture corporate jets, you can total the manufacturing costs. Sometimes your variable cost per item will be zero, however. If you're a consultant, for example, you sell hours of your time. But there may not be an hourly cost you pay because you consult an hour.

Your fixed costs are just all those costs you pay regardless of whether you sell stuff or not. If you have to pay an employee a salary regardless of whether you're selling stuff, his or her salary is a fixed cost, for example. Your rent is probably a fixed cost. Things like insurance and legal and accounting expenses are probably also all fixed because they don't vary with fluctuations in your revenue.

Fixed costs, by the way, may change a bit from year to year or may bounce around a bit. So, maybe "fixed" isn't a very good adjective. People use the term "fixed" costs, however, to differentiate these costs from variable costs, which are those costs which do vary with income.

4. The "You Can Grow Too Fast" Formula

Here's a weird little paradox. One of the easiest ways for a small business to fail is by being too successful. I know. It sounds crazy. But it's true. In fact, I'll even go so far as to say that by far the most common reason for business failure that I see is business success.

"Oh, geez," you're saying, "this nut is talking in circles."

Let me explain. Whether you realize it or not, your business needs a certain amount of financial horsepower, or net worth, to do business. (Your net worth is just the difference between your assets and liabilities.) You need to have some cash in the bank to tide you over the rough times which everybody has at least occasionally. You probably need some office furniture and computers so that you can take care of the business end of the business. And if you make anything at all, you need adequate tools and machinery. This part all makes sense, right?

OK, now on to the next reality. If your business grows and continues to grow, you're going to need to increase your financial horsepower, or net worth. A bigger business, for example, needs more cash to make it through the tough times, more office furniture and computers, and more tools and machinery. Oh sure, you may be able to have a one-time spurt in size because you have more financial horsepower — more net worth — that you need. But — and this is the key part — you can't grow and continue to grow without increasing your net worth at some point. In other words, you can't sustain business growth without increasing your net worth.

Some of you are now saying things like "No way, man. That doesn't apply to me." I assure you that it does. The reality is this: Growing a business means more than just growing your sales and growing your expenses. You need to grow your financial net worth, too.

Before I give you the actual formula, I want to tell you one more thing. The most important thing you can take away from this discussion is this bit of knowledge: There is a limit to the growth rate at which a business can sustain growth.

Back to the chase. As long as your creditors will extend you additional credit as you grow you business — and they should as long as you're profitable and as long as you don't have cash flow problems — you can grow your business as fast as you can grow your net worth. If you can grow your net worth by 5% a year, you can only grow at an easily sustained rate of 5% a year. If you can grow your net worth by 50% a year, you can only (only?) grow at an easily sustained rate of 50% a year.

You grow your net worth in only two ways: One way is by reinvesting profits in the business, and the other way is by getting people to invest money in the business. If you're not in a position to continually raise money from new investors — and most small businesses aren't — the only practical way to grow is by reinvesting profits in the business. (Note that any profits you leave in the business rather than drawing them out — such as through dividends — are reinvested.) So, the simple answer to calculating what growth rate your business can sustain can be obtained by calculating this formula:

Reinvested Profits/Net Worth

I should say, just for the record, that this formula is a very simple "sustainable growth" formula. Even so, it offers some amazingly interesting insights. Let's say that you're a commercial printer doing $500,000 in revenues a year with a business net worth of $100,000, that the business earns $50,000 a year, but that you only leave $10,000 a year in the business. In other words, your reinvested profits are $10,000. In this case, your sustainable growth is calculated as follows:

$10,000/$100,000

Work out the numbers and you get .1, or 10%. In other words, you can grow your business by 10% a year (as long as you grow the net worth by 10% by reinvesting profits). For example, you can easily go from $500,000 to $550,000 to $605,000 and continue growing at this 10% rate. But you can't grow any faster than this. For example, you'll get into serious trouble if you try to go from $500,000 to $600,000 to $720,000 and continue growing at a 20%.

You can convert a decimal value to a percentage by multiplying the value by 100. For example, .1 times 100 equals 10%. You can convert a percentage to a decimal value by dividing the value by 100. 25% divided by 100 equals .25, for example.

By the way, the sustainable growth formula inputs are pretty easy to get once you have Quicken up and running. You can get your net worth figure off your balance sheet. You can calculate your reinvested profits by looking at your net income and deducting any amounts you pulled out of the business.

I'm not going to go through the mathematical proof of why this formula is true. My experience is that it makes intuitive sense to people who think about it for a few minutes. If you aren't into the intuition-thing or you don't believe me, get a college finance text book and look up its discussion of the sustainable growth formula.

One more item. I don't want to beat this sustainable growth thing to death, but let me close with a true and mercifully short story.

I've just seen another entrepreneur fail because he was successful. At first, he ignored the symptoms of fast growth. He needed another computer, so he bought it. He had to hire another person so he just did it. Cash flow was tight and getting tighter, but he ignored the problems. After all, he was making lots of sales and the business was growing. Sure, things were getting awkward, but he didn't have to worry, right?

Unfortunately, vendors were always getting paid later and later. This went on for a few weeks until some vendors started insisting on cash payments and other vendors said "Hey buddy, no more sales until you pay us what you owe."

One Friday, he couldn't make his payroll. He then committed the unpardonable sin of borrowing payroll tax money — something you should never ever do.

Finally, he had lots of bills to pay and not only no cash to pay the bills but no cash in sight. Employees quit. Vendors said, "No more — and we mean it this time." And this is what ultimately killed the business. When the telephone company cuts off your telephone service, you're pretty much in serious trouble. When your landlord locks you out of your business location, you're pretty much out-of-luck.

The paradox in all this is that the guy had a successful business. He just spread his financial resources too thin by growing too fast.

5. The First "What Happens If..." Formula

One of things that's really curious about small businesses is that small changes in revenue, or income, can have huge impacts on profits. A retailer cruising along at, say, $200,000 in revenue and struggling to live on, say, $20,000 a year never realizes that boosting the sales volume, say, 20% to $250,000 may increase his profits by 300% to $60,000.

In fact, if there's only one thing you take away from this little discussion, it's this weird little truth: If your fixed costs don't change, small changes in revenue can mean big changes in profits.

If you want to see how all this works, I'll step you through an example and provide a secret formula. For starters, let's say that you're currently generating $100,000 a year of revenue and are making $30,000 a year in profits. Let's also say that your revenue per item sold is $100 and your variable cost per item sold is $35. (In this case, your fixed costs happen to be $45,000 a year, but that isn't all that important to the analysis.)

Accountants like to whip up little tables that describe these sorts of things, so the following table gives the current story on your imaginary business:

Description	Amount	Explanation
Revenue	$100,000	You sell 1000 dohickeys at $100 a pop
Variable Costs	(35,000)	You buy 1000 dohickeys at $35 a pop
Fixed Costs	(45,000)	All the little things: rent, your salary, and so on
Profits	$30,000	What's left over

The preceding table shows the current situation. But let's suppose that you want to know what will happen to your profits if revenue increases by 20% but your fixed costs don't change. Mere mortals, not knowing what you and I know, might assume that a 20% increase in revenue would produce a roughly 20% increase in profits. But we know that small changes in revenue can produce big changes in profits, right?

To estimate exactly how a change in revenue effects profits, you use the following secret formula:

Percentage * Revenue * (1 – Variable cost per item/Revenue per item)

Using the example data provided earlier — and I'm sorry this is starting to resemble those story problems from 8th grade math — you make the following calculation:

.20*$100,000*(1 – 35/100)

Work out the numbers and you get 13000. What does this mean? It means that a 20% increase in revenue produces a $13,000 increase in your profits. As percentage of profits, this $13,000 increase is more than 40%. ($13,000/$30,000 equals 43.33%)

To summarize, in this case, a 20% increase in revenues results in more than a 40% increase in profits.

Let me stop here and make a quick observation. In my experience, entrepreneurs always seem to think they need to grow big to make big money. They concentrate on doing things that will double or triple or quadruple their sales. Their logic, though, isn't always correct. If you can grow your business without having to increase your fixed costs, small changes in revenues can produce big changes in profits.

Before I stop talking about this first "What Happens If..." formula, I should quickly describe where you get the inputs you'll need for the formula. The percentage change input is just a number you pick. If you want to see what happens to your profits with, say, a 25% increase in sales, you use .25.

The revenue input is just your total revenue. You can get it from your Profit & Loss Statement.

The revenue per item sold and variable costs per item sold figures work the same way as described for the break-even formula. Rather than repeat myself, I'll assume that you've either just read that formula description or you can read it next.

6. The Second "What Happens If..." Formula

Maybe I shouldn't tell you this, but financial guys like me have a prejudice about sales guys. It's not just because good sales guys usually make more than good financial guys. It's really not. Honest to goodness.

Here's the prejudice: Financial guys think sales guys always want to reduce prices.

The sales guys see it a bit differently. They say, in effect, "Hey, dude, you worry too much. We'll make up the difference in additional sales volume."

It's an appealing argument. You just undercut your competitor's prices by a healthy chunk and make less on each sale. But because you sell your stuff for so cheap, your customers will beat a path to our door.

Just for the record, I just love a good sales guy. I think a good sales guy is more important that a good financial guy. (I use the term *guy* here as non-gender specific. A guy can be a male or a female.)

But, that painful admission aside, I have to tell you that there's a problem with the "Cut the prices, we'll make it up on volume" strategy. If you cut your prices by a given percentage — like 10%, say — you usually have to have a much bigger percentage gain in revenue to break even.

Let me show you what I mean and how this all works. Again, suppose that you have a business that sells some dohickey or thingamajig. Let's say that you're generating $100,000 a year of revenue and are making $30,000 a year in profits. Let's also say that your revenue per item, or dohickey, sold is $100 and your variable cost per item, or dohickey, sold is $35. Your fixed costs, as you may remember, happen to be $45,000 a year. But, again, it isn't all that important to the analysis. Here's another of those little tables that summarize the current situation.

Description	Amount	Explanation
Revenue	$100,000	You sell 1000 dohickeys at $100 a pop
Variable Costs	(35,000)	You buy 1000 dohickeys at $35 a pop
Fixed Costs	(45,000)	All the little things: rent, your salary, and so on
Profits	$30,000	What's left over

Then, one month, business is particularly bad. Joe-bob, your sales guy, comes to you, all bummed out, and says, "Boss, I've got just a killer idea. I think we can cut prices by 15% and get a truly massive boost in sales."

You're a good boss. You're a polite boss. Plus, you're intrigued. So, you think a bit. The idea has a certain appeal. You start wondering how much of an increase in sales you need to break even on the price reduction.

You're probably not surprised to read this, but I have another secret formula that can help. Using the formula shown below, you can calculate how many items — dohickeys in our example — you need to sell just to break even on the new, discounted price. Here is the formula:

(Current profits + Fixed costs)/(Revenue per item – Variable cost per item)

Using the example data provided earlier, you make the following calculation:

($30,000 + $45,000)/($85 – $35)

Work out the numbers and you get 1500. What does this mean? It means that just to break even on the 15% price reduction — *just to break even* — Joe-bob needs to sell 1500 dohickeys. Currently, per the last table shown, Joe-bob is selling 1000 dohickeys a year. As percentage, then, this jump from 1000 dohickeys to 1500 dohickeys is exactly a 50% increase.

OK, I don't know Joe-bob. He may be a great guy. He may be a wonderful salesperson. But here's my guess. Joe-bob isn't thinking you guys will enjoy a 50% increase in sales volume. (Remember, with a 15% price reduction, you need a 50% increase just to break-even!) And Joe-bob almost certainly isn't thinking about a 75% or 100% increase in sales volume — which is what you need to make serious money on whole deal, as shown in the following table:

Description	1500 units sold	1750 units sold	2000 units sold
Revenue	127500	148750	170000
Variable Costs	–52500	–61250	–70000
Fixed Costs	–45000	–45000	–45000
Profits 30000	42500	55000	

In summary, you can't reduce prices by, say, 15%, and then go for some penny ante increase. You need to huge increases in your sales volume to get big increases in your profits. If you look at the preceding table you can see that if you can double the sales from 1000 dohickeys sold to 2000 dohickeys sold, you'll almost double your profits. This assumes your fixed costs stay level, as the table shows.

I should quickly describe where you get the inputs you'll need for the formula. The profit figure can come right off the Quicken Profit & Loss statement. The fixed costs figure just tallies all your fixed costs. (I talked about this in the paragraphs that describe how to estimate your break-even point.) The revenue per item is just the new price you're considering. Finally, the variable cost per item is the cost of the thing you're selling. (I've talked about this before, too.)

Please don't construe the preceding discussion as proof that you should never listen to the Joe-bobs of the world. The cut-prices-to-increase-volume strategy can work wonderfully well. The trick, however, is to massively increase your volume. Sam Walton, the late founder of Wal-Mart, used the strategy and became at one point the richest man in the world.

7. The Economic Order Quantity (a.k.a., Isaac Newton) Formula

Isaac Newton invented differential calculus. This is truly amazing to me. I can't imagine someone just figuring out calculus. I could never, in a 100 years, figure it out.

The neat thing about calculus — and no, we're not going to do any here — is that it lets you calculate optimal values for equations. One of the coolest equations it can do this for is a formula called the economic order quantity, or EOQ, model. I know this all sounds terribly confusing and totally boring, but stay with me for just another paragraph. (If you're not satisfied in another paragraph or so, skip to the next secret formula.)

Let's say you buy and then resell — oh, I don't know — let's say you buy and resell 2000 cases of vintage French wine every year. What the EOQ model does is let you decide whether you should order all 2000 cases at one time, order a one case at a time, or order some number of cases in between one case and 2000 cases.

Another to say this same thing is that the EOQ model lets you choose the best, or optimal, reorder quantity for items you buy and then resell.

If you're still with me at this point, I figure you want to know how all this works. You need to know just three pieces of data to calculate the optimal order quantity: the annual sales volume, the cost of placing an order, and the annual cost of holding one unit in inventory. You then plug this information into the following formula:

$$(2 * \text{Sales volume} * \text{Order cost})/\text{Annual holding cost per item}$$

I've already supposed that you buy and resell 2000 cases a year, so that's your sales volume, Let's say that every time you place an order for the wine, you need to buy a $800 round-trip ticket to Paris (just to sample the inventory) and pay $200 for a couple nights at a hotel. So, your cost per order is $1,000. Finally, let's say that with insurance, interest on a bank loan, and the costs of maintaining your hermetically-sealed, temperate-controlled wine cellar, it costs about $250 a year to store a case of wine. In this example, then, you can calculate the optimal order quantity using this formula:

$$(2 * 2000 * \$1000)/\$100$$

Work through the numbers and you get 200. This means that the order quantity that minimizes the total cost of your trips to Paris *and* of holding your expensive wine inventory is 200 cases. You could, of course, make only one trip to Paris a year and buy 2000 cases of wine at once, thereby saving travel money, but in this case you would spend more money that you save on holding more of your expensive wine inventory. And while you could reduce your wine inventory carrying costs by going to Paris every week and picking up a few cases, your travel costs would then go way, way up.

Now there's a little problem with the EOC formula from the Mac user's perspective. Your Mac's calculator, unfortunately, doesn't have a square root key. So if you have to use the Mac's calculator, you'll need to back into the number. You can do this by trying to square different numbers and then seeing which squared number equals the number for which you want to calculator a square root. In the Wine business, for example, if you tried squaring 200 (by entering 200*200=), you would learn it equals 40,000. Once you know this, you also know the square root of 40,000 equals 200. If this is too clunky for you, consider pulling that pocket calculator out of your desk. It probably provides a square root key. If you use this later approach, I suggest you use the time you save to write Apple and tell them to beef up the Calculator accessory.

8. The Rule of 72

The Rule of 72 isn't exactly a secret formula. It's more like a rule of thumb. Usually, people use it to figure out how long it takes some investment or savings account to double in value. It's a cool little trick, however. And it has several useful applications for business people.

What the rule says is that if you divide the value 72 by an interest rate percentage, your result is approximately the number of years it'll take to double your money. If you can stick money into some investment that pays 12% interest, for example, it'll take roughly 6 years to double your money since 72/12 equals 6.

The rule of 72 isn't exact, but it's usually close enough for government work. If you invest $1000 for 6 years at 12% interest, for example, what you really get after six years isn't $2,000 but $1,973.92.

If you're in business, you can use the rule of 72 in a couple other ways, too. If you want to forecast how long it'll take inflation to double the price of some item, you can just divide 72 by the inflation rate. If you own a building that you figure will at least keep up with inflation and wonder how long it'll take to double in value if inflation runs at 4%, for example, you just divide 72 by 4. When you do, you get 18, meaning it'll take roughly 18 years for the building to double in value. Again, the rule of 72 isn't exactly on the money, but it's dang close. A $100,000 building increases in value to $202,581.65 over 18 years if there's 4% annual inflation.

Another way business owners can use the rule of 72 is by forecasting how long it'll take to double your sales volume given some annual growth rate. For example, if you can grow your business by, say, 9% a year, you'll roughly double the size of the business in 8 years because 72/9 equals 8. (I'm becoming kind of compulsive about this, I know, but let me again say that the rule isn't exact but very close. If a $1,000,000-a-year business grows 9% annually, its sales equal $1,992,562.64 after eight years of 9% growth. This really means that the business will generate roughly $2,000,000 of sales in the ninth year.)

INDEX

Notes

Notes

Notes

Notes

Notes

Notes

Order Form

Order Center: (800) 762-2974 (8 a.m.-5 p.m., PST, weekdays) or (415) 312-0650

For Fastest Service: Photocopy This Order Form and FAX it to: (415) 358-1260

Quantity	ISBN	Title	Price	Total

Shipping & Handling Charges

Subtotal	U.S.	Canada & International	International Air Mail
Up to $20.00	Add $3.00	Add $4.00	Add $10.00
$20.01-40.00	$4.00	$5.00	$20.00
$40.01-60.00	$5.00	$6.00	$25.00
$60.01-80.00	$6.00	$8.00	$35.00
Over $80.00	$7.00	$10.00	$50.00

In U.S. and Canada, shipping is UPS ground or equivalent.
For Rush shipping call (800) 762-2974.

Subtotal _____

CA residents add
applicable sales tax _____

IN and MA residents add
5% sales tax _____

IL residents add
6.25% sales tax _____

RI residents add
7% sales tax _____

Shipping _____

Total _____

Ship to:

Name _____

Company _____

Address _____

City/State/Zip _____

Daytime Phone _____

Payment: ❑ Check to IDG Books (US Funds Only) ❑ Visa ❑ Mastercard ❑ American Express

Card# _____ Exp._____ Signature_____

Please send this order form to: IDG Books, 155 Bovet Road, Suite 310, San Mateo, CA 94402.

Allow up to 3 weeks for delivery. Thank you!

IDG BOOKS WORLDWIDE REGISTRATION CARD

RETURN THIS
REGISTRATION CARD
FOR FREE CATALOG

Title of this book: Quicken 5 For Macs For Dummies

My overall rating of this book: ❑ Very good [1] ❑ Good [2] ❑ Satisfactory [3] ❑ Fair [4] ❑ Poor [5]

How I first heard about this book:

❑ Found in bookstore; name: [6]　　　　　　　　　　　　　❑ Book review: [7]

❑ Advertisement: [8]　　　　　　　　　　　　　　　　　　❑ Catalog: [9]

❑ Word of mouth; heard about book from friend, co-worker, etc.: [10]　　❑ Other: [11]

What I liked most about this book:

What I would change, add, delete, etc., in future editions of this book:

Other comments:

Number of computer books I purchase in a year:　❑ 1 [12]　❑ 2-5 [13]　❑ 6-10 [14]　❑ More than 10 [15]

I would characterize my computer skills as: ❑ Beginner [16] ❑ Intermediate [17] ❑ Advanced [18] ❑ Professional [19]

I use ❑ DOS [20]　❑ Windows [21]　❑ OS/2 [22]　❑ Unix [23]　❑ Macintosh [24]　❑ Other: [25]_____
　　　　　　　　　　　　　　　　　　　　　　　　　　　　　　　　　　　　　(please specify)

I would be interested in new books on the following subjects:
(please check all that apply, and use the spaces provided to identify specific software)

❑ Word processing: [26]　　　　　　　　　❑ Spreadsheets: [27]

❑ Data bases: [28]　　　　　　　　　　　　❑ Desktop publishing: [29]

❑ File Utilities: [30]　　　　　　　　　　　❑ Money management: [31]

❑ Networking: [32]　　　　　　　　　　　　❑ Programming languages: [33]

❑ Other: [34]

I use a PC at (please check all that apply): ❑ home [35]　❑ work [36]　❑ school [37]　❑ other: [38] _____

The disks I prefer to use are ❑ 5.25 [39]　❑ 3.5 [40]　❑ other: [41]_____

I have a CD ROM:　❑ yes [42]　　❑ no [43]

I plan to buy or upgrade computer hardware this year:　❑ yes [44]　❑ no [45]

I plan to buy or upgrade computer software this year:　❑ yes [46]　❑ no [47]

Name: _____　Business title: [48] _____　Type of Business: [49] _____

Address (❑ home [50] ❑ work [51]/Company name: _____)

Street/Suite# _____

City [52]/State [53]/Zipcode [54]: _____　Country [55] _____

❑ **I liked this book!** You may quote me by name in future
IDG Books Worldwide promotional materials.

My daytime phone number is _____

**IDG
BOOKS**

THE WORLD OF
COMPUTER
KNOWLEDGE